D1452506

The philosophy of Joss Whedon

Butler Community College

THE PHILOSOPHY OF
JOSS WHEDON

The Philosophy of Popular Culture

The books published in the Philosophy of Popular Culture series will illuminate and explore philosophical themes and ideas that occur in popular culture. The goal of this series is to demonstrate how philosophical inquiry has been reinvigorated by increased scholarly interest in the intersection of popular culture and philosophy, as well as to explore through philosophical analysis beloved modes of entertainment, such as movies, TV shows, and music. Philosophical concepts will be made accessible to the general reader through examples in popular culture. This series seeks to publish both established and emerging scholars who will engage a major area of popular culture for philosophical interpretation and examine the philosophical underpinnings of its themes. Eschewing ephemeral trends of philosophical and cultural theory, authors will establish and elaborate on connections between traditional philosophical ideas from important thinkers and the ever-expanding world of popular culture.

SERIES EDITOR

Mark T. Conard, Marymount Manhattan College, NY

BOOKS IN THE SERIES

The Philosophy of Stanley Kubrick, edited by Jerold J. Abrams
Football and Philosophy, edited by Michael W. Austin
Tennis and Philosophy, edited by David Baggett
The Philosophy of the Coen Brothers, edited by Mark T. Conard
The Philosophy of Film Noir, edited by Mark T. Conard
The Philosophy of Martin Scorsese, edited by Mark T. Conard
The Philosophy of Neo-Noir, edited by Mark T. Conard
The Philosophy of Spike Lee, edited by Mark T. Conard
The Philosophy of David Lynch, edited by William J. Devlin and Shai Biderman
The Philosophy of Horror, edited by Thomas Fahy
The Philosophy of The X-Files, edited by Dean A. Kowalski
Steven Spielberg and Philosophy, edited by Dean A. Kowalski
The Philosophy of Charlie Kaufman, edited by David LaRocca
The Philosophy of the Western, edited by Jennifer L. McMahon and B. Steve Csaki
The Philosophy of Science Fiction Film, edited by Steven M. Sanders
The Philosophy of TV Noir, edited by Steven M. Sanders and Aeon J. Skoble
Basketball and Philosophy, edited by Jerry L. Walls and Gregory Bassham
Golf and Philosophy, edited by Andy Wible

THE PHILOSOPHY OF
JOSS WHEDON

Edited by Dean A. Kowalski
and S. Evan Kreider

THE UNIVERSITY PRESS OF KENTUCKY

Copyright © 2011 by The University Press of Kentucky

Scholarly publisher for the Commonwealth,
serving Bellarmine University, Berea College, Centre
College of Kentucky, Eastern Kentucky University,
The Filson Historical Society, Georgetown College,
Kentucky Historical Society, Kentucky State University,
Morehead State University, Murray State University,
Northern Kentucky University, Transylvania University,
University of Kentucky, University of Louisville,
and Western Kentucky University.
All rights reserved.

Editorial and Sales Offices: The University Press of Kentucky
663 South Limestone Street, Lexington, Kentucky 40508-4008
www.kentuckypress.com

15 14 13 12 11   5 4 3 2 1

Cataloging-in-Publication data is available from the Library of Congress.

ISBN 978-0-8131-3419-2 (hardcover : alk. paper)

This book is printed on acid-free paper meeting
the requirements of the American National Standard
for Permanence in Paper for Printed Library Materials.

Manufactured in the United States of America.

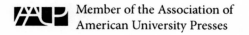 Member of the Association of
American University Presses

Contents

Part 3. "I'm All of Them, but None of Them Is Me": The Human Condition

Foreword

Tim Minear

Recently an interviewer asked me if I was aware I was being "studied in universities." One imagines oneself in a petri dish. She was, of course, referring to work in which I had been involved over the years. Specifically, what is known as "The Whedonverse"—the universe comprising the creations of Joss Whedon.

The matter and energy that make up this 'verse include movies, comic books, television series, and now web series. In the case of *Firefly,* literally a 'verse within the 'verse. In the case of the *Buffy* musical and *Dr. Horrible's Sing-Along Blog,* music. Songs. Three-minute dramatic units crammed with character information that help tell the larger story. Verse and chorus within the 'verse.

For my part, of the four network television series that constitute a particular constellation of the Whedonverse, I was intimately involved with three of them: *Angel, Firefly,* and *Dollhouse.*

Here's the thing you need to know about making a television series—it's chaos. Beyond the puzzle of simply trying to make one story track, you're trying to make twenty-two stories track. Track with themselves and with each other. Twenty-two hours of story. Roughly the equivalent of ten feature films.

Obviously for an endeavor this complex, one must never begin before mapping out with absolute precision every detail.

Except, that's never how it works. You fill in the map afterward. At best, you're starting with some landmarks and orange cones to guide the way. You think you're going to find a route to the West Indies and end up somewhere in Santa Monica. Or Pylea, for that matter.

The "process" looks something like this: While you're figuring out the story that's inevitably late, you're rewriting the one that's shooting; while you're rewriting the one that's shooting—and prepping the one you still haven't figured out—you're editing (and often rewriting) the one you just shot; while you're editing the one you just shot, you're doing the FX and sound mix of the one you just locked. At every step of the process, you're getting notes from the producers and the other writers (this is known as "collaboration") and notes from the studio and network (this is known as "interference").

In the years when we were making both *Buffy* and *Angel*, it was not only about making the short- and long-term narratives on one show work; we always had to take into account what the guys on the other show were doing. Sometimes this meant nixing a promising episode idea because it was too similar to what was happening on the sister show that week. On other occasions, that overlap was embraced as a happy confluence of events and a crossover might result. I think now specifically of "Fool for Love"/"Darla." I had sought out Joss on the *Buffy* set to pitch episode seven of season two of *Angel*. I would be directing an episode for the first time, and I wanted to explore Darla's backstory in flashback. I figured something simple for my first time—the Boxer Rebellion on a TV budget. When I approached Joss with this idea, he said he liked it, but unfortunately *Buffy* was going to be doing Spike's backstory that very night. Some of that backstory would cross with Angel/Darla's backstory. A comic beat. A shared double-take. A "two-hour *Buffy/Angel* event" was born.

During year four of *Angel* and the last years of *Buffy*, Joss and I were also busy launching *Firefly*. For a time, there were always three stories being broken, three episodes being prepped, three episodes being shot, three episodes in postproduction. All at once. It was, in a word, nuts.

But out of such smashing and bashing and chaos, universes are born. Even ordered universes. Universes in which one might find coherent strains of philosophical thought. The hidden hand of the Creator. The Creator's voice.

To be sure, in television as in other collaborative art forms there may be multiple voices. But in really good television there's a single voice, a single vision. The rest of us are trying our best to do that cat's act.

Funny fact. After my first year at Mutant Enemy, people started to notice that Joss, David Greenwalt, and yours truly all had a similar way of speaking. We'd all affected the same weird cadence—possibly unnatural to all of us, as no one could quite remember how it started. I retain some of that affectation to this day. Years later, I was making a show called *The Inside*. As it happened, we were shooting on the old *Buffy* stages. My office had been Joss's office back when Mutant Enemy was headquartered there. One day Joss came to visit me. An assistant in the office had no idea who Joss was. After Joss left, this assistant remarked, "Who was that guy? He talks just like Tim."

The voice of the Whedonverse is distinctly Joss's voice. The ideas that run through its various incarnations are reflections of his conscious and unconscious thought. Art is a way to work out ideas and problems. Of bringing order to chaos. Through chaos. Often while doing a funny voice.

What follows are the works of other writers putting our 'verse into some kind of order. Occasionally with a funny voice. And I, for one, thank them for it.

Surrounded by the chaos of my desk in Los Feliz, California—

Tim Minear

Introduction

Dean A. Kowalski and S. Evan Kreider

Creature of the night? Look elsewhere for your meal. Demon goddess? There will be no apocalypse today. Fascist galactic government or soulless mind-controlling corporation? No willing subjects dwell within. This book is not for any of you. This book is for those who seek the salvation of the world, the truth of the signal, and the freedom of humanity; it is for Scoobies, Champions, Browncoats, and Echo-inspired former Dolls only.

Now that we have your attention, recall Joss Whedon's recent comment about *Dollhouse:* "We're trying to create something that's more than the sum of its parts. And not just in an 'Oooh, we're heavy with mythology' way. Dare I say we're reaching for something more philosophical?" Of course, Whedonites everywhere have always known that Joss's body of work, from the earlier *Buffy the Vampire Slayer* and *Angel* to the later *Firefly/Serenity,* and *Dr. Horrible's Sing-Along Blog,* was rife with philosophical musings. *Dollhouse* was thus merely extending a previously existing trend. Indeed, the single biggest challenge for this volume was deciding on a focus, given the enormous variety of philosophical issues that pervade Joss's illustrious body of work. In the end, we decided on a hybrid approach. Though the articles throughout do cover a great range of topics, certain common themes start to emerge. In particular, many of our authors focus in some way or another on Joss's implicit contribution to the age-old philosophical exploration of the nature of the "good life," in respect to happiness and fulfillment, relationships and community, authenticity and autonomy, and the like. By considering the essays within this text in light of the good life, we hope that you, our readers, will better appreciate the contribution that Joss makes to this classic philosophical discussion.

The first part—"'You Can't Take the Sky from Me': Freedom and Its Limits"—contains four essays. David Baggett's "*Firefly* and Freedom" can-

1

vasses Jean-Paul Sartre's existentialist account of human free choice and moral value, and, using "Objects in Space" as a case study, explores the extent to which Whedon affirms Sartrean positions. Baggett argues that, although Whedon regularly emphasizes the significance of human freedom, various examples from *Firefly* speak against interpreting Joss as a thoroughgoing existentialist. In "'Just Get Us a Little Further': Liberty and the Frontier in *Firefly* and *Serenity*," Amy H. Sturgis furthers Baggett's exploration of Whedon's treatment of human freedom. She introduces Isaiah Berlin's distinction between positive and negative liberty to argue that Malcolm Reynolds consistently acts in accordance with the latter. In this way, Whedon's *Firefly* is representative of many science fiction stories influenced by Frederick Jackson Turner's "frontier thesis" of American westward expansion. Impositions upon negative liberty invariably involve rights violations. Joseph J. Foy employs the social contract theorists Thomas Hobbes and John Locke in his essay, "The State of Nature and Social Contracts on Spaceship *Serenity*," to shed light on the moral and legal interactions between the Browncoats, Alliance, Reavers, and spaceship *Serenity*. He then argues that Whedon's depictions of the social arrangements aboard *Serenity* are best understood via Lockean principles, thereby reaffirming Joss's broader commitments to community, rights, and justice. In "*Dollhouse* and Consensual Slavery," S. Evan Kreider uses the *Dollhouse* series to explore the moral legitimacy of consensual slavery. Kreider employs the ideas of Thomas Mappes, John Stuart Mill, and John Locke to elucidate several different points of view within the series, as voiced by its various characters. He then argues that Joss's own view, as implied in the show, is an even stronger version of Locke's position: the idea of freely entering into contractual slavery seems incoherent.

The second part—"'Live as Though the World Were as It Should Be': Ethics and Virtue"—contains five essays. In "Plato, Aristotle, and Joss on Being Horrible," Dean A. Kowalski utilizes examples from *Toy Story, Angel, Firefly,* and *Dr. Horrible* to highlight the differences between Plato's and Aristotle's ideas about the good life. He then goes on to argue that Whedon is best interpreted as affirming an Aristotelian view of the good life, most notably in his depictions of community and friendship, picking up on themes introduced near the end of Foy's essay; ultimately, then, Plato and Aristotle help us to better understand Whedon and his corpus. In "Aristotle, Kant, Spike, and Jayne: Ethics and Character in the Whedonverse," Jason D. Grinnell explores the classic philosophical issue of moral motivation. Grinnell introduces us to the problem of moral motivation and its potential conflicts with self-interest through the works of Plato, and then provides a possible solution by way of Aristotle's virtue ethics, in which a virtuous character is largely its own reward. In this framework, Grinnell traces the moral development of Spike and Jayne, each of whom begins his respective character arc as a villain, but each of whom also ends up a hero through a long path of moral development. This coheres with themes argued for in Kowalski's essay in that becoming a certain kind of person is both good in itself and good for you. In "Companions, Dolls, and Whores: Joss Whedon on Sex and Prostitution," Tait Szabo tackles the controversial moral issue of prostitution, and in doing so picks up on some of the themes introduced by Kreider. By exploring the way in which prostitution in one form or another is represented in shows such as *Firefly* and *Dollhouse,* Szabo argues that such a profession could be morally legitimate in the right form and under the right circumstances. *Firefly*'s Inara Sera and *Dollhouse*'s Caroline/Echo are nothing if not assertive and resourceful. In "Fashioning Feminism: Whedon, Women, and Wardrobe," Patricia Brace explores how Whedon tends to depict—literally—his female characters. She analyzes Joss's shows within a feminist framework. Focusing primarily on the characters of Willow, Buffy, and Cordelia, Brace argues that we can best understand Whedon's work from a third-wave feminist point of view, in which clothing and fashion are a reflection of and contribution to a woman's personal empowerment. In "Heroes and Villains: Morality, the Will to Power, and the Overman in the Work of Joss Whedon," Gary Heba, with an assist from Robin Murphy, analyzes Joss's corpus in Nietzschean terms to explore the extent to which he affirms moral values at all. The authors trace the development of Nietzsche's ideas and show how this development is reflected in the development of several of Joss's characters, including Buffy, Faith, Angel, Spike, River, and Echo. They then argue that Joss's work implies an extension of Nietzsche's ideas, in which some traditional but still life-affirming moral values can be maintained while placed within a new framework that is almost subversively nihilistic. Like the authors of the previous essays, then, Heba and Murphy attempt to convey the balancing act between opposing philosophical ideas that Joss often attempts in his narratives.

The third and last part—"'I'm All of Them, but None of Them Is Me': The Human Condition"—contains four essays. In "Seeking Authenticity in the Whedonverse," Joseph J. Foy and Dean A. Kowalski also explore the competing themes of ethical subjectivity and objectivity in the Whedon-verse. They initially apply Heidegger's ideas of authentic human existence regarding values, goals, and projects to distinguish the characters of Dr. Horrible and Captain Hammer. They go on to assess Whedon's heroes—Buzz Lightyear, Buffy, Angel, Simon—in an attempt to provide a coherent account of authenticity across Joss's corpus. Eschewing a straightforward Sartrean analysis, they argue that Whedon is best understood along Socratic and Rawlsian lines. But do we possess the kind of genuine freedom to autonomously choose among various conceptions of the good? In the Whedonverse, the heroes are constantly struggling against some inner demon or pesky prophecy. Employing the Jasmine story-arc from *Angel*, Susanne E. Foster and James B. South use their "'Look What Free Will Has Gotten You': Isolation, Individuality, and Choice in *Angel*" to present a classic philosophical dilemma: human choice may be completely free of constraint, but arbitrary and ultimately meaningless, or it may be meaningful, but ultimately unfree. They argue that the possibility of meaningful and free choice nevertheless remains—in the Whedonverse and for the rest of us—as exemplified near the end of the arc via Angel's loving sacrifice on behalf of Connor's well-being. In "Aiming to Misbehave at the Boundary between the Human and the Machine: The Queer Steampunk Ecology of Joss Whedon's *Firefly* and *Serenity*," Lisa Hager presents a novel (and much underappreciated) way to look at how Whedon tends to juggle various competing ideas in his narratives. She begins by showing us how Joss's unique brand of steampunk in *Firefly* and *Serenity* provides a potential solution to the conflicts between civilization and nature, and man and machine, that have plagued us since at least the Industrial Revolution. Hager argues that by featuring the ship *Serenity* herself as a sort of character in the show, a member of the crew, and a living environment for the crew, Joss is implicitly blurring these artificial distinctions and creating a middle ground in which man and machine can live in harmony. Roger P. Ebertz, in "Shepherd Book, Malcolm Reynolds, and the Dao of *Firefly*," argues that Joss conveys another, but non-Western notion of harmony in *Firefly/Serenity*. Ebertz interprets the interactions on spaceship *Serenity* as a brand of unique community driven by the dynamic of harmonious opposites. In this way, *Firefly* exemplifies the Chinese concepts of yin, yang, and Dao, and, in turn, serves as a depiction of living well. In this way, he closes the circle begun by Baggett: There's no place else to be now that we have found *Serenity*—which the Browncoats have known all along.

The book ends with an appendix that lists all of the episodes from *Buffy the Vampire Slayer, Angel, Firefly,* and *Dollhouse*. We include this because the essay authors refer to many different episodes, and we thought that an episode list would prove helpful in placing the authors' points in context. The appendix ends with a listing of Joss's film credits as either director or screenwriter.

Finally, readers should be made aware of the fact that this volume is laden with examples from *Angel, Firefly, Dr. Horrible,* and *Dollhouse*. This doesn't mean Buffy and the Scoobies are completely absent, of course. However, there already exist various scholarly books about *Buffy* (two quality examples of which are edited by one of our contributing authors). Accordingly, we chose to extend Whedon scholarship by focusing on other narratives. In this way, on the one hand, Whedonites can better appreciate Joss's corpus by examining how certain themes have continued and evolved post–*Buffy the Vampire Slayer;* on the other hand, Whedonites can also learn about themes that have emerged in the later (or other) parts of the Whedonverse, with an eye to better comprehending Joss's corpus overall.

So, what might be *the* philosophy of Joss Whedon? The vastness of the Whedonverse makes daunting any attempted answer. Further, as you can already see, Joss's corpus is diffuse with many different ideas, not all of which are easily reconciled. Nevertheless, Joss seems preoccupied with the question posed by Socrates long ago: "What kind of life should one live?" Socrates believed that persons with any sense at all will grasp the important force of this question (*Gorgias,* 500b). Joss seemingly agrees. The following pages testify to Whedon's constant exploration of the "messiness" of the human condition—the constant balancing act we experience between competing ideas and beliefs about being human.

Joss asks: To what extent may an individual permissibly exercise her freedom to become the kind of person she wishes? His answer seems to be: A great deal, but not to the point of completely losing herself or harming her close friends. Moreover, Joss asks: To what extent should an individual conform to current societal norms and fashions for the sake of fitting in? His answer seems to be: Almost none at all—personal and moral growth of genuine individuals is preferable—but some contrarian behaviors nevertheless remain impermissible, and life completely alone is not preferable. And Joss asks: To what extent may a government, in the name of social stability and safety, permissibly impose its mandates on individual citizens? His answer seems to be: Not much, but life with no government at all isn't really living either.

But at this point, perhaps, we should follow Joss's lead and stop there. That is, we are happy to offer a few initial insights about what to look for in the pages to come, but this must be balanced with our wish to not give too many away. Furthermore, Socrates warned that learning cannot truly occur by simply pouring facts into another's head (*Republic,* 518b). The learner herself must be active and take responsibility for what she knows. Joss believes that "you cannot stop the signal"; if so, then we should not stop looking for it.

Part 1

"You Can't Take the Sky from Me": Freedom and Its Limits

Firefly and Freedom

David Baggett

Take my love, take my land
Take me where I cannot stand
I don't care, I'm still free
You can't take the sky from me
Take me out to the black
Tell them I ain't comin' back
Burn the land and boil the sea
You can't take the sky from me
There's no place I can be
Since I found Serenity
But you can't take the sky from me
—"The Battle of Serenity," theme song of *Firefly*

Written by Joss Whedon and performed by Sonny Rhodes, the theme song of *Firefly* alerts readers to the central role of freedom in this short-lived but brilliant series. The sky represents a place of freedom; after the war is lost and the land is taken, the sky remains as the refuge of freedom. The freedom that the sky represents is primarily a social sort of freedom: liberation from the controlling hand of the Alliance. The result of losing the Unification war was that some, like Mal (Nathan Fillion), along with Zoe (Gina Torres), his trusted partner in the war, largely removed themselves from what they considered a corrupt society. Unwilling to cooperate with wrongful authorities or tyrannical powers, they opted out of the mainstream "civilized" society, refusing to give their tacit assent to its systemic injustices and corrupt rule of law. Having lost his faith in God and government, Mal moved to the periphery of the "society," the outskirts of the solar system—the rim, or outer, planets. Forging a new community on the spaceship *Serenity*, cobbling together a living through various activities, some nefarious in the eyes of the law, Mal and his crew try to remain under the radar screen of the Alliance, even while harboring a couple of fugitives from the law.

The show's mixed genre as a space Western lends itself and adds texture to the premise. Set in the future, the series depicts the characters on *Serenity* fighting for survival on a brutal new frontier and scraping together a living, profoundly distrustful of authority. Whedon came up with the idea for the show after reading Michael Shaara's 1975 Pulitzer Prize–winning *Killer Angels*, a novel about the Battle of Gettysburg. While Whedon wasn't at all enthralled with the Confederacy's defense of slavery—though rights of self-determination (a Confederacy mantra) are thematically important in *Firefly*—it was the idea of the losers in a war that captured his attention.[1] There have been efforts at mixing the genres of science fiction and Westerns before, of course: *Gene Autry and the Phantom Empire, The Adventures of Brisco County, Jr., Star Trek, The Wild Wild West, Battlestar Galactica*, to name a few. Ubiquitous Western vernacular, combinations of fiddles, guitar twangs, and symphonic sounds, various codes of behavior, rugged individualism, revolvers, layers of rustic western dust, muted earth tones, settlers of all kinds, boots and vests and horses, retro Wild West accents, all juxtaposed with holograms and spaceships, give *Firefly* a distinctively space-Western look and sound.[2]

This essay focuses most especially on one particular episode of *Firefly*, probably the most philosophical of them all, "Objects in Space." By Whedon's admission, this episode is his attempt to capture key ideas of the existentialist writings of Jean-Paul Sartre (and of Albert Camus' *Myth of Sisyphus*). Whedon describes Sartre's philosophical fictional work *Nausea* as "the most important book I have ever read." *Nausea* is much more about what might be labeled "metaphysical freedom," freedom internal to each person, than political freedom (from tyranny, for example). The connection between these kinds of freedom isn't always obvious. Sartre, though a firm believer in the autonomy of the individual will, embraced a socialist view of government; whereas other strong believers in individual freedom insist that laissez-faire or free market economies are the most consistent outworking of a strong prior belief in metaphysical freedom. Whedon himself, a social progressive in many respects, has been argued by some to be committed, in his work, to a libertarian understanding of society.[3] This essay won't try settling which economic or political picture is most consistent with existentialist freedom. It will, however, spend some time looking at Whedon's portrayal of Sartre's account of freedom in *Nausea,* the extent to which Whedon affirms existentialist views about choice and value, and the overall adequacy of Sartre's vision.

Nausea

Nausea is a brooding novel written as the journal of Antoine Roquentin, a young historian in the throes of existential angst. Horrified by his own existence and by the vacuity of experiences, he comes to see life as devoid of any inherent significance. He's profoundly cognizant of the transitory nature of life and the unavoidable, encroaching, impending reality of death. The dilemma of the protagonist is not intended by Sartre as a commentary on or to be a function of Roquentin's idiosyncratic, antisocial, and misanthropic personality; rather, his dilemma is supposed to represent the human condition per se, the existential reality we all face, whether we realize it or not. Ordinary objects, events, and places lack any intrinsic meaning or import, so there is no meaning to be discovered, a dominant Sartrean theme, making *Nausea* an almost canonical existentialist text. Sartre considered it his greatest achievement, and it contributed to the body of work for which he was awarded the Nobel Prize for literature in 1964, though he declined the award, declaring it a product of a bourgeois institution.

Encountering the meaninglessness of life and its attendant angst and disorientation, irremediably bored by life, Roquentin feels his freedom threatened: "I am no longer free. I can no longer do what I will."[4] The "sweetish sickness" of nausea colors all he does and afflicts him to the core, depriving him of all his zest and passion for life as he desperately searches for meaning. The darkness pervades every aspect of his life, from his sexual liaisons to his historical research. He comes to see this nausea as the result of a recognition that we are here by sheer accident; that we experience bare existence and imagining anything else is an effort to avoid this fact; that meanings and values are not universal or imposed, but at most invented and freely adopted. Neither the future nor the past exists; only the present. No grand metaphysical theory or cosmic lawgiver exists to make sense of life; what determines reality is our own consciousness and ability to be aware of facts and feelings and sensations. What determines the meanings of our lives is no preexisting pattern or purpose for our being here; rather, we find ourselves existing, need to come to terms with the contingency and reality of that existence, and must forge our own meanings, unconstrained by any larger cosmic guide than our own internal consciousness.

"Objects in Space"

"Objects in Space" is the *Firefly* episode largely inspired by *Nausea*. As Rhonda Wilcox puts it, it is "a story Whedon unquestionably used for spiritual, intellectual, and philosophical exploration—non-Christian existentialism."[5] In the episode, a bounty hunter named Jubal Early (Richard Brooks) comes after River Tam (Summer Glau), a member of Mal's crew.[6] River had been abducted by the Alliance, which then treated her as a means to their corrupt ends, violating her in horrific ways, but in the process making her capture and return to the Alliance a lucrative proposition for an unprincipled bounty hunter like Early. Her experiences also left her disoriented, confused, childlike, dysfunctional, and at times bordering on pathological, with a take on reality unique at best, radically skewed at worst. Her instability and potential danger to the crew, and what to do about it, preoccupy the crew members at the beginning of this episode, but by the end of the episode, River is accepted, at long last, as a full-fledged member of the crew.

Early and River share a distinctive viewpoint: they seem particularly sensitive to and aware of their surroundings. River is privy to the private, unarticulated thoughts of crew members, and both wonder about the meanings and functions of objects. Early considers features of his gun unconnected with its intended function as a weapon, such as its weight and aesthetic features, whereas River exudes a childlike wonder when considering objects. In a crucial scene, a gun appears to her as a harmless object of beauty (a branch, specifically), and she says: "It's just an object. It doesn't mean what you think." She seems aware of its bare existence, unmediated by meanings imposed by considerations of its features or functions. Early, too, has a sense, less innocent though, of the solidity and reality of objects and asks philosophical questions about what imbues objects, events, or places with meaning or significance. And he seems, as Lyle Zynda perspicaciously observes, acutely aware of arbitrariness and incongruities in human life.[7] Early, like Roquentin, seems overwhelmed at times with the absurdity of his surroundings in particular and of life in general, yet he presses on with his ignoble mission.

Consider River's perception of the gun that happens to belong to the character Jayne (Adam Baldwin). Despite that the gun's designer may have intended it to be a weapon, it need not be used as one. It could make a decoration or doorstop or paperweight. The gun is not intrinsically a weapon; it's a bare object whose meaning is malleable. River sees it as an innocent object of beauty. In her subjective experience and conscious apprehension of it, that is indeed how it appears and, in some sense, what it is. Although

Early and River take their unique perspectives in different directions, each seems gripped with existential insights that would make Sartre proud.

In *Nausea,* Roquentin comes to terms with the implications of a godless, meaningless world by feeling empowered. He comes to the existentialist realization that the inherent lack of meaning in the world offers him the chance to create his own meanings by his autonomous expressions of will. Rather than allowing his nausea over the insignificance of life to lead him to undervalue the present, he decides to create what meaning he can by throwing himself into an artistic endeavor and by recognizing that the meanings he constructs and projects are the only meanings he will find. He has to invent them, though, not discover them—a common existentialist refrain.

Mal, too, subsequent to the loss of his faith that the good guys will win or that God will ensure that all will come out well in the end, refuses to quit. He goes on, despite his loss of faith, although he's in a dark place through much of the series and most of the film *Serenity.* It's been suggested that Shepherd Book (Ron Glass), a preacher on board Mal's ship, represents an aspect of Mal's past he lost, namely, his faith. When Book asks to pray before a meal, Mal says it's fine, as long as he doesn't do it out loud. Mal's experience in Serenity Valley made him lose faith in a reliable providence. The problem of evil, we could say, was the undoing of his religious convictions.

As a teenager, having lost his own faith, Whedon was given Sartre's book, which proved so significant because it gave Whedon a way to come to terms with his newfound atheism. Sartre is famous for his atheism, of course, as is Camus (who also influenced Whedon), although not all existentialists have been atheists (Dostoevsky, Kierkegaard, Marcel, and Jaspers, for example).[8] In Sartre's view, it's the absence of any deity that leads to the basic existential reality of our coming to exist first, our meaning and purpose coming later through our volitional choice. Since we aren't created in God's image, according to some prepackaged plan or purpose, there is no meaning to discover for our lives, only meaning to invent through passionate commitment and artistic creation.

Is Whedon an Existentialist?

And this brings us to Whedon himself, although it's with some trepidation we should broach the subject of Whedon's own views and convictions. Whedon is a purveyor of some particularly memorable pieces of popular culture, and his philosophical views are neither altogether transparent nor eminently important. By his own admission, he is neither an intellectual nor a philosopher. As William Irwin writes: "Some literature, for example

Nausea, may be philosophy, and it is theoretically possible that some element of popular culture could be philosophy, but to my knowledge, no instance yet exists. Until and unless someone manages to create a piece of popular culture that is also philosophy (or vice versa), we must limit ourselves to interpretations that give the philosophical significance of popular culture."[9] Even if Irwin is right, though—and plenty of philosophers would disagree with him—he concedes that works of popular culture can be philosophical, from the movies of Woody Allen to those of Alfred Hitchcock; in fact, something of a cottage industry has arisen among philosophers arguing about just how philosophical popular movies and television shows can be. Still, Whedon is usually better at asking than answering the big questions his dramatizations raise. Generally, popular culture should be used as a springboard to consider various philosophical questions rather than as a source of great philosophical insight; nonetheless, with that said, let's go ahead and at least tentatively explore whether Whedon's the existentialist he thinks he is.

Lyle Zynda's excellent piece on "Objects in Space" accentuates the existentialist influences on Whedon's story. A key theme in his analysis is the way objects in this episode are, as described earlier, imbued with meaning rather than possessing meaning on their own. Neither their existence nor their essence is necessary; without value, meaning, or function, there is no reason for a thing to be the way it is. Both Early and River, in very different ways, imbue the objects around them with meanings, either innocent or horrific. The meanings aren't intrinsic to the objects; rather, they're given to the objects by people like us, which in a real sense says something special about the kind of creatures we are. There are some limits to the meanings with which we can imbue objects, but within those limits (which Sartre refers to as their *facticity*), there is always a free choice about how to operate.[10] River sees the gun as a harmless branch; in patent contrast with her innocent, wide-eyed wonder at things, Early, like Roquentin, sees objects as alien and alienating, producing the sort of anguish and dread of which existentialists speak. For if value is conferred, then objects in and of themselves lack such value, and this can be profoundly disorienting and disillusioning. Existentialists often attempt to move on from there, insisting that on the other side of the disorientation and disillusionment is a range of opportunities to forge meaning and find significance in bold, creative ways. Early, however, does not seem to have found a very satisfactory way of processing his insights, whereas River is beginning to be able to do so much more effectively.

An intriguing question at this juncture, however, is what the basis is for deeming River's creative impositions of form and efforts at finding meaning objectively better than Early's. Clearly (per his DVD commentary), Whedon sees River's as the better response, but does existentialism contain sufficient resources to undergird such a value judgment? Existentialists may wish to insist that it does, but consider the role of volition, or choice, in their theory. If our valuations are based on free choice, doesn't this imply that they are arbitrary—not in the sense of an individual lacking reasons for her personal preference, but in the sense of no objective fact of the matter existing? If our choices aren't merely what we *happen to value*, but determinative of what *is valuable*, isn't there an ineliminable arbitrariness about our valuations? How can an existentialist avoid this conclusion? This is often where an appeal to an absolute standard, like God, is thought to be useful, but even here the appeal is thought susceptible to an analogous challenge. The "Euthyphro Dilemma," harkening back to an early Socratic dialogue, asks if God values something because it's valuable or if it's valuable because God values it. If the former, then the value of the thing is independent of God's valuation; if the latter, then anything at all could be valuable just because God chooses to value it, leading to all sorts of arbitrariness and vacuity objections and to depictions of God as a capricious tyrant. So when the will is thought to function at the foundation of our valuations, arbitrariness seems to result. This is a potential problem as much for the existentialist as for the divine command theorist.

But Whedon himself, and by extension Mal, most assuredly doesn't seem to think of morality as purely subjective. Examples are legion, but consider the following: despite that Mal has lost much of his idealism and that his name, in Latin, means "bad," he retains great decency, recognizing that people aren't property, that it's morally wrong to take advantage of an innocent person who's vulnerable to exploitation or harm. He rejects the cynical moral perspective that everyone uses everyone, adamantly opposes slavery, does some things just because they're the right thing to do, and demonstrates loyalty to and love for his crew.[11] Similar conclusions can be made about Whedon, whose work is replete with the value of love and friendship, especially when these ties are bonded by choice and camaraderie (per *Buffy* and *Angel*).

Now, one could venture to offer an existentialist analysis of Mal's or Whedon's ethics, suggesting that this set of values has been freely chosen and, once chosen, has become in some sense binding and authoritative for them (merely because they continue to choose them). But this analysis strains credulity; the much better explanation is that such recognition of objective values is beyond what an existentialist ethic can alone justify. Consider the sheriff's words in "Train Job": "These are tough times. A man might get a job, he may not look too close what that job is. But a man learns all the details of a situation like ours, then he has a choice." To which Mal replies, "I don't believe he does." The most straightforward explanation of such a sentiment is that Mal is a firm believer that it would have been wrong, and not his moral prerogative, to refrain from returning the lifesaving drugs to the people at Paradiso, despite the potential cost to himself and his crew. Mal, like Whedon, may have lost his faith, but not his humanity, basic decency, and essential moral compass. Perhaps this is why Badger still sees in Mal not a captain of a spaceship but a duty-bound sergeant. Just beneath the surface is the old sergeant, with his homilies and stories, glory and honor. In the desperation of his circumstances, his ethics have a pragmatism about them at times, but even here he's consistent with some of the most memorable of characters from Westerns.[12] In refusing to lose himself after losing his faith (the way the Operative does in the movie *Serenity*), Mal does echo an existentialist motif, namely, that after the disillusionment of loss comes liberation and the chance for new meanings; but Mal's moral paradigm also contains leftover remnants from earlier in his life, including the recognition of objective moral truth.

If Whedon, like Mal, retains convictions about promoting justice or defending the helpless, what can we make of his commentary on "Objects in Space"? Before exploring this question, consider another way in which Whedon departs from existentialism. When Roquentin in *Nausea* comes across existing things, he feels nausea; when Whedon, as a teenager reading *Nausea*, becomes aware of the fact of existence, he feels exhilaration. Something about the objective existence of things, despite the ways in which we imbue them with meaning ourselves, enthralled him. This led Agnes Curry, with perhaps tongue partially in cheek, to ask if Whedon is becoming a Thomist. It's Aquinas who thought of existence as the central piece of a thing, and ultimately God as the "pure act of existence, and finite creatures as following from God's unlimited actuality."[13] Whedon, in his commentary, says that "what makes objects so extraordinary is the fact of them, the very fact of them. It's mind-boggling. I believe that whether you have faith or not—to think about consciousness, our ability to understand that these things exist and to think about the fact of existence." If Whedon isn't becoming a Thomist, he's at least sounding awfully non-Sartrean in his enthralled recognition of the fact of existence. For Whedon, existing things have a rapture to them; apprehending them for him was an epiphany, not a crisis, as Curry points out. Again, Whedon, though moved by Sartre, goes in a rather different direction.

So what do we say of Whedon's payment of homage to Sartre? Plato argued that artists don't know their own craft very well, especially when (or perhaps how) they are doing it. So what Whedon believes he is doing and what he is actually doing need not be the same thing. Then again, though, Whedon is a highly intelligent fellow. Perhaps he was taken with the idea of being an existentialist but doesn't really believe in it thoroughly. On this account, "Objects in Space" is simply a return to the ideas by which he was initially mesmerized but now no longer fully accepts. In the end, perhaps Whedon is an existentialist about some things but not others; and demands for consistency, as mentioned earlier, are unrealistic.[14] Or maybe existentialist thinking is more tempting when it comes to physical objects (human artifacts especially), but is much less tempting when it comes to natural kinds and value theory. So perhaps some physical objects are just that: objects; then we place meaning, value, and purpose on them. Perhaps human artifacts, unlike natural kinds, have no essences after all. In other words, tables and chairs, which are human constructions, may not inherently possess essential properties the way a molecule of water possesses the property of being H_2O, which defines it in some stronger sense.[15] So even if chairs and tables (or chair- and table-shaped collections of atoms) don't exist in the same sense as an atom of gold, it doesn't follow that neither natural kinds (like the atoms making up those chairs and tables) nor human persons feature essences, defining properties of their identity. In the case of human beings, their identity or essential nature, if they possess one, would not be reducible to their atoms arranged body-wise (unlike a chair, for example, which arguably is just a collection of atoms arranged chair-wise), but something above and beyond that. Aristotle, for example, would be inclined to understand their nature "teleologically," according to their natural telos or aim or goal: their nature, for example, as rational creatures. But Sartre, of course, was famous for denying that human beings had essences; rather, our choices alone define us. This issue of essences arises again in the next section.

A final possibility is that Whedon, when it comes to moral values, re-mains, like most of us, a work in progress. Like some of his most memorable characters, he seems acutely aware of the gap between the way things are and how they ought to be, but somewhat at a loss as to what to do about it. There is in him a compelling tension that often plays out on the screen, between idealism and pragmatism, between light and darkness, between right and wrong. When he creates a sinister character as loveable as Dr. Horrible—with designs on using his freeze ray to stop and then rule the world with the girl with whom he can't quite muster the courage to make an "audible connection"—or a character as conflicted and tortured yet winsome as Mal, or when he paints a beautifully inverted picture of a Companion blessing a minister, it shows how goodness and badness, saint and sinner, are often juxtaposed. It's not just the white and black hats; good and evil run through each of our hearts. And rather than seeking to resolve the tension or eliminate it altogether, he lets the tension do its work. If a foolish consistency is the hobgoblin of small minds, Whedon's mind is huge. A hero can have feet of clay; the bad guy can have charming and attractive features. Appearances can be deceiving; the prostitute can have a heart of gold, and the hero can be egomaniacal. This is far from a dogmatic insistence on seeing everything in stark black-and-white; life's often just too messy for that. This doesn't deny objective morality, but it does complexify the task of sorting it all out and makes pat answers unacceptable and a lack of epistemic humility a vice.

Freedom and Value: Human and Divine

So freedom, on an existentialist analysis, is important. It's our choice how we choose to interpret the situations in which we find ourselves, how to react to those situations, whether to remain in those situations, whom to go to for advice. But as important and legitimate as all of these existentialist points may be regarding freedom, freedom seems to have its limits in what it can accomplish. Although our choices may be able to imbue a chair or gun with meaning, they can't volitionally control whether or not atoms have essential features, human beings have a telos, or, extending the discussion to moral value, whether or not cruelty or torture are right. Choice can't make just anything at all right or acceptable or valuable. However, if Zynda is right, existentialists like Sartre indeed hold that value is merely based on free choice; therefore, value must be arbitrary on their analysis. Generalizing the point about imposing value and imbuing meaning, if value per se is merely a function of free choice, it would be our volitional prerogative and power to make something, within the general confines of facticity, mean anything at all or to make nearly any action morally right or wrong. To see more clearly why, let's delve a bit more into what freedom really is. On an existentialist analysis, it's a basic fact of our existence, something about which we can be surer than just about anything else. It's autonomy of will, something from which we can't escape, something that defines us, and something for which we are responsible.[16] Perhaps most ultimately, it's the locus of value.

But *is* this the only or best way to make sense of the relationship between value and freedom? Just because we *can* make a decision does not mean we're morally *permitted* or *obligated* to do so; once more, this is one of the notorious limitations of an existentialist analysis. Likewise, just because we have the technology to do something doesn't mean it ought to be done. Technological mastery too easily becomes our dominant ethos and exemplar of truth, shaping our understanding of nature, society, and the human being. The Alliance chose to cut into River's brain time and again, but their ability to do so didn't make their actions right. As we saw earlier with the Euthyphro Dilemma, it would seem that even if God himself were to choose to command child torture for fun, it wouldn't make child torture right. To think otherwise is to invest in free will more importance and significance than it's rightly thought to possess. The mistake of a certain kind of existentialist is the same as that of a certain divine command theorist: investing in volitional choice a sort of valuational authority it doesn't have.

Interestingly, though, this notion of freedom as the capacity to do or value practically just about anything at all is a relatively modern notion of freedom. There's a much more ancient understanding of freedom that paints a very different kind of picture. But harkening back to it requires a departure from both an ultravoluntarist divine command theory where divine freedom is concerned, and from an understanding of existentialism predicated on a modern conception of radical freedom. On a "premodern" conception (and certain modern conceptions) of freedom, some moral choices aren't really choices, but "no-brainers" that are sufficiently obvious to all rational persons. A person's doubts about the wrongness of child torture, for example, do not raise questions about the propriety of child torture as much as they raise concerns about such a person's sanity. For human nature, a deliverance of reason, or our natural telos (goal or end), makes it clear what the moral path requires. A wholesale departure from this understanding of freedom-as-acting-in-accord-with-our-essence raises a serious question about the trajectory of society. Once a society loses its convictions in objective moral truth and in free will constrained by who we are as human beings, what guarantee or even reason to believe is there that feeding the poor, empowering the disenfranchised, or lifting up the downtrodden will continue to be values a society extols? Just because individuals can and will continue doing so is no guarantee to suggest that societies as a whole will, for if the choice to do so is just a personal (existential) preference reflective of nothing more ultimate, then it lacks authority. Although it takes time, that loss of moral authority seeps into the fabric and plausibility structures of a culture. It hasn't always been an accepted fact that all people are equal; many ancients rejected such a notion, and more recently Nietzsche was vociferous in his opposition to it. For a society deeply imbibing notions of freedom as liberation from constraint and coercion, while resting on the largely nonteleological moral metaphysics of modernity and jettisoning convictions about a transcendent source of the good to which the will is naturally drawn, what can be said to be inherently irrational or abominable?

The point here isn't to be alarmist, but to raise a genuine question: What *is* a proper locus of value? It's not uncommon nowadays to hear a sector of the population rail against old-fashioned religious conviction as the source of all manner of evil, and surely plenty of evil deeds have been done in God's name. *Serenity* features such a character in the Operative (though Whedon's epistemic humility makes him far from a Richard Dawkins). But isn't it an equally interesting question what range of malicious deeds are likely to result from a rejection of traditional moral foundations, a loss of conviction about human teleology, and a view of freedom that isn't predicated on the natural ends toward which rational people are drawn? What will spare us from the logic of bioethicists who deem Down syndrome babies or congenitally deformed infants as unfit for living, or social engineers harboring hopes for a resurgence of a eugenics movement, the sorts of horrific visions we could easily conceive the Alliance entertaining?[17] Some followers of Nietzsche, arguably, would chalk up resistance to such ideas to a "slave morality" informed by the Christian myth; Nietzsche rightly saw that a rejection of that sort of transcendently grounded understanding of morality would eventually have big implications. He would say that Mal and Whedon haven't rejected enough of their past; they should give up fighting for the weak and helpless and realize that the evolution of mankind is leaving such unfortunates behind.[18]

Ultimately, again, questions about what to do with all this are the kind Whedon is good at raising. What he, like all of us, needs to do is set about trying to take such questions with dreadful seriousness. If we have reason to think that human beings have a nature or essence or teleology after all, then it would seem that such a thing should inform our understanding of and bolster our convictions in objective morality. If God exists and has a stable nature or character—like perfect love on the classical monotheistic model—then those who think that God provides the objective foundation of morality shouldn't fear the Euthyphro Dilemma.[19] For God, as God, neither would nor could command the torture of kids for fun because it would be contrary to his nature. He could no more issue such a command than decide not to exist. And if God has such a perfect nature, or if human beings have a stable nature that defines what it means to be human after all, or both, then the existentialist account of freedom seems inadequate. For any real moral constraints on us would not be objectionable limitations on us, but, instead, ways in which to realize our highest potential.

Some philosophers, from Stoics to Kantians, would argue that moral truth in general or the essential equality and dignity of persons in particular (as encapsulated in the Universal Declaration of Human Rights, for example) is sufficiently obvious that there's little cause for concern about our society losing such convictions anytime soon. But ideas have a history and a power to them, and it's tempting to attribute to, say, intuition or some other transparent moral apprehension what, in fact, is a recognition that came about only after a protracted evolution of moral thought that included seminal, transformative ethical paradigm shifts along the way. With the rejection of a metanarrative postulating a transcendent source of moral authority, and the resultant loss of conviction in human teleology, it's not altogether clear that the modern existentialist-inspired conception of freedom will prove able either to sustain itself or to provide the bulwark against moral abuses and tyrannies that some think it will. And it's certainly far from clear that Mal's final words in *Serenity* about the primacy of love will win the day. Even if Joss *does* become a Thomist.

Notes

Thanks to Dean Kowalski, Mark Foreman, and Stephanie Deacon for helpful comments on an earlier draft of this essay, and special thanks to Mark for introducing me to *Firefly* and to Stephanie for the *Firefly* and *Dr. Horrible* marathons.

1. As Evelyn Vaughn notes: "Remember how often the show is called a space Western? What some people prefer not to recognize about the Western genre, whether in episodes of *Gunsmoke* or *The Lone Ranger*, is that the majority of its archetypes hail from the Old South, the losing side of the Civil War, as surely as do Mal and Zoe" (see Vaughn, "The Bonnie Brown Flag," in *Serenity Found: More Unauthorized Essays on Joss Whedon's* Firefly *Universe*, ed. Jane Espenson, with Leah Wilson [Dallas: BenBella Books, 2007], 190–91). Whedon makes clear his negative attitude toward slavery in "Our Mrs. Reynolds" and even more explicitly in "Shindig" (see ibid.).

2. Fans of Whedon know that he relishes mixing genres: noir and detective stories; horror and teenage-girl-coming-of-age stories; and now this. At one point when he wanted to mix noir elements with Westerns in *Serenity*, he found precedent for such a blend in *Pursued*, *The Furies*, and *Johnny Guitar*.

3. See P. Gardner Goldsmith, "Freedom in an Unfree World," in *Serenity Found*, 55–65.

4. Jean-Paul Sartre, *Nausea* (New York: New Directions, 2007), 9.

5. Rhonda V. Wilcox, "I Do Not Hold to That: Joss Whedon and Original Sin," in *Investigating* Firefly *and* Serenity: *Science Fiction on the Frontier*, ed. Rhonda V. Wilcox and Tanya R. Cochran (New York: Tauris, 2008), 158.

6. Jubal Early, in fact, was a Confederate soldier who also happens to be an ancestor of Nathan Fillion.

7. Lyle Zynda, "We're All Just Floating in Space," in *Finding Serenity: Anti-heroes, Lost Shepherds, and Space Hookers in Joss Whedon's* Firefly, ed. Jane Espenson (Dallas: BenBella, 2004), 91.

8. An older but useful book about existentialism and religion is David E. Roberts's *Existentialism and Religious Belief* (New York: Oxford University Press, 1959).

9. William Irwin and Jorge J. E. Gracia, *Philosophy and the Interpretation of Pop Culture* (New York: Rowman and Littlefield, 2007), 56.

10. Recall again the series' theme song: Mal can't do much about powerful entities "burning the land" or "boiling the sea," but what he chooses to do about them and his powerlessness regarding them is not beyond him; in this respect, he is still free.

11. Relevant episodes demonstrating such traits of Mal's include "Heart of Gold," "Shindig," "Our Mrs. Reynolds," and "The Train Job."

12. As Eric Greene writes: "It is more accurate to say [Mal] believed in nothing that was abstract, only in what was immediate. Like many a pragmatic hero in the American Western, Mal is compelled almost exclusively by practical considerations, immediate survival needs, and personal loyalties. Mal is primarily instinctual rather than ideological" (Greene, "The Good Book," in *Serenity Found*, 83).

13. Agnes B. Curry, "Is Joss Becoming a Thomist?" http://slayageonline.com/essays/slayage16/Curry.htm.

14. Even Sartre himself arguably couldn't be a fully consistent existentialist because his view seemingly entails that it is bad or wrong to live in bad faith.

15. Although this is an interesting and provocative idea, reminiscent in certain respects of Trenton Merricks's intriguing denial of the existence of things like chairs (see his *Objects and Persons* [New York: Oxford University Press, 2003]), existentialists may be committing a modal mistake here, spuriously inferring from the contingency of objects their lack of essential properties.

16. An interesting side note: In much of the current philosophical literature on free will, the biggest challenge to it is scientific materialism. Existentialists are often the ones most vocal in assigning greater primacy to the subjective sense of freedom than to what seems a deliverance of a naturalistic worldview according to which we're complicated organic machines invariably determined to do all we do. In "Free Will in a Deterministic Whedonverse," Thomas Flanson embraces the view that the dominant metaphysical view in Whedon's fictional worlds is a deterministic one. In support of this, he adduces psychological evidence for determinism, the viability of prophecies in Whedon's fictional worlds (like *Buffy* and *Angel*), and effective predictions (in *Firefly*, such as when Mal predicts Saffron's betrayal and the like). One could respond to Flanson by pointing to the enduring metaphysical challenges in answering philosophical questions about free will that science alone seems ill-equipped to answer; to the potential consistency of prophecies and libertarian free will (for an informed and accessible recent analysis of this, see Dean Kowalski's "*Minority Report,* Molinism, and the Viability of Precrime," in his edited volume *Steven Spielberg and Philosophy: We're Gonna Need a Bigger Book* [Lexington: University Press of Kentucky, 2008], 227–47); and to the fact that the truth of the proposition "if we are determined, then predictions of human behavior are viable" doesn't entail that "if predictions of human behavior are viable, then we are determined" (see Flanson's essay in *The Psychology of Joss Whedon: An Unauthorized Exploration of Buffy, Angel, and Firefly*, ed. Joy Davidson [Dallas: BenBella, 2007], 35–49). (Whether

Joss must be interpreted as a determinist remains to be seen, however, and probably requires a separate essay.)

17. A real-life, particularly apt illustration of a governmentally imposed effort aimed at making people better through morally dubious, even hideous, technology is the eugenics movement of the nineteenth and twentieth centuries. Sir Francis Galton coined the term "eugenics" in 1883, but intellectual precursors of the movement go back further—even Plato thought that reproduction should be monitored and controlled by the state. In the name of enhancing the procreation of the genetically advantaged, compulsory sterilization of those deemed inferior was thought justified. In the United States, Woodrow Wilson supported eugenics and, in 1907, helped to make Indiana the first of more than thirty states to adopt legislation aimed at compulsory sterilization of certain individuals. Hitler's infamous efforts to maintain a "pure" German race, killing tens of thousands of the institutionalized disabled while rewarding "Aryan" women who had large numbers of children, and engaging in mass genocidal practices toward the Jews—whom he considered inferior morally, spiritually, artistically, and physically—are perhaps the best-known atrocities arising from this perverse mentality.

18. In the *Dollhouse* series, in the episode "Omega," Joss rejects a Nietzschean type of nihilism by having Echo refuse to "transcend" with Alpha. This only furthers the argument that Joss is not a nihilist about ethics and value. There are objective standards insofar as slavery or preying on the innocent is wrong.

19. Jerry Walls and I give a much more thorough treatment of the Euthyphro Dilemma in our *Good God: The Theistic Foundations of Morality* (New York: Oxford University Press, 2011), esp. chap. 2.

"Just Get Us a Little Further"

Liberty and the Frontier in *Firefly* and *Serenity*

Amy H. Sturgis

In July 2007, I had the pleasure of lecturing to a select international group of outstanding graduate students in the arts at a summer seminar sponsored by the Institute for Humane Studies and held on the campus of the University of California, Los Angeles. The seminar was titled "Cinematic and Literary Traditions of Liberty." Much to my delight, my first presentation directly followed an appearance by Tim Minear, the executive producer of and a writer for *Firefly*. Minear spoke about his career, most notably his work on *Firefly*, before showing and providing commentary on one of the episodes he wrote for the series, "Out of Gas." I followed with a talk on the tradition of frontier literature from Frederick Jackson Turner's "frontier thesis" idea through Western fiction and science fiction, concluding with its contemporary incarnation in the genre-crossing cinematic texts of *Firefly* and *Serenity*.

"Tends to Gum up the Works": Intruding on Personal Liberties

One of Minear's comments seemed of particular relevance to my own interests. He noted that "Out of Gas"—an episode that serves both to underscore the love story between Captain Malcolm Reynolds (Nathan Fillion) and *Serenity* and to provide the tales of how Wash (Alan Tudyk), Kaylee (Jewel Staite), Inara (Morena Baccarin), and Jayne (Adam Baldwin) first came to the Firefly-class ship—includes a scene of which he is particularly proud, one that offers, in his words, the "most libertarian" moments of the episode. The scene uses a metaphor to suggest Minear's message about individual liberty and governments' tendencies to impede it. Young Kaylee, on board *Serenity* for the first time, repairs the engine by solving a reg couple problem that had eluded the ship's official (and soon to be replaced) engineer, Bester (Dax Griffin). As Kaylee removes the offending part, she explains: "Your reg couple's bad. . . . Don't really serve much of a purpose anyway. Just tends to gum up the works when it gets tacked. . . . So I figure, why even have it?"

If gumming up the works represents obstructing an individual's freedom, it follows that the works themselves—the other parts of the engine—represent liberty. In "Out of Gas," Minear implies that such liberty is easy to take for granted if one possesses it, and its true value may only be apparent when one loses it. Thus, when the captain of the salvage ship (Steven Flynn) dismissively tells Mal that the engine's catalyzer is a "nothing part," Mal responds: "It's nothing til you don't got one. Then it appears to be everything." In fact, Mal knows that without the proper functioning of the works, "we don't breathe." Through his script, Minear seems to say that liberty is as precious and necessary for individuals as air.

The reg couple metaphor subtly echoes Mal's sentiments in the Joss Whedon–penned pilot episode, "Serenity," when Mal says: "That's what governments are for. Get in a man's way." Minear elaborates on this notion when discussing another of the episodes he wrote, "Bushwhacked": "The second half was about civilization becoming *so* civilized that it becomes this collectivist, bureaucratic behemoth that can't get anything done, and it's trying to control you too much."[1]

On *Serenity*, the way to free the engine is for Kaylee to remove the unnecessary component that cannot get anything done on its own and serves only to hamper the proper workings of the other engine parts. In the *Firefly* and *Serenity*-'verse, heroes such as Malcolm Reynolds likewise seek to be liberated from the Alliance authority that obstructs the workings of their daily life and their exercise of individual liberty. Since they cannot throw out the Alliance like a bad reg couple—Mal and Zoe (Gina Torres) tried in the War of Unification, after all, and failed—their only option is to go where Alliance control is weakest: the frontier. The Border and Rim worlds. The black.

As I discuss in the following pages, these ideas mark *Firefly* and *Serenity* as frontier narratives in more ways than one, inheritors of the frontier thesis of the scholar Frederick Jackson Turner as well as the frontier metaphors of science fiction. Moreover, *Serenity*'s crew, and especially her captain, desire a particular kind of individual liberty on the frontier. This conception of freedom is what the philosopher Isaiah Berlin has termed "negative liberty," the desire for noninterference, or freedom from obstacles—in other words, the state of a Firefly-class engine without its reg couple.

"Them as Feel the Need to Be Free": Turner's Frontier Thesis

It is not often that a historian presents a scholarly paper at a professional conference and changes the world. (I am a historian, and I know of what I speak.) At the tender age of thirty-one, however, the University of Wisconsin historian Frederick Jackson Turner managed to do just that. He presented his essay "The Significance of the Frontier in American History" to his colleagues at the American Historical Association's national meeting, which was held during the Chicago World's Fair in 1893, and its ideas soon changed not only academic but also popular perceptions of the United States and its unique character. Even today, more than a century later, scholars who specialize in U.S. and western history often frame their arguments in the context of Turner's famous frontier thesis.

In his paper, Turner suggests that what made the United States different from other nations, including the European countries that colonized its lands before it gained independence, was the experience of the frontier. In Turner's words, "The existence of an area of free land, its continuous recession, and the advance of American settlement westward, explain American development."[2] While recognizing that many factors contributed to the evolution of the United States, Turner argues that the existence of the frontier was the single most important factor influencing the American national character. He claims that the institutions and practices that became synonymous with American identity, from democracy and capitalism to social and geographic mobility, have their roots in the country's long-term experience with the frontier—an experience unique to the United States.

Of the qualities he identifies as indicative of so-called American exceptionalism, one of the most important is what he considers to be the "striking characteristics" of "the American intellect": "That coarseness and strength combined with acuteness and inquisitiveness; that practical, inventive turn of mind, quick to find expedients; that masterful grasp of material things, lacking in the artistic but powerful to effect great ends; that restless, nervous energy; that dominant individualism, working for good and for evil, and withal that buoyancy and exuberance that comes with freedom—these are traits of the frontier, or traits called out elsewhere because of the frontier."[3]

Whether we agree or disagree with the historical accuracy of Turner's assessment, we can see the enduring power of the frontier hero archetype he described as it is imagined and reimagined in popular culture. The Western characters portrayed by actors such as John Wayne and Clint Eastwood have embodied many of these characteristics, as have fictional science fiction heroes such as Han Solo. Perhaps no non-Earth-born character better exemplifies Turner's "American intellect," however, than Captain Malcolm Reynolds.

We know from "Our Mrs. Reynolds" that Mal is a child of the frontier, born on the Rim world of Shadow and raised by his rancher "momma" and "about forty hands." Turner describes the frontier as "the outer edge of the wave—the meeting point between savagery and civilization."[4] In *Serenity*, Mal identifies himself and his crew in such a position: "So here is us, on the raggedy edge." Tim Minear uses similar language to Turner's, explaining that he wrote the episode "Bushwhacked" about "civilization," "savagery," and "how our people [on *Serenity*] inhabit a space between those two extremes."[5]

Mal's colloquial manner of speech, which contrasts sharply, for example, with the educated language used by Inara or Simon (Sean Maher), reflects his coarseness, as does the lack of polish he exhibits in formal society ("Shindig"). His strength is highlighted multiple times, from his survival of the Battle of Serenity Valley ("Serenity") to his endurance despite terrible wounds ("Out of Gas," *Serenity*) and torture ("War Stories"). His "acuteness and inquisitiveness" lead him to outsmart his foes ("Serenity," "Trash") and observe and understand more than others ("Bushwhacked," *Serenity*). His practicality and inventiveness aid him in securing and completing the various jobs, legal and illegal, that support his ship and crew and their life at the "corner of No and Where" ("Objects in Space"). Furthermore, when speaking to Simon in "Serenity," Mal admits to a "restless, nervous energy," promising, "We never stop moving." As long as his ship is "still flying," "it's enough."

At the heart of Mal's character, like those of Turner's "American intellect," are individualism and a love of freedom. He has to live on the frontier of space because it is the only setting in which he can exercise his liberty—or, in his words from "Out of Gas," "live like people." In that episode, he outlines his goals to his first mate, Zoe: "Small crew, them as feel the need to be free. Take jobs as they come—and we'll never be under the heel of nobody ever again. No matter how long the arm of the Alliance might get . . . we'll just get us a little further."

Part of this drive to go "a little further," to be sure, comes from the fact that the Alliance is a creature that craves control. As Zoe points out in "Ariel," the Core planets reflect constant governmental sterility, surveillance, and restriction: "It's spotless, it's got sensors, and when there ain't sensors, there's Feds." The only way to elude such pervasive control is to go under or beyond the proverbial radar.

But another part of this drive comes from the fact that Mal and Zoe were on the losing side of the War of Unification. To them, the Alliance is not simply a bureaucracy run amok, but an occupying enemy force. It is difficult to imagine how they could cope, watching their worlds be remodeled to fit the Alliance agenda, living side by side with those who had vanquished them; after all, Mal seems unable to get through even one Unification Day anniversary without violence.

From the beginning, Joss Whedon modeled his story on the experience of the defeated Confederate soldiers after the U.S. Civil War, many of whom fled to the frontier rather than resume life at home under Union domination. (Thus, in "The Train Job," Mal taunts his former enemies with his variation on a Confederate refrain: "I'm thinking we'll rise again.")[6] Whedon admits that after he read Michael Shaara's Pulitzer Prize–winning Civil War novel *Killer Angels,* he knew the kind of series he wanted to write: "It was about the minutiae of the soldiers' lives. And I wanted to play with that classic notion of the frontier: not the people who made history, but the people history stepped on."[7] Frederick Jackson Turner would say that providing a haven for "the people history stepped on" is one of many ways the frontier has played a central role in U.S. history. And just as the American West provided a "continent-sized safety valve" for former Confederates to escape Union authority and reinvent themselves, so the outskirts of space provide a haven for former (or not-so-former) Browncoats.[8]

If *Firefly* and *Serenity* are Western narratives in the Turnerian sense, it is fitting that in the film *Serenity,* Mal predicts the end of his frontier in terms of fences: "Every year since the war the Alliance pushes further out, fences off another piece of the 'verse. Come a day there won't be room for naughty men like us to slip about at all." In fact, three years prior to Turner's presentation of his influential paper, a U.S. government census report declared the U.S. frontier officially closed. The open West had been filled up by farmers and families, their churches and schools, and, of course, their government. Turner's thesis, then, was less a celebration of the frontier than a eulogy for it. Even in Turner's lifetime, it seemed that the free range was no longer free.

"Crowded in My Sky": The Frontier and Science Fiction

Frederick Jackson Turner looked to the past, to the U.S. West, to see the frontier as an opportunity for liberty. Since then, science fiction authors have used the metaphor of the frontier to consider the story of freedom in the future. The scholar and critic Gary K. Wolfe notes that the fascination of science fiction comes directly from the fascination with the West as "not quite uncharted or even unsettled, but still an arena for the kind of heroic individualism that increasingly seemed to be disappearing in the urbanized and industrialized East. With the closing of the frontier, the popular audience sought promises of yet new areas to explore, and science fiction gained popularity as a kind of literature that not only offered new frontiers but did so without sacrificing the technological idealism that had equally come to characterize industrial America."[9]

Carl Abbot, professor of urban studies and planning at Portland State University, explores the relationship between the U.S. West and science fiction in his *Frontiers Past and Future: Science Fiction and the American West*. Abbot traces the frontier science fiction story back to the pulps of the late nineteenth century. This corresponds, as Wolfe says, to the actual "closing of the frontier" in the United States. It also corresponds roughly to the time in which Turner's "frontier thesis" was gaining popular acclaim and widespread acceptance.

Countless works of science fiction draw a connection between the frontier and freedom. Perhaps the archetypal novel in this vein is Ray Bradbury's *The Martian Chronicles* (1950), which revisits the story of the U.S. West through the metaphor of Mars. Bradbury makes it clear that a primary, if not the primary, force behind the settlement of Mars is Earth people's—specifically Americans'—desire to escape the control of their overweening government and seek individual liberty: "To get away from wars and censorship and statism and conscription and government control of this and that, of art and science!"[10]

In his book, Abbot credits Robert A. Heinlein novels for young readers (the so-called "Heinlein juveniles") with introducing him to and cementing his lasting interest in science fiction. It is appropriate to consider Heinlein—known widely in the genre as the award-winning "Dean of Science Fiction"—because his works repeatedly suggest that the only place one might pursue true liberty is at the margins, the outskirts, the frontier. Many of his juveniles repeat this message. For example, the young hero of *Farmer in the Sky* (1950) becomes a pioneer of Jupiter's moon Ganymede. Despite the intensive labor of cultivating the surface of the moon, he chooses to remain there, where he can pursue his own dreams, rather than return to an Earth of government rationing and want. In achieving the stars (not always through accepted means), the protagonist of *Starman Jones* (1953) escapes an Earth characterized by an oppressive legal caste system in which the professions are closed to all but a fortunate few.

It is Heinlein's adult novel *The Moon Is a Harsh Mistress* (1966), however, that appears most relevant in the context of *Firefly* and *Serenity*. In this work, Heinlein retells the story of the American Revolution, casting the moon in the role of the colonies and the Earth in the role of Great Britain. Heinlein borrows the liberation rhetoric from the American and French Revolutions and gives a self-confessed rational anarchist the role of guiding the conflict and mentoring the rebels. By contrasting the oppressive, narrow-minded, and rigid Earth dwellers with the adaptive, innovative, and liberty-loving "Loonies" of Luna, the lunar colony, Heinlein updates Turner's thesis, suggesting that the frontier creates opportunities for the development of freedom that do not exist in established, entrenched communities.

In the ending of the novel, Heinlein takes this idea one step further: once Luna is independent, its leaders establish a governmental bureaucracy that promises to become as stifling as Earth's. Mannie, one of the surviving heroes of the revolution, already looks to the next frontier as an escape. He notes that "quite a few young cobbers have gone out to Asteroids. Hear about some nice places out there, not too crowded. My word, I'm not even a hundred yet."[11] Bradbury and Heinlein, like Whedon, base their future frontiers on the historical examples of past frontiers. Moreover, Bradbury's characters, and especially Heinlein's, just like Mal and his crew, seem to appreciate that individuals must go into space—and, once there, increasingly farther out to the borders of civilized space, to the frontier—to exercise meaningful liberty.

Mercedes Lackey, herself a prolific author of speculative fiction, questions whether or not Mal and his comrades really do find freedom on the edge of space, however. In "*Serenity* and Bobby McGee: Freedom and the Illusion of Freedom in Joss Whedon's *Firefly*," Lackey claims that if you asked Mal about his freedom, he would explain that he "is absolutely free," that he is "getting away with whatever he wants to." His liberty is an illusion, she asserts, because in truth "his 'freedom' exists only because he and his crew, on the one hand, are too small to bother with, and on the other, provide the Alliance with a service it would otherwise have to pay for."[12] The Alliance's resources are stretched thin after the Pyrrhic victory of the War of Unification, she says, and therefore apprehending Mal and his small crew while they are involved in petty misbehavior represents a waste of precious resources; for that matter, the kind of black market deals with which the captain and his comrades are involved help to cement, not undermine, Alliance control by meeting the needs of settlers on the frontier and discouraging rebellion.

Far be it from me to anticipate Mal's exact answer to any question; I expect it would depend a great deal on who did the asking. He does not, however, act like a man who believes himself at complete liberty. On the contrary, he seems very aware of the many ways in which his choices are limited. Although Badger (Mark A. Sheppard) double-crosses him in "Serenity," Mal chooses to run rather than stand on principle because he feels the Alliance breathing down his neck. As *Serenity* draws close to the heavily surveilled Core planet in "Ariel," his orders reflect his caution: "No one's setting foot on that fancy rock. I don't want anyone leaving the ship. Come to think of it, I don't want anyone looking out the windows. Or talking loud." In "Serenity," it seems that he mourns his loss of freedom when Zoe observes that the Reavers, like Mal and his crew, are "pushing out further every year, too." Mal replies that it is "getting awful crowded in my sky."

Moreover, I am not convinced that the Alliance would pay for the services the *Serenity* crew members provide if they failed to offer them, from the delivery of concentrated foodstuffs ("Serenity") to the sale of wobble-headed geisha dolls ("Trash"). The Alliance does not seem overly bothered about the health of its people on the Border and Rim worlds. Even when its forces are present in Paradiso in "The Train Job," they are unconcerned that vital medication for the locals has been stolen. In fact, when homesteaders are massacred in "Bushwhacked," Mal mocks the idea that the Alliance would care: "Alliance? Right, 'cause they're gonna run right out here lickety-split, make sure these taxpayers are okay." In addition, it is highly unlikely that the small jobs Mal and his kind perform are enough to satisfy the outlying worlds and keep them from rebelling. The ongoing, implied parallel with the U.S. Civil War suggests that it is much more likely that the labor-intensiveness of the settlers' lives, the scarcity of their resources, and the recent memory of the bloody defeat of the Independents are far more powerful factors in their lack of overt rebellion.

Most importantly, though, it seems that the location of Mal's crew is at least as important as its size. Until his final, dramatic gesture in *Serenity,* Mal wishes to evade Alliance attention, and he does this by seeking out the frontier—in Wash's words from "Out of Gas," "without running afoul of any Alliance patrols. Or a single living soul, for that matter." Mal confirms that this is his plan: "Way it should be." He goes to great lengths to avoid any interaction with the Alliance. "Safe" offers an illustration of how deep this wariness runs; despite the fact that Shepherd Book (Ron Glass) is gravely wounded and likely dying, Mal initially rejects the idea of approaching an Alliance cruiser in order to request medical assistance. When he must visit a Core planet or Alliance ship, he is fully cognizant of his peril.

To put it another way, Mal seems to sum up his position in *Serenity:* "I mean to live. I mean for us to live. The Alliance won't have that, so we go where they won't follow." Only on the frontier of space, beyond the long arm of the Alliance, can Mal and his crew pursue the freedom to live their lives as they please.

"I Do Not Hold to That": Isaiah Berlin and Negative Liberty

In his essay "The Birth of Greek Individualism," the political philosopher Isaiah Berlin reminds us of Aristippus of Cyrene, who considered himself to be a perpetual stranger and who, according to Socrates, wished "'neither to rule nor to be ruled.'"[13] Both the archetypal cowboy and spaceman are also strangers wherever they go. But it is Aristippus's desire neither to control others nor to be controlled that most resonates in the character of Malcolm Reynolds. In *Serenity,* the Operative warns Mal that he cannot beat—and, presumably, replace—the Alliance. Mal responds: "I got no need to beat you. I just wanna go my way." Mal does not resist the Alliance because he wishes its power could be in different hands; he resists the Alliance because he believes that no one should wield such power over others.

To understand the kind of freedom Mal and his crew seek, we should turn to Isaiah Berlin and his famous essay "Two Concepts of Liberty," which he first delivered as his inaugural lecture as Chichele Professor of Social and Political Theory at Oxford University in 1958. In this essay, Berlin identifies two distinct kinds of liberty: negative liberty, or noninterference, and positive liberty, or self-realization. To put it another way, negative liberty is being left alone to make your own choices without external constraints. Positive liberty is being empowered, or liberated, to achieve self-mastery, to become a certain kind of person. The two may be characterized as freedom *from* (negative liberty) and freedom *to* (positive liberty).

Through *Firefly* and *Serenity,* and especially through the character of Mal, Joss Whedon and his fellow creators such as Tim Minear appear to articulate a yearning for negative liberty—a yearning for the removal of the metaphorical reg couple from the equally metaphorical engine. Mal does not want people to hinder him from choosing his own direction. Mal's desire to go his own way, of course, does not guarantee an ideal life, or even a safe one. Illness might strike him. A key part of *Serenity* might malfunction. He might misjudge a local market and invest in merchandise that no one wants to buy. None of these possibilities interferes with his negative liberty. As Berlin explains: "You lack political liberty or freedom only if you are prevented from attaining a goal by human beings. Mere incapacity to attain a goal is not a lack of political freedom."[14]

In a 'verse with negative liberty, no equality is assured: some people will be as honest as Kaylee, while others will be as dishonest as Saffron (Christina Hendricks); some will begin life as wealthy as the Tams (Sean Maher and Summer Glau), while others will begin life as poor as the miners on Paradiso; some will inherit thriving cities, while others will inherit unbroken wilderness. Still, Mal seems content to try to build a life on his own—or rather, as he explains in "Our Mrs. Reynolds," with a private association of "people who trust each other, who do for each other and ain't always looking for the advantage. There's good people in the 'verse. Not many, lord knows, but you only need a few."

Since negative liberty makes no guarantees of anything (including choices), some might say that it would set up a world that resembles a Hobbesian nightmare—that is, in which life is "solitary, poor, nasty, brutish, and short."[15] Joss Whedon, however, implies that people are capable of living together in cooperation and community, of exercising individual liberty in moral and meaningful ways. The crew and passengers of *Serenity,* those "people who trust each other," are a case in point. Mal repeatedly proves that, of his own free will, he recognizes a particular standard of ethics to which he holds himself (as when he returns the crates he stole from Paradiso once he realizes they contain much-needed medicine in "The Train Job") and others (as when he refuses to let Jayne return to the crew until the mercenary shows genuine remorse and shame for betraying Simon and River in "Ariel"). Whedon seems to say that, left to their own devices, diverse people have the ability to come together to create family and build cooperative and compassionate lives together—by choice and without coercion.[16]

Mal fought as an Independent in the war, and after his side lost the conflict, he tried to live as independently as he could anyway, along with a company of "them as feel the need to be free." Whedon does more than support Berlin's notion of positive liberty through the poster child of Malcolm Reynolds, however. Whedon also offers a critique of the outcomes of positive liberty. At first blush, the concept of positive liberty seems a good, even noble thing, as it promotes the opportunity for people's lives to begin on a level playing field, determined by their choices and not by external forces—political, economic, or social. But for this to happen, there must be a degree of interference by some in the lives of others in order to create, for example, an equality of conditions for all people.

Here lies the problem. Who, then, gets to interfere, and when? As Berlin explains, this difficulty extends back to the very definition of who we are: "The real self may be conceived of as something wider than the individual (as the term is generally understood), as a social 'whole' of which the individual is an element or aspect: a tribe, a race, a Church, a State, the great society of the living and the dead and the yet unborn."[17] In other words, any institution created to promote positive liberty faces a slippery slope that leads away from the individual and toward the group. Rather than providing the opportunity for you to become the best you possible, then—after all, it would be incredibly difficult to tailor policies to each separate person—it might provide the means to make you the best Christian, or the best Australian, or the best socialist, or the best civilized human being. Those who control the institution control the definition of "best," of course—and control the people who must be made to fit this definition.

Those who wish to create a certain result, no matter how praiseworthy (equality, justice, etc.), face a serious challenge. What if others do not want this same outcome? Berlin shows how the impetus to create "freedom" can in fact lead to tyranny, when some are convinced that they know what is best for others: "Once I take this view, I am in a position to ignore the actual wishes of men or societies, to bully, oppress, torture them in the name, and on behalf, of their 'real' selves, in the secure knowledge that whatever is the true goal of man (happiness, performance of duty, wisdom, a just society, self-fulfillment) must be identical with his freedom—the free choice of his 'true,' albeit often submerged and inarticulate, self."[18] To put it simply, the idea of positive liberty offers a license to those who wish to impose their vision of an ideal world on others for their own good.

Whedon and company present damning indictments of such thinking. Those in power within the Alliance government apparently believe they are doing what is best for everyone, including the Rim and Border worlds that fought kicking and screaming against unification with them. It is clear from the comments of River's teacher (Tamara Taylor) in *Serenity* that she believes the Independents had to be forced to be free, "so everyone can enjoy the comfort and enlightenment of true civilization." River defends the Browncoats and their desire for noninterference, saying, "People don't like to be meddled with." The teacher's response implies that anyone who resists the Alliance's style of civilization simply does not know how to think and should be taught. It is telling that, the next moment, the audience sees the teacher plunging her stylus into River's forehead, before the scene cuts to Alliance scientists plunging very real needles into River's brain. Both moments underscore powerfully the invasive violation that is the result of Alliance "civilization" and its attempts to "teach people how" to think.

Note that this scene is not a criticism of the spirit of true education. It is, however, an indictment against the bully Berlin sees hiding behind the idea of positive liberty, the coercive power that can "ignore the actual wishes of men or societies." The teacher, as a representative of the Alliance agenda, cannot admit that the Independents merely held a contrasting perspective or embraced an alternate vision of the good life. If they disagreed with the Alliance, the only conclusion she can draw is that they are unthinking. The fact that the Independents wanted something different from what the Alliance wanted is proof, in Alliance eyes, that they did not, could not, comprehend what was best for them. If they truly had understood, then they would have chosen for themselves exactly the life that the Alliance has chosen for them. This is what Berlin means when he says that such powers "bully, oppress, torture them [the people] in the name, and on behalf, of their 'real' selves." Whedon, like Berlin, seems to fear how good intentions in this framework easily could lead to very bad ends.

Whedon does not stop there with his implied criticism. In *Serenity,* the Operative (Chiwetel Ejiofor) wishes for a "world without sin," which certainly sounds like a worthy goal. When Mal claims to give it to him at the end of *Serenity,* what he in fact shares is a firsthand account of those good intentions gone devastatingly wrong. The Alliance tried to free the population of Miranda from aggression by forcing G-23 Paxilon Hydroclorate on them through their air supply. The desired effect would have been a case study in positive liberty; the people would have been liberated from aggression and thus freed to realize their more peaceful and harmonious selves. Instead, the unintended effect was the death of most of the population and the transformation of the few survivors into monsters.

Mal does not criticize the means the Alliance uses. The moral of the story, after all, is not simply to avoid G-23 Paxilon Hydroclorate. Instead, Mal criticizes the ends of the Alliance: "They will try again. Maybe on another world, maybe on this very ground, swept clean. A year from now, ten, they'll swing back to the belief that they can make people . . . better. And I do not hold to that." Note that he does not condemn an individual's personal choice to try to make himself or herself better; he condemns the decision of one group to impose their vision of "better" upon others.

The scholars J. Michael Richardson and J. Douglas Rabb assert that Mal's journey from the events of *Firefly* to those of *Serenity* represents a shift in his freedom. In the former, they claim, he is "constantly forced to choose the lesser of two evils," but in the latter, he realizes "a genuine freedom which prevents more evil from entering the world."[19] Certainly Mal does grow as a character from the episode "Serenity" to the film *Serenity,* but this development need not appear as drastic as the shift painted by Richardson and Rabb. If we view Mal's actions and choices through the lens of Berlin's two concepts of liberty, they seem more consistent—and so, too, does his understanding and experience of freedom.

Mal desires negative liberty, and he seeks it when he can on the frontier. He understands that pursuing positive liberty, as the Alliance does, opens the door for some to make decisions on behalf of others. For Mal, pursuing his own goals and resisting actively those who wish to impose theirs on him or others constitute a choice for true freedom. He repeatedly proves willing to accept the ramifications of his decisions in *Firefly*; in *Serenity*, he demands that those in the Alliance face the repercussions of theirs.

"Out to the Black": Final Thoughts

In his "Two Concepts of Liberty," Isaiah Berlin sums up the difference between those who seek negative liberty and those who seek positive liberty: "The former want to curb authority as such. The latter want it placed in their own hands."[20] This ably characterizes Captain Malcolm Reynolds and his crew on one side and the representatives of the Alliance on the other, respectively. It is no surprise that Mal's attitude (as embodied in *Firefly*'s theme song) is "Take me out to the black / Tell them I ain't comin' back," because, as science fiction authors such as Robert A. Heinlein have suggested, an individual must go into space—and, once there, increasingly farther out to the borders of civilized space—to have the opportunity for freedom. If we consider space as a metaphor for the U.S. West—and Joss Whedon invites us to do so by drawing heavily on John Ford's classic 1939 Western *Stagecoach* for the form and substance of *Firefly* and *Serenity*—then we can see how Mal's "dominant individualism" reflects Frederick Jackson Turner's understanding of the frontier.[21]

It seems that government meddling is not a problem as easy to solve as a bad reg couple in an engine. When one cannot change the system as it is, however, one can try to escape it. Matthew B. Hill offers a fitting insight into the philosophy of Joss Whedon and his collaborators as it relates to liberty and the frontier: "Mal, River, and the rest of *Serenity*'s crew are, for the most part, too insignificant to defeat the Alliance and restore 'freedom' to the 'Verse; they do not (often) kill the bad guy at high noon, they do not destroy the Death Star or topple the Emperor, they do not wipe out and scalp Comanche kidnappers. . . . Instead, Whedon offers us a world in which the most effective and appropriate response to such trauma is to 'light out for the territory.'"[22]

Notes

Many thanks to Larry M. Hall, Andrew P. Morriss, and Dean A. Kowalski for their helpful comments during the preparation of this essay.

1. Tim Minear, quoted in Abbie Bernstein, Bryan Cairns, Karl Derrick, and Tara Di Lullo, Firefly: *The Official Companion*, vol. 1 (London: Titan, 2006), 84.

2. Frederick Jackson Turner, "The Significance of the Frontier in American His-

tory," in *The Frontier in American History*, by Turner (New York: Holt, Rinehart and Winston, 1965), 1.

3. Ibid., 37.

4. Ibid., 3.

5. Tim Minear, quoted in Bernstein, Cairns, Derrick, and Di Lullo, Firefly: *The Official Companion*, 1:94.

6. For that matter, Whedon explains that he penned the theme song for *Firefly*, "The Ballad of Serenity," "so that it could be sung as a Civil War lament." Joss Whedon, quoted in Abbie Bernstein, Bryan Cairns, Karl Derrick, and Tara Di Lullo, Firefly: *The Official Companion*, vol. 2 (London: Titan, 2007), 33.

7. Quoted in Emily Nussbaum, "Must-See Metaphysics," *New York Times*, September 22, 2002, and June 28, 2010, www.nytimes.com/2002/09/22/magazine/must-see-metaphysics.html?pagewanted=3.

8. Bruce Bethke, "Cut 'Em off at the Horsehead Nebula!" in *Serenity Found: More Unauthorized Essays on Joss Whedon's* Firefly *Universe*, ed. Jane Espenson (Dallas: BenBella, 2007), 182. Interestingly enough, contemporary scholarship suggests that Joss Whedon's 'verse has managed to fill in some of Turner's omissions concerning the subject of the frontier. In her essay "Frederick Jackson Turner Overlooked the Ladies," for example, the historian Glenda Riley claims that Turner's analysis turns a blind eye toward the contribution of women to the story of the West (*Journal of the Early Republic* 13 [Summer 1993]: 216–30). Robert L. Lively, however, finds that the opposite is true for Whedon in "Remapping the Feminine in Joss Whedon's *Firefly*." In his (re)imagined West, Lively explains, Whedon "is attempting to redefine and remap the possible roles of the females he sees in the genre, so that they are actors and active participants in cutting a place for themselves on the frontier" (in *Channeling the Future: Essays on Science Fiction and Fantasy Television*, ed. Lincoln Geraghty [Lanham: Scarecrow Press, 2009], 196). Patricia Nelson Limerick, in her essay "What on Earth Is the New Western History?" highlights Turner's lack of attention to nonwhite peoples in the West, including Native Americans (in *Does the Frontier Experience Make America Exceptional?* ed. Richard W. Eutlain [Boston: Bedford/St. Martin's, 1999], 109–13). Scholars agree that, metaphorically at least, Whedon addresses Native America through the characters of the Reavers, but they disagree about how successfully he does this. Agnes B. Curry asserts that Whedon perpetuates stereotypes of American Indians, while J. Douglas Rabb and J. Michael Richardson argue that he deconstructs and thus subverts them (Curry, "We Don't Say Indian: On the Paradoxical Construction of the Reavers," *Slayage: The Online International Journal of Buffy Studies* 7, no. 1 [25] [Winter 2008], http://slayageonline.com/essays/slayage25/Curry.htm; Rabb and Richardson, "Reavers and Redskins: Creating the Frontier Savage," in *Investigating* Firefly *and* Serenity: *Science Fiction on the Frontier*, ed. Rhonda V. Wilcox and Tanya R. Cochran [New York: Taurus, 2008], 127–38.)

9. Gary K. Wolfe, "Frontiers in Space," in *The Frontier Experience and the American Dream: Essays on American Literature*, ed. David Mogen, Mark Busby, and Paul Bryant (College Station: Texas A&M University Press, 1989), 248. Before Joss Whedon mixed science fiction and Western genres, other works of television and film blended the two

in TV series such as *The Wild Wild West* (1965–1969) and *The Adventures of Brisco County, Jr.* (1993–1994) and in movies such as *Westworld* (1973) and *Outland* (1981).

10. Ray Bradbury, *The Martian Chronicles* (New York: William Morrow, 1997), 42.

11. Robert A. Heinlein, *The Moon Is a Harsh Mistress* (New York: Orb, 1977), 382.

12. Mercedes Lackey, "*Serenity* and Bobby McGee: Freedom and the Illusion of Freedom in Joss Whedon's *Firefly*," in *Finding Serenity: Anti-heroes, Lost Shepherds and Space Hookers in Joss Whedon's* Firefly, ed. Jane Espenson (Dallas: BenBella, 2004), 66.

13. Quoted in Isaiah Berlin, "The Birth of Greek Individualism," in *Liberty: Incorporating Four Essays on Liberty*, by Berlin (Oxford: Oxford University Press, 2002), 312–13.

14. Isaiah Berlin, "Two Concepts of Liberty," in *Liberty: Incorporating Four Essays on Liberty*, by Berlin (Oxford: Oxford University Press, 2002), 169.

15. Thomas Hobbes, *Leviathan* (Oxford: Oxford University Press, 1996), 84.

16. In so doing, Whedon mirrors the findings of scholars of new institutional economics such as Terry L. Anderson and Peter J. Hill, who find that the wild, wild West of the U.S. frontier was not so wild after all, as they turn their attention "from the autonomous strivings of traditional heroes to the cooperative efforts of communities" (Anderson and Hill, *The Not So Wild, Wild West* [Stanford: Stanford University Press, 2004], 9). For a fascinating study of how frontier individuals and communities built effective institutions in the absence of the state, see Andrew P. Morriss, "Hayek and Cowboys: Customary Law in the American West," *NYU Journal of Law & Liberty* 35 (2005), www.law.nyu.edu/ecm_dlv3/groups/public/@nyu_law_website__journals__journal_of_law_and_liberty/documents/documents/ecm_pro_060884.pdf.

17. Berlin, "Two Concepts," 179.

18. Ibid., 180.

19. J. Douglas Rabb and J. Michael Richardson, *The Existential Joss Whedon: Evil in Human Freedom in* Buffy, Angel, Firefly *and* Serenity (Jefferson: McFarland, 2007), 140, 149.

20. Berlin, "Two Concepts," 212.

21. Fred Erisman, "*Stagecoach* in Space," *Extrapolation* 47, no. 2 (2006): 249–58.

22. Matthew B. Hill, "'I Am a Leaf on the Wind': Cultural Trauma and Mobility in Joss Whedon's *Firefly*," *Extrapolation* 50, no. 3 (2009): 502.

The State of Nature and Social Contracts on Spaceship *Serenity*

Joseph J. Foy

In the *Firefly* episode "War Stories," Shepherd Book (Ron Glass) makes the wry observation that "a government is a body of people, usually, notably un-governed." A critique of the unchecked power of the state and a cynical take on the potential for abuses, Book's comment reflects a strain of anti-elitism and anti-institutionalism that can be traced throughout the Whedonverse. Whether providing a critique of covert government and military operations like that of the Initiative in *Buffy the Vampire Slayer,* or of the corporate and legal clout of Wolfram and Hart and its clientele in *Angel,* Joss Whedon con-sistently pits the struggles of the individual resisting illiberal concentration of authority in the hands of state, bureaucratic, and corporate powers. In the space-Western series *Firefly* and its companion film, *Serenity,* Whedon transforms these personal battles into ones with overtly political connota-tions. More than just offering a reactionary critique against the expansion of state power, Whedon suggests that living a quality life of one's choosing is dependent on the proper political ordering of a just society. Moreover, this essay argues that *Firefly/Serenity* serves as a microcosm for Whedon's pervasive commitment to Lockean ideals of government and individualism.

"I Ain't Goin' Anywhere near Reaver Territory"

The political commentary woven throughout *Firefly* is one that focuses on the need for liberal (i.e., individual freedom from external control) protections against a political regime. The Alliance, clearly a bureaucratic-authoritarian model of the state, is also expansive, comprised of the extensive merging of government, market, and security forces. The Alliance embodies Enlight-enment notions of a political system based on objective principles carried out by technocratic experts. In such systems, diversity, individualism, and democracy become hindrances to the state's effectiveness to develop and enforce policy. This is where the authoritarian nature of the Alliance begins to emerge. Captain Malcolm "Mal" Reynolds (Nathan Fillion) and the crew of spaceship *Serenity* embody a rejection of this type of authority, seeking instead to carve out a personal sphere of individual autonomy and empowerment. They discover that this goal is slowly but steadily being threatened by the expansion of Alliance control; they ultimately decide (in *Serenity*) that liberating themselves commits them to the liberation of all.

The frontier narrative that serves as the backdrop for *Firefly* provides insight into the philosophical message Whedon delivers throughout. The Core planets, Sihnon and Londinium, are highly developed socially, politically, and economically, as are the more central planets like Ariel. Here the Alliance has established full administrative control, providing order and stability. Farther out in the system, planets are much less developed, and struggles for survival among various colonies are marked by greed, corruption, and lawlessness, not unlike the American frontier during the early days of westward expansion. This gradual distancing from civilization in the "Outer Rim" planets calls to mind the often-used term "state of nature," a thought experiment designed to demonstrate the conditions of human existence outside of government. Theorists who invoke this hypothetical situation do so in an attempt to understand why people would rationally accept a common political authority—perhaps even one like the Alliance.

References to the "state of nature" in *Firefly* call to mind the writings of one thinker in particular, Thomas Hobbes. In *The Leviathan,* Hobbes describes life in the state of nature as one of general equality in terms of personal abilities; although some individuals might be physically stronger and others more wily or cunning, when taken together, these differences are not considerable. The result is everyone fending for themselves and their own interests, resulting in a state of perpetual conflict, "a war . . . of every man, against every man." In such a state there is no space for the development of industry, culture, education, arts, letters, or of a peaceful society—no opportunity for a quality life. Humanity would thus abandon the leisurely pursuits of the mind, property, or comfort, and commit entirely to the competition for dominion over each other. Without a common power to deter our selfish impulses, competition results in violent clashes, making life in such a state "solitary, poor, nasty, brutish, and short."

Whedon provides a particularly vivid depiction of a Hobbesian state of nature—and why it ought to be avoided—through a group of humans known as "Reavers." Completely removed from the rule of the dominant social and political order, Reavers live like savages, nightmarishly symbolizing the most horrific potential of humanity. In the pilot episode "Serenity," Zoe (Gina Torres) describes to Simon (Sean Maher) what to expect from a Reaver attack: "If they take the ship, they'll rape us to death, eat our flesh and sew our skin into their clothing. And if we're very, very lucky, they'll do it in that order." Absent an authority strong enough to deter them, the Reavers, stripped of any sense of humanity, engage in perpetual war against anyone they encounter. In "Bushwhacked," Shepherd Book claims that Reavers are just men who have been outside society far too long. Mal disagrees, however, arguing that "Reavers ain't men. Or they forgot how to be. Now they're just . . . nothing. They got out to the place of nothing. And that's what they became."[1]

The Reavers are admittedly an extreme example. Nevertheless, life in the Outer Rim remains otherwise dangerous. In "Serenity," the crew tries to sell illegally salvaged goods to Patience (Bonnie Bartlett), the de facto head of a settlement colony on Whitefall moon, who once shot Mal over "a legitimate conflict of interests." Patience and her gang ambush the crew, fully intending to take the goods without paying. Mal, anticipating her treachery, deployed Jayne (Adam Baldwin) for remote cover fire, which helps him and Zoe fight off the ambush. It is only through strength, skill, and cunning—traits they must utilize throughout the series—that Mal and his crew receive their payment, symbolizing the lawlessness of the largely ungoverned frontier.

Whedon makes clear that the selfish nature of human beings—be it savage or merely greedy—makes ungoverned existence tenuous. Perhaps (contra Hobbes) some may be inclined to act ethically. Mal may be a criminal by the legal standards imposed by the Alliance, but he still attempts to live by an ethical code in which he treats others with mutual respect (as is implicit in his comments to Simon at the end of "Serenity"). Whedon invariably portrays Mal's Alliance-defined "criminal" activities as justified acts of disobedience in the face of unjust hierarchies of authority. Mal stops short of harming the innocent (in "The Train Job," he returns the stolen medicine to the people of Paradiso), while the actions of the other men are done for personal gain regardless of the cost to others.[2] Unfortunately, Mal seems to be the exception: the 'verse is replete with the likes of the nefarious crime-lord Adelei Niska (Michael Fairman), ruthless con-artists like Saffron (Christina Hendricks), petty smugglers like Tracey Smith (Jonathan M. Woodward), self-indulgent and exploitive land barons like Ranse Burgess (Fredric Lane) and Magistrate Higgins (Gregory Itzin), and corrupt officials like Lt. Womack (Richard Burgi). Their self-serving villainy harms others who are forced into perpetual vigilance to guard against them. In this respect, Whedon suggests, as does Hobbes, that some form of common authority is necessary in order to provide order and peace. Absent a political power that has the capacity to suppress the corrosive effects of human nature, life is defined by "continual fear and danger of violent death." Per Hobbes, the stronger the government, the less we must worry for our livelihoods.

"That's What Governments Are For . . ."

On a Hobbesian analysis, established governments like the Alliance are justified in establishing order by any means necessary. In *The Leviathan*, Hobbes defines what he considers to be the rights of sovereign governments, which include the right of the state to have full authority over its subjects. The people living under the authority of such a state have no right to protest, alter, or abolish such a state because to reserve that right would threaten the ability of the ruler to preserve the order for which it was initially established. A right to abolish the state risks casting society back into the state of nature through civil war and a struggle for dominance. We submit to the Leviathan to save us from ourselves; and because we (and more importantly, others) cannot be trusted to act decently, we empower the sovereign to act for us. Thus, once established, this common authority has the right to define all aspects of life within the state. There is no recourse for its subjects to countermand, challenge, change, or cancel its actions. The only liberty a subject rightfully enjoys, therefore, is the ability to act freely in a manner consistent with the power of the sovereign.[3]

Hobbes's assertion of the ultimate authority of the state is predicated on principles of legal positivism, which hold that all laws are crafted by a sovereign government and that there need not be any connection between the law and abstract principles of morality. Hobbes writes: "To this war of every man against every man, this is also consequent; that nothing can be unjust. The notions of right and wrong, justice and injustice have there no place. Where there is no common power, there is no law: where no law, no injustice."[4] So, because Hobbes holds that morality and ethics are defined entirely by the state itself, it becomes nonsensical to argue whether the laws of the state are consistent with notions of justice. The Hobbesian sovereign has the authority to define all aspects of morality, what is socially permissible, and all aspects of spirituality and personal belief. There is no notion of justice external to the state, and as such, subjects are bound by the regulations the sovereign establishes.

Hobbes's notion of a social contract to establish political control is also present in the 'verse. Whereas the Hobbesian contract is an implied agreement between the ruler and the ruled, in *Firefly* it comes in the form of the armistice to end the Unification War between the Browncoat resistance and the Alliance. The signing of this treaty sets the foundational agreement between the state and its citizens. In accordance with the writing of Hobbes, rather than an agreement among the people to form a government for mutual benefit, the terms of this particular contract are between the state and the people submitting to its authority. The Browncoats lost the war and are now forced to submit to the rule of the Alliance.

This insight leads to a Hobbesian critique of Mal and his crew. Once the sovereign power has been established, "he that dissented must now consent with the rest; that is, be contented to avow all the actions he shall do, or else be justly destroyed by the rest."[5] Mal's involvement with the Browncoat resistance in the Unification War was a failed attempt to defy the rule of the Alliance. After the Battle of Serenity Valley, tantamount to the Browncoats' last stand, and the signing of the armistice, the Alliance establishes full control of the system. Mal and the rest of the resistance fighters are forced to submit to the authority of the state. His defiant acts of rebellion in the form of illegal transport of goods (and, in the case of the Tams, people) are violations of the sovereign authority of the state, making Mal and the crew of *Serenity* the real villains, not the Alliance.

"So Me and Mine Gotta Lie Down and Die?"

But, of course, Mal is not Whedon's villain, signaling Joss's philosophical departure from Hobbes. Hobbes and Whedon disagree about what kind of government to empower upon leaving the state of nature. Hobbes advocates a limitless government of unchecked authority to maintain order and peace— nothing less can prevent our return to the hellish state of nature. Citizens can only hope that the state will perform actions aimed at maximizing the happiness of all. Whedon believes this hope is unfounded, as demonstrated by his depiction of the Alliance. Joss's portrayal of it implicitly shows that such an illiberal concentration of power leads to unacceptable tyranny that is destructive to the ends of a good life. It is in this respect that the use of the frontier narrative serves a secondary purpose for deconstructing the philosophical messages within Whedon's series. *Firefly* employs the sci-fi–Western genre pioneered by the original *Star Trek* series. Unlike *Star Trek*, however, which offers a view of the Federation as a benevolent force helping to tame the savage frontier of space, Whedon flips the script in order to critique the expansion of civilization and the threat it poses to the possibility of carving out a space to form a unique sense of personal identity.[6]

Whedon seemingly believes that a state like the Alliance has little regard for the innate value of individual humanity. Individuals are to be contained and controlled rather than nurtured and allowed to autonomously develop. This is illustrated in the "training" of River Tam (Summer Glau). The Alliance recruits River, an extraordinarily gifted student already enrolled in high-level courses in physics, to "the Academy" at the age of fourteen. Over a period of three years, the Alliance prepares her to become an assassin and spy—a path she does not freely choose—using a series of psychological, surgical, and medical treatments meant to enhance her natural gifts. To enhance her latent psychic abilities, Alliance surgeons remove River's amygdala, preventing River from filtering her emotions and altering how she perceives reality. Within months of joining the Academy, she displays signs of deep psychological distress, caused in part by her learning about the Alliance's involvement in performing experiments that lead to a massive holocaust on a settlement planet called Miranda. Doctors at the Academy also use a drug called Delcium to make her dreams more vivid and enhance her nightmares.[7]

In *Serenity,* an exchange between Mal and the state assassin known merely as "the Operative" (Chiwetel Ejiofor) elucidates a broader problem with the Hobbesian perspective. After wiping out the Haven colony, a place Mal and his crew would have gone to seek solace, the Operative confronts Mal: "If your quarry goes to ground, leave no ground to go to. . . . Or did you think none of this was your fault?" Mal responds by saying that he doesn't "murder children," but the Operative responds coldly: "I do. If I have to." The Operative exterminated an entire civilian population, including Shepherd Book, to try to get to the crew of *Serenity* and track down River. For him such action is justified because it serves a perceived state interest to maintain order and authority. If River, a person with psychic capabilities who was let near top-level scientists and government officials, were to reveal what she had learned in the Academy, a revolution would result, casting the population into the chaos of the state of nature. Thus, the Operative deems no action unjust that is designed to preserve the state's ability to maintain order and stability.

Most illuminating of all was the covert development and testing of the gas Pax, designed to suppress emotion and have a calming effect on human populations. Consistent with the Hobbesian principles of the state's role in maintaining order and peace, the Pax would have prevented conflict and violence. However, the testing of the gas on the planet Miranda resulted in a mass holocaust. People exposed to the Pax simply lost concern for anything at all—including taking care of their basic needs—until they wasted away. The use of the Pax resulted in the death of more than 90 percent of the planet's population, leaving only a small fraction whose adverse psychological response to the gas was one of extreme rage and aggression (the first Reavers). The Alliance experimented on its own people, which resulted in mass deaths and the creation of monsters that torment, kill, rape, devour, and destroy. Yet, it is not clear that a Hobbesian view of the state would condemn such actions.

Examples of the oppressive brutality of Alliance rule abound. While the goals and methods of the Alliance are different than those of the Reavers, they are, in reality, as vile and inhumane. Certainly the Alliance may not be as outwardly savage as the cannibalistic Reavers, who wear clothing sewn from the skins of their victims, but no degree of sterilization can remove the injustices heaped upon the civilian populations by the state. What happens to River and the Haven community is unjust, as is the mass slaughter of the people of Miranda through secret testing by the Alliance. Individuals consent to be governed by a state to be freed from such brutality and fear for their lives and livelihood. Because the Hobbesian state permits such activities, it harbors counterintuitive entailments that undermine its possible justification.

"Under the Heel of Nobody Ever Again"

In contrast to a Hobbesian all-powerful state, Whedon (implicitly) gives us spaceship *Serenity*. In this intimate commonwealth, individuals are given personal space to define and seek out the kind of quality life they desire without imposing on others to do the same. *Serenity*, under the leadership of Captain Malcolm Reynolds, calls to mind the social contract theories of John Locke, who advocates all people sharing in an obligation to advance and protect the rights of others. Locke argues for the establishment of a rights-protective regime that would allow all individuals the ability to pursue happiness so long as it did not impede upon the rights of others. Although limits are imposed upon the individual in such a system—meaning that one is not completely free to do whatever she wants whenever she wants to—Locke's view of the state rejects a theory of total unity that imposes an absolutist structure that regulates everyone's life to the same end.

Like Hobbes, Locke bases his theories on a conception of the state of nature. However, unlike Hobbes, Locke believes that in nature, human beings are endowed with inalienable rights, including "life, liberty, health, limb, or goods of another" of which no government, group, or individual may justly deprive them.[8] These rights are prepolitical in that they exist prior to the formation of any kind of social order. However, Locke does not assume that, absent some form of civil authority, everyone would simply conform to the laws of nature. He identifies the possibility of a person who, in "transgressing the law of nature . . . declares himself to live by another rule than that of reason and common equity . . . of men, for their mutual security." Such a person becomes a threat not just in a single instance, but a potential threat to the "whole species, and the peace and safety of it." When such transgressions occur, an individual would be justified in taking action against the offender, but not all individuals would have the strength or ability to execute the warranted response. Yet, even in responding to these transgressions, the actions of the state must conform to the principles of natural rights. As such, Locke provides a direct counter to the legal positivism suggested by Hobbes. Rather than rights being created solely out of, and in conformity with, the rule of the state, the rule of the state must be made to conform to the laws of nature.[9]

Thus, although Locke concedes that citizens have the duty to obey the laws and authority of the state, he rejects the Hobbesian notion that state authority is absolute. Instead, the legitimate authority of the state is derived from the consent of the governed (democracy), which provides the continued possibility of legitimized forms of dissent and difference. If the state begins to close off genuine paths for resistance and reconciliation, it erodes the sanctity of the contract, threatening unjust usurpations of the natural rights of its citizens. In such cases, when the laws of the state do not deserve obedience because they do not conform to the inherent rights of individuals, and when the possibility of correcting such injustice is closed to the individual, then disobedience to civil law might be justified. This recasts the "criminal" actions of Mal and the crew of Serenity as defensible in light of the oppressive nature of the Alliance. They are violating unjust civil laws, but with a commitment to the maintenance of natural rights that are beyond the power of the state to violate. It is particularly revealing that the illegal jobs the crew often takes on involve the theft of food, basic materials, and medical supplies from the Alliance to be delivered to settlement populations in desperate need of the provisions. The Alliance is keeping necessities from its own citizens either intentionally as a means of imposing its will, because of corruption by local officials, or because of the inability of the state to properly distribute these goods. Therefore, the criminal activities become necessary acts of disobedience to serve a higher justice than that afforded by the laws of the state. To that end, Mal and the crew of Serenity demonstrate a commitment to the Lockean principle of noncompliance with unjust laws.[10]

Moreover, even if there were a mechanism to denounce or correct state actions, the incredible power of the Alliance to control the flow of information all but eliminates the possibility of someone doing so. Because the Alliance has essentially removed the existence of Miranda from the collective consciousness of everyone in the system, even if actions to correct the misdeeds of the state were warranted, no one has the information that might motivate them to act. In *Serenity*, River uses the ship computers to show Miranda to Mal, leading Kaylee (Jewel Staite) to ask, "How can it be there's a whole planet called *Miranda* and none of us knowed that?"[11] Mal responds with a story he had heard about Miranda being nothing but an uninhabitable "black rock" because terraforming did not take, which proved to be a false rumor, and Wash (Alan Tudyk) explains that there is no record of it on the Cortex. The power of the state to keep the truth from its people about what really happened on Miranda demonstrates the incredible potential for a state that is able to control all aspects of information and ultimately create a form of reality and a system of belief among its citizens. As Mal notes, "Half of writing history is hiding the truth." And when the truth can be kept from the people by a state with a full monopoly on information, then questions of justice and injustice give way to the false consent to authority manufactured by the all-powerful state. Whedon, for his part, clearly conveys the idea that such state-sanctioned acts should be condemned.

If nonconformity to law does not yield a necessary correction of unreasonable action by the state, citizens under a Lockean conception of the social contract maintain a right to revolution, to cast off the bonds of the unjust state and establish a new, just civil order. This is precisely what Mal does when he risks his own life in a final confrontation with the Operative in an effort to broadcast the Alliance's holocaust on Miranda to the entire 'verse, which would lead to a revolution against the unjust state. Prior to this overt revolutionary overthrow, Mal and his crew opt for establishing their own form of civil government outside the unjust order imposed by the Alliance. On board spaceship *Serenity*, there exists a contract based upon diversity and mutual respect of one another's rights. When those rights are threatened by the actions of some, whether on the ship in moments of conflict between crew members or by people outside of *Serenity*, Mal—who seems to embody the Lockean principles of political justice—and his cohorts are quick to step in and establish an end to the conflict and reassert the rights of each crew member.[12]

The notion that there is a form of social contract among the crew of *Serenity* is exemplified by the exchange between Mal and Simon after the rescue on Jiangyin. Simon expresses surprise that Mal would return for him and his sister given the threat they pose to the entire crew. Mal tells him that he came back for them because they are a part of the crew. Simon starts to argue, knowing that Mal does not even care all that much for the doctor and his mentally unstable sister, and Mal ends the conversation by saying: "You're on my crew. Why are we still talking about this?"

As captain, Mal protects his crew as part of the contract that exists on spaceship *Serenity*. When that contract is violated, Mal serves an important role in punishing transgressions. In "Ariel," when Jayne betrays the Tams for personal profit, Mal holds him in the airlock of the ship and threatens to blast him into the blackness of space. Jayne argues with Mal that his actions had nothing to do with the captain, but Mal disagrees: "You turn on any of my crew, you turn on me! But since that's a concept you can't seem to wrap your head around then you got no place here! You did it to me, Jayne, and that's a fact." Jayne is a member of the crew only insofar as he is willing to abide by the commitment to the common defense and protection of the rights and security of all. When he threatens to endanger others, Mal similarly threatens to terminate the implied contract that affords Jayne protection and membership within the community.[13] This example reveals that the Lockean form of social contract exists among those on board *Serenity*. When crew members remain committed to the rights and protections of each individual, they are each afforded a personal space to live the life that they choose for themselves. When they do not, Mal justly responds to punish the violators.

The Lockean form of social contract that governs life aboard *Serenity* allows for each member of Mal's motley crew—whether they are a preacher like Book, a Companion like Inara (Morena Baccarin), a female engineer trying to redefine femininity like Kaylee, a hired gun like Jayne, an elite and educated professional like Simon, a stalwart soldier and her lighthearted pilot husband like the Washburnes, or a brilliant and talented psychic who suffers severe psychological distress like River—to live and interact and work together. They do not all have to get along, and quite often they don't, but the crew on the spaceship *Serenity* are each given a sphere of autonomous space to define themselves and live the life they want while giving others the space to do the same. Likewise, unlike the imposed order the Alliance forced people like Mal to accept under the terms of armistice, the crew members of Serenity all voluntarily choose their life aboard the ship and could also leave the arrangement at any time.[14]

"Since I Found Serenity"

The unanswered issue in all of this is, How might citizens revolt against a much larger and more powerful authority such as the Alliance? The Brown-coat resistance was an attempt to overthrow the oppressive forces of the state that ended in failure. Are dissenters left with no recourse but a life of crime? Just as Locke notes that in a state of nature not all individuals would have the strength or ability to defend themselves against transgressions of the law of nature, so also is it the case that a revolution—even with just cause—would fail in light of the asymmetrical power of the state versus the people. What recourse do citizens have in such a case?

On one level, Mal's attempt to escape the influence and control of the Alliance reflects another aspect of Locke's political writings. In the *Second Treatise*, Locke argues that when a person reaches the age of legal autonomy, "then he is a free man, at liberty [to choose] what government he will put himself under, what body politic he will unite himself to." If one did not wish to abide by the rule of the commonwealth under which he was born, he could simply sell his property and find a new commonwealth. In a manner of speaking, that's exactly what Mal does when he purchases *Serenity* and hires his crew. With the all-encompassing rule of the Alliance, there is no other commonwealth outside of the jurisdiction of the state, and so they have to create their own. They enter into a new form of commonwealth together aboard the ship, defined by the principles of the Lockean social contract. As suggested by the show's theme, there is no place Mal could be free to be himself and to live the life he desired other than aboard *Serenity*. The expansion of the Alliance farther and farther into the Outer Rim, however, begins to close off the possibility of Mal's form of personalized resistance. As Mal notes in *Serenity:* "Come a day there won't be room for naughty men like us to slip about at all. This job goes south, there well may not be another. So here is us, on the raggedy edge."

Once the presence of the Alliance begins to threaten even the possibility of escape aboard *Serenity*, Mal's personal resistance is forcibly transformed into public opposition. However, because he is confronting the nearly all-powerful Alliance, an armed revolution will not suffice. Instead, his dissent mirrors that articulated by the democratic theorist Guillermo O'Donnell, who argued that the best way for citizens to oppose the illiberal nature of bureaucratic authoritarianism was not through armed, revolutionary struggle, but through an "unconditional commitment to democracy."[15] Social justice, O'Donnell argues, depends on the commitment of individuals protecting and furthering the rights of each even in the face of more powerfully organized threats. By exposing Miranda, the Pax holocaust, and the creation of the Reavers, the crew of *Serenity* brings openness and transparency to the closed, authoritarian regime that defines the Alliance. No longer is the Alliance able to control society through the centralized manufacturing of a false political narrative. It is through an unyielding commitment to the principles of justice, rights, and democracy that Mal and his crew dismantle the ruling authority in a manner that the armed resistance of the Browncoats was unable to achieve.

The Lockean critique of state power and authority present in *Firefly* and *Serenity* offer insight into the liberalism of Whedon's body of work more broadly speaking.[16] The covenant that exists between the crew members of *Serenity* allows for diversity to exist within community in the same way that similar diverse associations work in other aspects of the Whedon corpus. Whether depicting the Scoobies in *Buffy the Vampire Slayer* or the members of Angel Investigations in *Angel,* Whedon often presents as heroic and enviable the relationships among individuals that are based on diversity, mutual cooperation, and respect, and the trust that is formed out of a commitment to the protection of all. In *Firefly,* the emphasis on individual rights and personal autonomy are given overtly political connotations in his space Western, suggesting that the ability of one to live the good life as defined autonomously by the individual (and not imposed in a top-down system of power and authority) is dependent on the proper ordering of society and government. Through *Firefly,* Whedon suggests that while a common civil authority is necessary to maintain order and protect the rights of citizens, when that authority commands such an expansive sphere that it usurps the rights held by individuals, it violates the principles of political justice. In such instances, acts of disobedience against the illiberal state are warranted.

Most important, Mal provides a lesson about the nature of rights and the ability of each of us to live the kind of life we desire. In order to have the personal space to seek that which makes us happy, we must commit ourselves to protecting the rights of others to do the same, as the justifications used to deprive the rights and liberties of others might easily be turned against us. *Firefly* is, therefore, less a dystopian portrayal of humanity's future as it is a critical reflection on politics today. As citizens, we must remain committed to the rights of all individuals to define and live a quality life for themselves, regardless of who that person is or what beliefs he or she holds. Tolerance and diversity are essential to a free, democratic society, and we must guard against the dismantling of the private sphere by social, political, or economic forces that try to impose a life not chosen by the individual. We may not always like or agree with the lives others choose, but we must remain committed to the process that allows for disagreement and difference to exist. For, as Whedon noted about the fictive future presented in *Firefly,* "nothing will change . . . technology will advance, but we will still have the same political, moral, and ethical problems as today."[17]

Notes

I would like to thank Jonathan Hausen for his diligent research assistance, insights, and efforts on behalf of this project. His contributions proved invaluable, and I offer my sincerest gratitude for his work. It was a privilege working with him and sharing ideas and reflections about politics and the Whedonverse.

1. Throughout the television series, the Reavers are treated by some as "campfire stories" or poetic nonsense (officially the Alliance does not acknowledge their existence, claiming that the folktales are used by criminals to cover up their illegal activities), but most people seem to know the myth of a race of humans who were driven insane by the vastness of "the black" on the Outer Rim. In *Serenity*, of course, we learn differently. The Reavers are among the small fraction of Miranda's population who reacted with extreme rage and aggression to G-23 Paxilon Hydroclorate gas (the Pax) administered through the ventilation system of all buildings by the Alliance. There might be an inclination to dismiss the Reavers as being representative of any state of nature given this external stimulus that led to their creation. They do not embody the state of nature because their origin is unnatural. However, it might be that the affected population that became violent due to the Pax was merely giving in to a more base aspect of human nature, an urge to kill and take from others for their own selfish desires. This might explain the psychological regression to primitive violence displayed in witnesses of Reaver attacks, as was the case with the young man recovered from the salvaged ship in "Bushwhacked." These "second-generation" Reavers are so psychologically traumatized that they mutilate themselves and begin hunting others. That Mal seems to know of other, similar incidents leads us to believe that this is not an uncommon result. Ultimately, whether or not Reavers are a depiction of the true nature of humanity or the vilest of its unchecked potential is less important than what they represent. Thus, what matters here is not the origin of the Reavers so much as the existence of the Reavers outside of any defined aspect of civilization or legal authority.

2. Joss Whedon and Tim Minear help to clarify one notable exception to Mal's commitment to the protection and dignity of human life in the DVD commentary provided for "The Train Job." Near the end of the episode, Mal confronts one of Niska's henchmen, Crow (Andrew Bryniarski), who is bound and defenseless. Mal attempts to give him back the advance Niska paid for the stealing of supplies from Paradiso and send him back to deliver a message to his boss that the crew of *Serenity* would not take these much-needed supplies from the people who needed them. Crow tells Mal that he should keep the money to use for his funeral because Crow will hunt him down and kill him no matter where he may attempt to run. Mal unhesitatingly kicks Crow in the chest, sending him flying into the intake valve of the running engines on *Serenity* before bringing the next henchman forward. Whedon and Minear explain that this was a change that they made to the story line after Fox demanded "larger than life" villains, which caused them to opt for a more action-oriented scene between the two so that Mal could demonstrate how to treat "the life of big giant thugs who threaten us."

3. Thomas Hobbes, *The Leviathan* (London: Penguin Classics, 1968), pt. 2, chap. 21, pp. 261–74. Hobbes's prose has been emended in accordance with modern style.

4. Ibid., 188.

5. Ibid., 230.

6. The transformation of the frontier narrative to one that criticizes the intrusiveness of society, the market, and the state is a part of a growing tradition in popular culture to view the "taming of the frontier" as being destructive. Modern frontier-films like *Dances with Wolves* (1990) and James Cameron's *Avatar* (2009) depict the caustic expansion of the hegemonic forces of civilization as dislocating traditional cultures and destroying authentic individualism by juxtaposing social norms and expectations against the liberating backdrop of the frontier. Films like these offer a message consistent with that provided by Whedon, providing critiques of the dismantling of a personal sphere of private action by the encroachment of the seemingly oppressive forces of society and globalization (see Joseph J. Foy, "Tuning in to Democratic Dissent: Oppositional Messaging in Popular Culture," in *Homer Simpson Marches on Washington: Dissent through American Popular Culture*, ed. Timothy M. Dale and Foy [Lexington: University Press of Kentucky, 2010], 8–12).

7. "The R. Tam Sessions," *Serenity*, collector's ed. DVD (Universal City, Calif.: Universal Studios, 2007).

8. John Locke, *The Second Treatise of Government*, ed. Thomas P. Peardon (New York: Bobbs-Merrill, 1952), 5–6.

9. Concomitantly, Locke did not believe that natural rights principles would always provide a clear guide for resolving particular disputes when applied to specific cases. He describes the potential for conflict that is judged between two parties unable to achieve some kind of resolution between them to be such that a cycle of retribution develops into a state of war. This leads to the sort of "frontier-justice" evidenced in the Outer Rim planets in *Firefly*. For individuals to be the judge of who has wronged them and to determine what they feel to be an appropriate punishment in response can lead to a number of problems, not least of which is to determine when retribution is necessary and what level of response is just. Locke argues that "where there is [a civil] authority . . . from which relief can be had by *appeal,* there the continuance of the *state of war* is excluded, and the controversy is decided by that power."

10. That Mal believes justice and rights exist even in the state of nature is apparent by his commitment to a system of ethics simply because it is the right thing to do. At the end of the episode "Serenity," when Simon states his fear to Mal that the captain cannot be trusted, invoking a classic notion from Hobbes's view of the state of nature that Mal might come and kill him while he slept, Mal responds: "You don't know me, son, so let me explain this to you once. If I ever kill you, you'll be awake, you'll be facing me, and you'll be armed." This serves as a reminder of Mal's belief that even in the state of nature there are rules and that you ought not to shoot a man in the back.

11. Kaylee does have a vague recollection of there being a call for settlement because her father had talked about it, but there is no official record of the planet or its population's demise.

12. The contract aboard *Serenity* stands in stark contrast to the illiberal nature of the Alliance that cares little for the individual. It also counters the more oppressive intolerance of some of the more communitarian settlements along the Outer Rim. For instance, in the episode "Safe," Simon and River are kidnapped by a group of men who need Simon's medical expertise to tend to the sick in their town. At the same time, Book is severely wounded during a job, and Mal decides that they must seek off-world medical assistance if they are to have a chance of saving his life. *Serenity* launches, leaving River and Simon to fend for themselves on Jiangyin. When River begins using her telepathic abilities to "read" people (especially prominent officials), she is accused of being a witch and is set to be burned at the stake. The community's intolerance of River's unique abilities nearly leads to her and her brother's deaths, even though the people had been benefiting from Simon's practice. When *Serenity* swoops down to save the siblings, Mal is confronted by one of the townspeople yelling that River is a witch. He merely responds, "Yeah, but she's *our* witch."

13. Likewise, in "The Message," Tracey, a longtime companion of Mal and Zoe from the war, boards the ship (without Mal's permission) and misleads his old comrades. When Tracey threatens the lives of crew members in an attempt to force Mal to flee from the Alliance, which would place them all in great peril, Zoe and Mal both end up shooting him to protect the rest of the crew. Finally, at the end of "Our Mrs. Reynolds," Mal tracks down Saffron (Christina Hendricks), the hired gun who threatened the lives of everyone on *Serenity* in an attempt to profit from the theft and resale of the ship to pirates. When she tries to seduce him again to save herself from potential harm, Mal tells her, "Saffron, you even think about playing me again I will riddle you with holes."

14. As Inara decides to do in "Objects in Space" and Book does when he departs the ship to serve as the Shepherd for Haven.

15. Guillermo O'Donnell, *Counterpoints: Selected Essays on Authoritarianism and Democratization* (Notre Dame, Ind.: University of Notre Dame Press, 1999), xiii.

16. For example, in the season-four "Jasmine-arc" of *Angel*, the goddess's promise of world peace comes at the price of everyone's free will. Angel and his team must liberate everyone from Jasmine's (Charisma Carpenter/Gina Torres) control if they are to recontinue with their conception of the good life. This idea has persisted in Whedon's corpus, including the graphic novel installations of *Buffy the Vampire Slayer*. In the four-part series "The Long Way Home," Whedon introduces a new enemy of Buffy's, General Voll, who seeks to use the power of the state (as well as the magical powers of Amy Madison and the underhanded genius of a skinless Warren Mears) to try to suppress and destroy the Scoobies. Meanwhile, in a second four-part series, "No Future for You," which came as a collaboration between Whedon and Brian Vaughn, the British socialite and rogue-slayer Lady Genevieve Savidge is enticed by the wicked Irish warlock Roden to attempt to assassinate Buffy and take her place as the "queen of the Slayers" in order to use their power for his own ends. They also face the "big bad," a mysterious figure named Twilight, whose group is often compared by the Scoobies to the season-four covert government group the Initiative, headed by Professor Maggie Walsh (Lindsay Crouse), which uses drugs to enhance their soldiers as well as keep them in line. Buffy

and her friends are attempting to battle these threats and various other evils on all fronts in order to preserve their lives and freedom from control.

17. "Re-Lighting *The Firefly,*" *Serenity,* collector's ed. DVD (Universal City, Calif.: Universal Studios, 2007).

Dollhouse and Consensual Slavery

S. Evan Kreider

Dollhouse is arguably one of Joss Whedon's most philosophically complex shows, covering topics from the metaphysics of personal identity to the politics of social control. What stands out as one (if not *the*) central moral issue of the show is the idea of consensual slavery. The "dolls," or "actives," appear to have agreed to their place in the Dollhouse, at least initially. As the show progresses, the legitimacy of this agreement, this contract, is called into question. However, Joss expertly avoids creating a simple polemic; as a master of polyphony rivaling Dostoevsky, Joss presents a wide variety of views on the subject, so that although it becomes clear by the end of season one that Joss is arguing that consensual slavery is not morally legitimate, we the viewers do come to see that it is a difficult issue that gives rise to a variety of perspectives, each with some strengths and weaknesses. In this essay, I explore the views on consensual slavery presented in *Dollhouse* and analyze them in terms of the philosophies of Thomas Mappes, John Stuart Mill, and John Locke, concluding that Joss's opposition to consensual slavery, while having something in common with the views of all three of these philosophers and being closest to those of Locke, ultimately rests on Joss's own independent arguments as demonstrated in *Dollhouse*.

Thomas Mappes: Voluntary, Informed Consent and the Idea of a Coercive Offer

As devoted viewers of the series know, the Dollhouse is an organization that makes use of agents called "actives" or "dolls," people who have seemingly agreed to have their own personalities and memories shelved for a period of five years, during which they are routinely imprinted with other personalities and memories so that they may perform missions for rich and powerful clients who can use them for anything from negotiating the release of hostages, to infiltrating cults, to spending romantic (or at least, sexual) weekends with the clients themselves. Among those who attempt, at least initially, to justify the Dollhouse's use of the actives are Adele DeWitt (Olivia Williams), the woman in charge of the Los Angeles branch of the Dollhouse, and Topher Brink (Fran Kranz), the resident computer expert and the man responsible for developing the technology that imprints the actives with their various personalities. For both Adele and Topher, the key issue is consent: they both argue that the Dollhouse's use of the actives is morally legitimate because the actives themselves consented to the arrangement in return for something. For example, in the opening scene of the series pilot, Adele talks with the show's protagonist, Caroline (Eliza Dushku)—or "Echo," as she comes to be known as an active—about the possibility of working as an active for the Dollhouse. Adele refers to it as an "offer," eventually asking Caroline, "Are you volunteering?" ("Ghost"). Topher similarly defends the arrangement against criticisms from Boyd Langton (Harry Lennix), Echo's handler, by pointing out that "they volunteered for this" ("Grey Hour").

Both Adele's and Topher's reasoning echoes that of the contemporary philosopher Thomas Mappes.[1] On Mappes's view, interaction between persons is morally legitimate so long as it does not violate the Kantian principle that we not "use" people, and we observe this principle by respecting their rationality and autonomy. According to Mappes's take on Kant's principle, people may enter into whatever arrangements and interactions with one another that they like, so long as no one's voluntary, informed consent is violated. It is possible to violate a person's voluntary, informed consent in two ways: deception or coercion. Deception involves violating the "informed" part of "voluntary, informed consent" by either outright lying to someone about what the arrangement involves, or using misleading information or half-truths, or withholding relevant information to which the person is entitled. Coercion, on the other hand, involves violating the "voluntary" part of "voluntary, informed consent," and it comes in two forms: occurrent coercion and dispositional coercion. Occurrent coercion is the use of force, such as literally physically forcing someone to do something, or using brainwashing or drugs to make it physically impossible for someone to think or choose for himself. Dispositional coercion is the use of threats, such as threatening to harm someone or harm someone she cares about in order to get her to do what you want.

As Mappes points out, dispositional coercion is the most complex of the above concepts. First of all, it is important to distinguish a mere unpleasant offer from a true threat. An offer has the form, "If you *do* what I am proposing you do, I will bring about a *desirable consequence* for you," whereas a threat has the form, "If you *do not do* what I am proposing you do, I will bring about an *undesirable consequence* for you," where the undesirable consequence is something that the person issuing the threat will actively inflict on the victim, or something to which the victim is entitled that the person issuing the threat will withhold from the victim.[2] For example, if a boss tells an employee, "If you do not have sexual intercourse with me, I will fire you," that is a threat. However, if one's neighbor says, "If you have sexual intercourse with me, I will treat you to dinner and a show," that is merely an unpleasant offer (unpleasant if we assume that one has no desire to take the neighbor up on it). Sometimes threats can be disguised as offers, but the underlying form is still that of a threat. For example, when the mob enforcer tells the shop owner, "If you pay me one thousand dollars per week, I'll make sure that nothing bad happens to your shop," it might sound like an offer on the surface, but what he is really saying is, "If you do not pay me one thousand dollars per week, I will make sure that something bad happens to your shop," which is clearly a threat. Furthermore, some situations are threatening even if the person issuing an offer doesn't intend it to be. For example, if a professor told a student, "If you have sex with me, I will give you an A," even if the professor genuinely intends that as an offer and not a disguised threat ("If you don't have sex with me, your grade may suffer"), the situation is inherently threatening, given the power imbalance between the professor and the student, and that it would be reasonable for the student to assume that declining the offer would result in negative consequences of some sort.

So how does the Dollhouse's arrangement with the actives hold up on Mappes's account? In the case of Sierra (Dichen Lachman), it's quite easy to see what's morally wrong: she is the victim of both occurrent coercion and deception and thus has not made a fully voluntary informed decision to become an active. As we learn in season two, she rejected the advances of a rich and powerful man who then had her drugged so that she would appear crazy—so much so that even she herself wasn't entirely sure about her own sanity—so that he could have her brought into the Dollhouse, allowing him to engage her services as often as he liked ("Belonging"). When she agrees to Topher's offer of a position in the Dollhouse in return for what essentially amounts to psychiatric care, her consent is neither fully voluntary due to the drugs making it impossible for her to think clearly (occurrent coercion), nor is it fully informed since she cannot accurately assess her own mental condition (deception).

On the other hand, the Dollhouse's arrangement with Madeline Costly/ November/Millie (Miracle Laurie) fares better on Mappes's account, at least by all available evidence. In her real life previous to joining the Dollhouse, Madeline lost her daughter and was unable to cope with the grief and guilt ("Needs"). The Dollhouse seems to have offered her a contract in return for the time to deal with her feelings, at least at an unconscious level. There does not seem to be any element of coercion, and so the genuine offer could be stated as, "If you work for us as an active, we will return you to your life at a later date, when you have recovered from your daughter's death and are ready to move on." We also get the opportunity to see Madeline fulfill her contract (albeit somewhat early, thanks to the intervention of Paul Ballard [Tahmoh Penikett], the FBI agent investigating the Dollhouse, who was for a time the next-door neighbor and short-term love interest to Madeline's sleeper agent identity "Millie"), at which time she seems perfectly happy with how the arrangement worked out—in fact, she acts like a satisfied customer, not a freed prisoner or slave ("Omega").

However, although Mappes's account (as far as it has been described above) can't identify anything obviously wrong based on explicit evidence from the show, one still wonders how informed the actives' decisions really were. For example, was Madeline told that, as an active, she might have to kill another human being? As viewers know, Adele does have November kill Sierra's handler after it is discovered that he was raping Sierra ("Man on the Street"). As another example, did Adele tell Anthony/Victor (Enver Gjokoj) that he would be servicing her romantically ("A Spy in the House of Love")? It seems unlikely that either of them was told any such thing, but frankly, the evidence simply isn't conclusive. Perhaps they were given an idea of the sorts of things they would have to do as actives, and perhaps they were told that homicide or sexual intercourse with their employers might be among them. However, one rather suspects not, and even Adele, in a conversation with Caroline, implies that those signing on to become dolls may not know exactly what they are getting themselves into: "Nothing is what it appears to be," she says cryptically, just before Caroline signs her contract ("Echoes").

Many of the actives' cases are even more complex than those of Sierra, November, or Victor. Caroline's case is particularly unclear. Caroline has engaged in terrorist activities against the Rossum Corporation, the organization behind the Dollhouse. Furthermore, her activities have resulted in a person's death, which is tantamount to felony murder.[3] She has been caught, and if she goes through the legal system, she will almost certainly face life in prison. The Dollhouse has saved her from the system and from the consequences of her own actions and does appear to be making a legitimate offer. Adele tells Caroline: "I'm going to make you an offer. . . . Your life for your life. I get five years, you get the rest. You'll be free" ("Echoes"). It might be tempting to try to interpret Adele's offer as a veiled threat—"If you don't work for me, I'll see to it that you go to jail"—but as Mappes makes clear, the person issuing the threat must be the one responsible for the negative consequence stated in the threat itself, and that simply isn't the case here, as Caroline herself is clearly responsible for any jail time she faces.

However, as Mappes points out, there may be genuine offers that still contain an element of coercion. These "coercive offers" are genuinely not threats, but they are made under circumstances in which the person has no other reasonable choice, and so the person making the offer is knowingly taking advantage of the other person's unfortunate circumstances. Mappes uses the example of "Ms. Opportunistic," who offers to pay the mortgage of "Mr. Troubled" in return for sexual favors. Mr. Troubled has no interest in Ms. Opportunity but has no other way to pay his mortgage and care for his children—he is unemployed, has no prospects, and no one else will give or loan him the money. Ms. Opportunistic is genuinely not threatening Mr. Troubled—after all, she is not responsible for his unfortunate circumstances—but her offer still contains an element of coercion precisely because it is opportunistic—she is taking advantage, and he has no other real options.[4]

In this light, the actives' agreements with the Dollhouse seem far more troubling. Sierra, even if she weren't already being coerced and deceived, is obviously being taken advantage of. The Dollhouse also appears to be taking advantage of November's unfortunate situation, although one might argue that she does have other reasonable options (for example, therapy, support groups, etc.). We also learn that the Dollhouse originally conscripted Alpha as a result of a short-lived policy of offering contracts to prisoners, which is certainly an opportunistic exploitation of the prisoners' bad circumstances ("Omega"). The idea of a coercive offer also seems to apply to Caroline's case. True, the Dollhouse is not threatening her; true, Adele is making Caroline a genuine offer. However, the offer does have the appearance of coercion as Adele seems to be taking advantage of Caroline's situation, and it could be said that Caroline really does not have any other reasonable option but to accept Adele's offer.[5] As Caroline says, "I told you all I want is to be left alone," to which Adele replies, "We both know we're past that" ("Echoes").

This is a reasonable case to make; however, it does not appear to be the case that Joss wants to make. First of all, notice the difference between Caroline's case and the case of Mr. Troubled. According to all the available evidence, Mr. Troubled finds himself in his unfortunate position through no fault of his own. This is precisely why it is called an *unfortunate* circumstance—it is the result of bad fortune, not a result of his actions. In Caroline's case, we cannot truly call her circumstances unfortunate since they are the direct result of her own actions. She committed acts of domestic terrorism that led to someone being killed. If she is facing jail time, then it is, to be quite blunt, her own fault. Caroline's situation is, ultimately, her own responsibility.

This becomes clear in the season-one finale, "Omega." Alpha, an active who has become a homicidal maniac/evil genius after accidentally being imprinted with multiple personalities (one of which is itself a multiple personality), has captured Echo and brought her to a remote location in which he has re-created the Dollhouse imprinting technology for the purpose of turning her into a fellow "ascended being" (as he calls it) whom he intends to call "Omega." He also captures an innocent bystander and imprints her with the original Caroline personality so that Omega may kill her in an act symbolic of her ascension.[6] Alpha argues that Echo/Omega ought to want to kill Caroline anyway, saying, "She's responsible for all of the terrible things you can't remember." When Caroline says, "I want back in my brain," Alpha responds, "You should have thought of that before you vacated the premises," adding: "She abandoned you! She walked out on you when you needed her most! Times got a little tough, the road got a little rocky, the seas got a little choppy, and she thought 'Hey, I'll go to sleep. Night-night, I'll see you in five years.' She left you to the jackals, to the wolves, to the predators!" Shortly thereafter, Echo agrees, saying to Caroline: "He may be crazy, but he's right. You walked away from me. You left me alone in that place," showing Caroline that when it all comes down to it, she is the one who bears primary responsibility for her situation.

In summary, Mappes's view gives us an excellent framework to consider some sides of the issue. Those characters who try to justify the Dollhouse's arrangement with the actives do so on the basis that the arrangement is supposedly voluntary. For actives such as Sierra, that is obviously not the case, which gives us the clear means to judge the Dollhouse's use of her as immoral. In other cases, though the arrangement may rest on a genuine offer, there may still be an element of coercion involved, making the arrangement morally distasteful at the very least. This may apply to November's and Echo's cases, and we certainly suspect that it applies to other actives—as one man-on-the-street interviewee puts it, "There's only one reason that someone would volunteer to be a slave, is if they [sic] is one already" ("Man on the Street"). However, it's also entirely possible that some actives are true volunteers, without any element of coercion. Indeed, for some people, accepting a contract as a doll is an attractive idea—as another interviewee puts it: "So being a Doll, you do whatever. And you don't got to remember nothing. Or study. Or pay rent. And you just party with rich people all the time? Where's the dotted line?" ("Man on the Street"). Since it does seem at least possible that some actives participate of their own free will, and since Caroline herself does not want to use the excuse of coercion, we still need another way to think of the Dollhouse if we are going to come to the conclusion that there is something intrinsically wrong with the Dollhouse's arrangement with the dolls.

John Stuart Mill and the Freedom Not to Be Free

In the context of Mappes, our analysis of the moral legitimacy of the Dollhouse contract focuses primarily on whether or not the agents of the Dollhouse are doing something immoral by making the offer to someone to become a doll. We may also ask whether or not the persons to whom the offer is made are doing something immoral by accepting the offer, whether or not the offer itself is morally legitimate. Indeed, some philosophers have argued that people do not have the right to agree to a contract to become a slave. John Stuart Mill is one such philosopher, and a brief overview of his ethical and political philosophies should suffice to show why he is against such contracts.

Mill subscribes to an ethical theory known as utilitarianism. Though the theory comes in many variations, the core idea of utilitarianism is that we ought to perform acts that in one way or another contribute to the greatest possible good; simply put, our actions should have good consequences, ones that make the world a better place on the whole. Specific utilitarians have different ideas about how to elaborate on this core idea; complicating things, there is some debate about Mill's exact definition of "good" in the aforementioned idea of the greater good. According to a standard reading—to which, for the purposes of this essay, I adhere—Mill is what is known as a hedonistic utilitarian. On this reading, Mill believes that pleasure is the only thing with intrinsic value, and thus all our actions ought to contribute in some way, directly or indirectly, to increasing the total amount of pleasure and happiness in the world, and likewise, reducing the amount of pain and suffering.

A common and reasonable concern about utilitarianism is that it would allow for the mistreatment of individuals if such mistreatment would serve a greater good. However, Mill argues that utilitarianism is compatible with a robust theory of individual rights. In *On Liberty,* Mill argues that "the sole end for which mankind are warranted, individually or collectively, interfering with the liberty of action of any of their number is self-protection. That the only purpose for which power can be rightfully exercised over any member of a civilized community, against his will, is to prevent harm to others. His own good, either physical or moral, is not a sufficient warrant."[7] Mill goes on to clarify this principle in terms of rights, claiming in essence that people have the right to do whatever they want as long as they are not violating the rights of others. They do have the right to do whatever they like so long as their actions affect only themselves. In this regard, Mill is strongly anti-paternalistic: he does not believe that society has a right to force individuals to act, or refrain from acting, in a way that harms themselves only.

Mill seems to make an exception in one case, however. Individuals do not have the right to give up their rights, as in the case of slavery contracts: "By selling himself for a slave, he abdicates his liberty; he foregoes any future use of it beyond that single act. He therefore defeats, in his own case, the very purpose which is the justification of allowing him to dispose of himself. He is no longer free, but is thenceforth in a position which has no longer the presumption in its favour that would be afforded by his voluntarily remaining in it. The principle of freedom cannot require that he should be free not to be free."[8] There is a great deal of scholarly debate about whether or not Mill is contradicting himself at any point of the above. If we once again stick to a standard—and charitable—reading of Mill, we might say the following: Mill is, first and foremost, a utilitarian. As such, he absolutely believes in the greater good. However, he also believes that as a practical matter, the best way to achieve the greatest good in any society is to allow as much personal freedom as possible, so long as people are not harming others. Paternalism, though perhaps well-intentioned, will always result in more harm than good, and so individuals should have the right to harm themselves. The only exception to this is that individuals should not have the right to give up their rights entirely as that would defeat the purpose of individual rights as the best means to the end of the greatest good.

If this reading is correct—or, at least, suitable for our purposes here—then it serves us well as a way of interpreting some of the viewpoints expressed in *Dollhouse*. In particular, Ballard and Boyd, despite playing on opposite teams, seem to express the idea that one's freedom cannot be used to give up one's freedom. Ballard, in particular, says in no uncertain terms: "I don't even care that these people signed themselves over to you. There is no provision for . . . for consensual slavery. It is wrong. You know it's wrong. You feel it in your bones" ("Briar Rose"). On another occasion, Ballard makes the point in stronger terms, arguing, "We're talking about people walking around who may as well have been murdered" ("Ghost"). Another of the man-on-the-street interviewees agrees with Ballard, claiming: "It's human trafficking, end of story. It's repulsive" ("Man on the Street").

Boyd expresses similar sentiments, though in a more veiled manner (and appropriately so, given that he works for the Dollhouse). On more than one occasion, Boyd points out the dolls' lack of freedom and the moral discomfort he feels about it. According to Boyd, the dolls are "a bunch of helpless children," and he says of Echo that "she's not even a person, just an empty hat" ("The Target"). During an assignment in which Echo is tasked to infiltrate a cult, an ATF agent asks Boyd whether Echo's qualifications are based upon her having escaped from another cult. "No, she didn't escape from anything," Boyd responds, obviously implying that he sees her as a slave of the Dollhouse.

The biggest problem with Mill's view (as reflected in Boyd and Ballard) is that, at best, it justifies a prohibition against using one's freedom to give up one's freedom *permanently,* but it does not give a strong argument against using one's freedom to give up one's freedom *temporarily* in return for more freedom later. Many of our agreements and compromises with other people involve just such a thing; for example, when I agree to sell something, I give up my freedom to use that thing, but I do so in return for the payment, which I presumably will use to further my own ends in some other way. Indeed, both Adele and Topher use this argument to further justify the Dollhouse's contracts with the dolls. A particularly telling example of this occurs during an exchange in which Echo attempts to escape (and free the other actives from) the Dollhouse and confronts them:

> TOPHER: When your contract is up, [you will] leave here, and go and do whatever you want. . . .
> ADELE: I eased your suffering.
> ECHO: Is that what you think you're doing here? . . . [You're] taking away basic human rights . . . the right to choose, feel, remember.
> ADELE: All relinquished by you to our care and discretion. ("Needs")

Adele and Topher make a collectively compelling argument. Caroline/Echo has indeed given up her freedom, but she has done so in return for more freedom—a life of her own instead of a life in prison. She really isn't in a position to criticize the Dollhouse on the grounds that they take away the actives' freedom if, in fact, it is a simple exchange for more freedom.

In summary, although Mill's view does help us understand the reasoning of some of the show's characters, it does not go far enough in showing what is wrong about the Dollhouse's contracts with the dolls. If the dolls were agreeing to give up their freedom permanently, that would be one thing, but they seem to be giving up their freedom only temporarily, and only some of their freedom in return for more freedom. However, Mill's arguments suggest an alternative and more profitable direction for arguments against the idea of consensual slavery. Mill's statement that we are not free not to be free suggests that there is a kind of logical contradiction implied by consensual slavery—that a contract to be a slave is not just immoral, but also impossible somehow. Unfortunately, Mill himself does not develop this line of thought. For that, we will be well served to shift our attention to another philosopher—namely, John Locke.

John Locke and the Social Contract

According to Locke, many of the moral rules that we live by can be conceived of as a system of agreements—that is, a social contract. Prior to such a contract, humans could be thought of as living in a state of nature, a state in which there is no formal society. As self-interested beings, humans in the state of nature are interested in their own survival. However, humans are not just self-interested, but also rational, and as such we recognize that others have the same interest in surviving as we do. In other words, reason allows us to recognize and respect the natural rights of others; among the most important of these are the rights to life, liberty, and property.[9]

However, our natural rights are not adequately protected in the state of nature, and thus the state of nature is in constant danger of degenerating into a state of war, a state in which people violate the rights of others by acts of violence (violating the right to life), enslavement (violating the right to liberty), and theft (violating the right to property).[10] In order to avoid the constant threat of the state of war, people join together and come up with a system of agreements that rational persons could agree to for their mutual benefit. In other words, they form a social contract, which, among other things, includes a system of moral rules against murder, slavery, theft, and so forth. As such, the primary purpose of the social contract is to protect the basic natural rights of all human beings to life, liberty, and property. Of course, an agreement without a means to enforce it is useless, and so some power must be created to enforce the social contract, and that power is the government, and its only legitimate exercise of power is to enforce the mutually agreed upon rules and laws that, among other things, protect our natural rights.[11]

It's already clear where slavery fits into this. Slavery involves the violation of another person's natural right to liberty. Legitimate social contracts are designed to protect natural rights, and so slavery could never be part of a legitimate social contract. When one person enslaves another, both have actually left the social contract and instead entered back into a state of war with one another.[12] Locke says: "For a man, not having the power over his own life, cannot, by compact, or his own consent, enslave himself to any one, nor put himself under the absolute, arbitrary power of another. . . . This is the perfect condition of slavery, which is nothing else, but the state of war continued."[13] Thus there is no morally legitimate contract for slavery since slavery involves the absence of any such contract. In that respect, a contract for slavery is not just immoral, but impossible—it is a logical contradiction.

With this in mind, we can make even more sense of Ballard's claim that "there is no provision for . . . consensual slavery" ("Briar Rose"). It is not merely that such a provision would be wrong; it is that there *can be no such provision at all.* Echo makes this clear in her conversation with Caroline:

> ECHO: Why don't you come home?
> CAROLINE: I did sign a contract.
> ECHO: I have thirty-eight brains, and not one of them thinks you can sign a contract to be a slave. Especially now that we have a black president. ("Omega")

Echo says "can," not "should," emphasizing the point that such a contract is not just immoral, but impossible—there is no such contract.

Thus, Locke's view seems closest to Joss's own, focusing as it does on the impossibility of a legitimate slavery contract. However, Joss's views appear to go even further than Locke's—the case of consensual slavery is in some respects even worse than Locke himself considered. In the final section, I show how we can interpret Joss as implicitly taking Locke's argument even further in order to show the deepest problem with the Dollhouse's contracts with the dolls.

Joss and the Option to Default

Joss raises two additional ideas in *Dollhouse* that seem to be missing from both Mill's and Locke's prohibition against consensual slavery. By addressing these two ideas, Joss not only improves upon the arguments of Mill and Locke, but also shows more clearly than either of them can what exactly is wrong about the Dollhouse's contract with the dolls.

First, in any legitimate contract, there is always some option to default—that is, an option to break the contract and face the consequences of doing so. This is true of many ordinary contracts, such as payment in return for cell phone services; the default in such a case may simply be the termination of services, or possibly the payment of additional fees or fines. Even Locke's idea of a social contract has a default option, as it were. If someone decides that he no longer wishes to participate in the social contract's rule against stealing, he has the option to break the contract by committing an act of theft as long as he is willing to face the consequences—most likely jail time. Of course, in most cases, it's not exactly a good idea to default on contracts, but the simple point here is that it is logically possible to do so.

Second (and closely related to the first), the key difference between an ordinary slave and a doll is that a slave retains some autonomy, at least in the metaphysical sense. A slave may give up the legal right to exercise his autonomy, but he does still have it: a slave is still capable of thinking and choosing for himself. For example, it is possible (if not necessarily desirable) for a slave to disobey orders, revolt, try to escape, and so forth. A doll, however, completely lacks autonomy in his doll state, and so is metaphysically incapable of doing any of the same things.[14] Both this and the previous consideration are brought out by a variety of examples from *Dollhouse*.

We've already seen Boyd's claims that the dolls lack autonomy. Furthermore, Laurence Dominic (Reed Diamond) tells the Dollhouse staff: "Don't think of them as children. Think of them as pets" ("Needs"). These observations make clear that the dolls are not autonomous individuals. Even the few choices that the dolls seem to be allowed are a façade of autonomy. They are routinely asked, "Would you like a treatment?" as though they really have a choice. When they are programmed, their handlers read from a script, "Do you trust me?" and the dolls are programmed to respond, "With my life." After a treatment, they are also programmed to ask, "Shall I go?" and are told, "If you like," but this, too, involves nothing more than the appearance of real choice.

The lack of autonomy, and the façade of free will that disguises it, is clearly brought out in the episode "Needs." Some of the actives—the aforementioned Echo, Sierra, November, among them—awaken one night with their original personalities restored, though still lacking their memories. During the course of the episode, the dolls attempt to escape the Dollhouse so that they can return to their normal lives—and regain their autonomy. When November does regain her memories and wants to go off separately from the rest of them, Sierra says, "That's why we left; we decide for ourselves now." Near the very end of the episode, Caroline appears not only to have escaped herself, but also to have freed the rest of the dolls. However, as we soon discover, the whole thing has been a ruse. Once they have achieved their goals, the dolls all fall asleep and are returned to the Dollhouse, with the memories of their adventures erased. The whole thing was an elaborate hoax perpetrated on the dolls by the Dollhouse on the recommendation of the house physician, Dr. Saunders (Amy Acker), who believed that the unconscious closure gained by their experiences would help the dolls to deal with various personal issues and better adapt to their positions as actives. Thus, even at the exceptional moment when the dolls appear to have regained some autonomy, they had no real autonomy at all.[15]

In conclusion, through these examples, Joss not only shows us what is wrong with the Dollhouse's contract with the dolls—the former robbing the latter of their metaphysical autonomy—but also improves upon Locke's arguments against slavery contracts. Such contracts are not legitimate because they are quite literally not possible. It is not merely that such contracts place the slave and master in a state of war, as Locke argues, but also that any legitimate contract must still leave all parties involved with some rights, including the option to default on the contract; the slave, giving up all his rights, has no such option. As a result, a slavery contract cannot be a real contract; or, in Echo's words once again, "I have thirty-eight brains, and not one of them thinks you can sign a contract to be a slave" ("Omega").

Notes

1. Thomas Mappes, "Sexual Morality and the Concept of Using Another Person," in *Social Ethics: Morality and Social Policy*, ed. Mappes and Jane S. Zembaty, 7th ed. (New York: McGraw-Hill, 2006), 170–83.

2. Ibid., 176.

3. Though of course she did not intend for her boyfriend to die as a result of their break-in at the Rossum-funded laboratory, a person is still legally responsible for what is called "felony murder" if someone dies as a result of a felony that the person has committed.

4. Mappes, "Sexual Morality," 181–83.

5. Complicating things further, there is a scene at the very end of "Echoes" that suggests that Adele and the Rossum Corporation have been aware of Caroline's activities all along and have been waiting for the right opportunity to make her an offer—opportunistic, indeed.

6. The Dollhouse imprinting technology allows for the recording and storage of an active's original/true personality, which is stored away during her tenure as a doll, making her a blank slate on which various artificial personalities may be imprinted. Alpha has stolen Caroline's original personality and imprinted it upon an innocent bystander so that Echo—the doll name for Caroline's body—can speak to her original personality directly.

7. Mill, John Stuart, *On Liberty*, ed. Elizabeth Rapaport (Indianapolis: Hacking, 1978), 9.

8. Ibid., 101.

9. John Locke, *Second Treatise of Government*, chap. 2, sec. 6.

10. Ibid., chap. 3, sec. 16ff.

11. Ibid., chap. 9, sec. 123ff.

12. Ibid., chap. 4, sec. 22ff.

13. Ibid., chap. 4, sec. 22–23.

14. Of course, Caroline is the exception: her body chemistry is apparently such that she is able to regain some degree of autonomy while a doll. For example, we see this clearly when Echo tells Adele, "It isn't finished," referring to her interrupted assignment with a wealthy video-game designer ("Man on the Street"). However, this is the exception rather than the rule: the vast majority of the dolls completely lack autonomy once put into the doll state, and so the argument against the standard Dollhouse contract still applies. In other words, the fact that, as chance would have it, Caroline is able to avoid some of the effects of her doll state does not make it any less reprehensible that the Dollhouse would offer to put her in such a state, or that she would agree to be put into it.

15. Though it falls outside of the scope of this article, it would be interesting to compare with Joss's other works. Certainly, the very idea of a vampire (as featured in *Buffy the Vampire Slayer* and *Angel*) involves having one's body used by others and the total absence of one's own autonomy in the meantime. Also, Jasmine (the "Big Bad" of season four of *Angel*) robs her followers of their autonomy, though in return for (supposed) happiness. Also, we learn in *Serenity* that the Reavers were the result of a failed experiment to make an entire planet's population more docile with an experimental drug.

Part 2

"Live as Though the World Were as It Should Be": Ethics and Virtue

Plato, Aristotle, and Joss on Being Horrible

Dean A. Kowalski

Gyges, the Lydian shepherd, appears nowhere in the Whedonverse. He is a literary artifact of the famed, ancient Greek philosopher Plato. With prose worthy of Joss Whedon's pen, Plato tells us how Gyges finds a gold ring: "One day there was a great storm and the ground where his flock was feeding was rent by an earthquake. Astonished by the sight, he went down into the chasm and saw . . . a brazen horse, hollow, with windows in its sides. Peering in, he saw a dead body. . . . It was naked save for a gold ring."[1] Fearing no Hellmouth, Gyges liberates the ring from the dead body and climbs out. Gyges serves as a thought-experiment for Plato. Through it, Plato argues that being morally good is its own unique reward, and that the good life cannot be led without becoming that sort of person. Joss Whedon is also concerned about the nature of good and evil, whether we ought to always do the right thing, and of what the good life consists. So, although Gyges is absent from the Whedonverse, the ideas he embodies infuse Whedon's impressive body of work.

This essay first delineates the interesting literary parallels between Plato and Whedon regarding their framing of questions pertinent to an examination of the good life. It then explains how Whedon's implicit answers to these questions more closely mirror those of Aristotle, Plato's famed pupil. Its overarching thesis is that exploring the Whedonverse for parallels to Plato and Aristotle is doubly beneficial. It provides an exciting platform from which to learn about Plato and Aristotle, and it also provides an enriched understanding of Whedon's corpus.

Magic Rings and the Temptations of Invisibility

Initially, the Gyges character appears to disprove Plato's hypothesis. Plato does this intentionally. If he can present the opposing side fairly and forcefully, but still refute it, he thereby establishes his preferred philosophical view. Plato utilizes his (historical) brother Glaucon as the mouthpiece of the opposing view. Glaucon doesn't actually believe the opposing side, but he has never heard it refuted either (358c–d). Glaucon hopes that Socrates, the main character of the *Republic* and the mouthpiece for Plato's preferred view, can finally provide the refutation he seeks.

Glaucon begins espousing the opposing side by reminding Socrates of the Gyges story. The shepherd soon discovers that when he turns the ring face one way, he becomes invisible; when he turns it back, he reappears. Emboldened by his invisibility, Gyges straightaway travels to the capital city. He seduces the queen and, with her help, kills the king; he assumes the throne and gains immediate access to great wealth and fame. The ring allows him to accomplish all of this without damaging his reputation. In fact, Gyges retains every appearance of being noble, generous, and kind. Glaucon hypothesizes that anyone would behave similarly to Gyges if given the chance. Consequently, Glaucon fears that people behave morally *only* because the negative consequences of not doing so—being thrown in prison or publically shunned—are comparably worse than what we might gain by satisfying our selfish impulses. Thus, doing the right thing or becoming morally decent is not its own, unique reward—it is merely a matter of pragmatics.

Whedon first employs the literary convention of invisibility in season one of *Buffy the Vampire Slayer*. In the episode entitled "Out of Mind, Out of Sight," Sunnydale student Marcie Ross (Marcie DuVall) becomes invisible as a result of being ignored by her classmates and teachers. Marcie soon takes advantage of her situation; she seeks harrowing revenge against those she believes responsible for her condition—the highly visible and popular students, including Cordelia (Charisma Carpenter). Yet Whedon suggests that becoming invisible is not necessarily desirable. Recall Giles's (Anthony Stewart Head) estimation of Marcie's behavior: she "has gone mad" due to "the loneliness, the constant exile" caused by her invisibility. However, Whedon also implicitly admits that the ramifications of invisibility are potentially staggering. The episode ends with Marcie joining a clandestine government program consisting of students who have become invisible at other schools; as the class is instructed to open their textbooks to the "Assassination and Infiltration" chapter, an unseen Marcie tantalizingly whispers, "Cool."

In the season-six *Buffy* episode "Gone," Whedon has Buffy's (Sarah Michelle Gellar) self-proclaimed "nemesises-ses" invent an invisibility ray. They intend to purposefully wield the power of invisibility, hoping to make themselves "unstoppable" foes of the Slayer. But so empowered, the trio straightaway travels to the local tanning salon simply to spy on naked women. Implicitly, Whedon affirms that the potential ramifications of invisibility are staggering, but not necessarily sinister. However, perhaps even buffoons such as Warren (Adam Busch), Andrew (Tom Lenk), and Jonathan (Danny Strong) would move on to more inspired dastardly deeds, thereby mirroring Marcie or Gyges (with Warren being the most likely candidate). Therefore, it remains unclear whether Whedon agrees with Glaucon about what invisibility scenarios demonstrate.

Glaucon intends to sway lingering skeptics like Whedon by modifying the invisibility thought-experiment to include *two* invisibility rings—one given to a morally good person and the other to an immoral person. Glaucon contends that we would soon have *two* unjust persons because "no one . . . would have such iron will as to stand fast in doing right or keep his hands off other men's possessions when he could . . . fearlessly help himself to anything he wanted . . . and in a word go about among men with the powers of a god" (360b–c). With this, Glaucon concludes (for the opposing view) that people act justly or morally only under compulsion. If even a morally good person would succumb to the temptations the ring represents, then justice cannot be its own unique reward, pursued for its own sake.

Whedon also entertains the possibility of a morally good character becoming invisible. The plot of "Gone" includes Buffy becoming invisible. She subsequently steals a parking-enforcement vehicle, manipulates a social services case worker overseeing her guardianship of her sister Dawn (Michelle Trachtenberg) and dictates an intimate encounter with the vampire Spike (James Marsters). During their romp, she confides that being invisible makes her feel liberated; there are "no rules to follow" and "no reports to file." So Whedon seemingly grants that a virtuous character, if invisible, would act in self-serving ways that she otherwise would not. However, it may be telling that Buffy acts out of character only temporarily, calling her "vacation from herself" a rather regrettable "giddy-fest."

Furthermore, recall the first-season episode of *Angel* entitled "In the Dark." Buffy sends a mystical ring to Angel (David Boreanaz) for safekeeping. A vampire wearing the ring cannot be destroyed, making powerful vamps like Angel or Spike invincible—proverbial "gods walking among men." (This accords with Angel's comment in "Consequences" that being a remorseless vampire walking among humans is to "feel like a god.") As it would be utterly disastrous if Spike possessed it, Angel dutifully hides the ring. Spike predictably travels to Los Angeles, abducts Angel, and employs a vampire-torturer to make Angel disclose its location. Yet Angel perseveres, and Spike never possesses it. Rather than keeping the ring for himself, Angel destroys it. Where Buffy succumbed to temptation, Angel did not. Thus, according to Whedon, it's not obviously clear that someone "walking among men with the powers of a god" would do so in any immoral or self-serving way, even temporarily.

Plato's Men, Whedon's Women

Hoping to persuade any remaining Whedon-like detractors, Glaucon's third thought-experiment for the opposing view is perhaps the strongest. It has two interlocking, main features. First, Glaucon proposes the possibility of a thoroughly immoral person who is so conniving, resourceful, and connected that he is able to deceive everyone into believing that he is thoroughly morally good. Should he ever slip, he has the wherewithal to eloquently, courageously, and convincingly defend himself (361a–b). But such slips will be rare: *appearing* thoroughly just, this person will have a reputation for virtue. This will allow him to hold public office and become a partner in any business. But *being* unjust, he will use his reputation to upend his opponents, grow rich, and help his like-minded, malevolent friends (362b–c).

Glaucon next proposes the possibility of a thoroughly morally good man who has been completely misunderstood by society. He has the (false) reputation of being completely immoral. In Glaucon's words: "He must be stripped of everything but justice, and denied every advantage the other [the unjust man] enjoyed . . . ; and under this lifelong imputation for wickedness, let him hold on his course of justice unwavering to the point of death" (361c–d). But perhaps death would be more like sweet release, because Glaucon further contends that "our just man will be thrown into prison, scourged, racked, his eyes burned out, and, after every kind of torment, be impaled" (361e). Somewhat reminiscent of Angel's plight in "In the Dark," Glaucon conveys imagery closer to the unspeakable hell-dimension of Quor-toth. He goes to these literary lengths to ensure that if the morally good person persists through such adversity, it must be because being just or virtuous is its own unique reward and not for any beneficial pragmatic consequence.

The main point of this thought-experiment is simply to ask: Which person would you choose to be? Glaucon fears that no one would choose to live a life like the misunderstood, thoroughly just person; it is more desirable to be the thoroughly unjust person only appearing to be morally good. If so, then Glaucon has gone a long way to establish the opposing view. Being morally good cannot be the kind of unique reward Socrates and Plato believe exactly because there are circumstances in which no one would want it. Thus the most desirable sort of life is not related to virtue and moral goodness in the way they believe.

The Buffy and Faith (Eliza Dushku) "body-switch" might be the closest Whedonesque parallel to Glaucon's third thought-experiment. In the *Buffy* episode "Who Are You?" Faith awakens from her coma to find serendipitously a package left to her by the deceased ex-mayor Richard Wilkins (Harry Groener). It includes a mystical device allowing the bearer to switch bodies with another. Faith switches bodies with Buffy. Buffy, now inhabiting Faith's body, is quickly apprehended by the Watchers' Council; she prepares to face summary judgment for Faith's misdeeds, including killing an innocent human being and allying herself with the demonically evil former mayor Wilkins. Faith, now inhabiting Buffy's body, is quickly comforted by Joyce Summers (Katherine Sutherland); she prepares for a life as the blond-haired Slayer, including amorous encounters with Buffy's new boyfriend, Riley (Marc Blucas). Buffy is chained, spat on, nearly executed, and faces life imprisonment—her true self misunderstood "to the point of death." Faith practices her Buffy impersonation in the mirror, ready to benefit from Buffy's deserved virtuous reputation and fully confident that she has the wherewithal to correct any slips in her performance. Where Faith represents Glaucon's unjust man believed to be virtuous and Buffy represents his misunderstood just man, and assuming these states of affairs continue indefinitely (even if they don't in the episode), we again are left wondering whether Faith or Buffy leads the more desirable life.

Plato unabashedly believes that the misunderstood but thoroughly just person leads the more desirable life. His response to Glaucon's challenge is rather involved, however, sprawling throughout much of the *Republic*. In rough outline, Plato hypothesizes that human nature is composed of three distinct aspects or elements. The first he calls the *appetitive*, as it is associated with our baser appetites for food, drink, sex, and monetary gain. The second is the *spirited*, associated with such higher emotions as pride, honor, and guilt. The third is the *rational*—the proverbial voice of reason. Furthermore, each element has a primary function, and, if performed well, a desirable character trait manifests. When the appetitive element functions well, the person becomes temperate. When the spirited element functions well, the person becomes courageous and loyal (to himself). When the rational element functions well, the person becomes wise. Becoming temperate, courageous, loyal, and wise is to achieve the pinnacle of human existence. By achieving this pinnacle, one leads the best human life, and true happiness obtains. For Plato, then, true happiness is a way to be and not a way to feel. This is why it is possible for the just person to lead the good life even if he or she is inappropriately shunned and left to excruciatingly suffer alone in prison.

Assuming that Plato is roughly correct about human nature, it's difficult to argue that reaching its pinnacle isn't intrinsically valuable. However, Plato wishes to show that being morally good is valuable for its own sake and good for a person. If the unjust person invariably suffers from some sort of inner conflict or psychological turmoil, as Plato sometimes suggests, then his position is very difficult to deny.[2] After all, if acting immorally invariably leads to gnawing personal unrest and thus unhappiness, it seems one is better off being morally good.

Whedon seems to grant the psychological dangers of immorality. Recall Faith's character arc. Like any Slayer, she is practically invincible. But she is unique in that she revels insatiably in her Slayer-laden abilities and has no qualms about fulfilling her desires. In fact, she initially believes that the life of a Slayer is simple: "want, take, have." Her appetitive element is in high gear. But once she inadvertently kills the deputy mayor—and despite her protestation to Buffy that she doesn't care that he's dead—Faith begins a downward spiral. The body-switch, by providing very intimate glimpses into Buffy's world, only hastens Faith's psychological plummet. Believing herself to be beyond the pale of redemption, she eventually asks Angel in "Five by Five" to kill her so as to end her torment. Thus, in some sense, Whedon agrees with Plato that being bad is not always good for one. It can lead to psychological conflict and misery.[3]

But it's unclear whether Whedon believes that Faith's fate is irresistible. Consider Saffron (Christina Hendricks) from *Firefly*. She gives no hint of becoming psychologically conflicted about fulfilling her selfish desires at the expense of others. Although neither invisible nor invincible, she is incredibly cunning, resourceful, and ruthless. The authorities do not deter her. She shamelessly attempts to swindle Mal (Nathan Fillion) and the crew of spaceship *Serenity* not once but twice. Her schemes commonly involve duping men into caring for her. She has been "married" many times, including to Mal. In "Trash," Saffron reunites with Durran Haymer (Dwier Brown)—the only "husband" she remotely cared for—only in order to relieve him of his prized Lassiter prototype laser pistol. Saffron's reunion with Haymer—a man who adored her—only serves to have him robbed and knocked unconscious. So, even if Faith's intimate exposure to Riley's love for Buffy solidifies Faith's psychological transformation, Saffron's reexposure to Haymer's love only solidifies her steely resolve. Thus it's not clear whether Whedon agrees that morally unjust people necessarily or invariably suffer inner turmoil.[4]

The Not-So-Evil Genius and the Not-So-Super Hero

We can't conclude from the mere fact that Whedon doesn't fully agree with Plato that Plato's solution is untenable. Moreover, Whedon would probably remind us—in some sort of clever, self-deprecating way—that he is neither an academic nor a philosopher, and so is unqualified to critique Plato in the first place.[5] Nevertheless, it seems that pursuing one more parallel between Plato and Whedon sheds important light on Whedon's vision of the good life. It also begins to explain more fully why Whedon diverges from the Platonic conception.

Whedon's sensational *Dr. Horrible's Sing-Along Blog* (2008) took the Internet by storm. In this short film, Whedon portrays two characters for our consideration: Dr. Horrible (Neil Patrick Harris) and Captain Hammer (Nathan Fillion). Dr. Horrible, the resident evil genius, believes that "the world is a mess and he just needs to rule it." He further contends that gaining entrance into the Evil League of Evil (E.L.E.) will facilitate his quest. His application is strong this year, complete with a letter of condemnation from the deputy mayor. However, Captain Hammer, the local superhero, thwarts Horrible at every turn; he has become the evil genius's nemesis. But the tides will turn with Horrible's nearly completed freeze ray. ("This is the one . . . stops time . . . tell your friends.") Captain Hammer, "corporate tool," will thwart him no longer. Of course, we learn all of this via Horrible's video blog, which he updates regularly.

To complete the freeze ray, Horrible requires Wonderflonium. Luckily, some is being locally transported via courier van; Horrible plots to commandeer the van by connecting it to a remote control. But Hammer—from nowhere—lands on top of the remote-controlled van, singing, "Captain Hammer's here, hair blowing in the breeze, the day needs my saving expertise!" Hammer incapacitates Horrible's remote transmitter but then jumps off the van to make time with a female admirer. As Hammer gets her phone number, the van careens down an alley heading straight for Penny (Felicia Day)—the girl of Horrible's dreams! Hammer abruptly jumps in front of Penny, launches her into a pile of garbage bags, and braces himself to stop the runaway van. At the last second, Horrible regains electronic control of it—"the remote control was in his hand!" The van stops only inches in front of Hammer's outstretched arms. As Penny wades through the bags of trash, she thanks Hammer for saving her. Gazing into Hammer's eyes, she becomes instantly smitten with her hero. Horrible cowers away in disbelief, but with the Wonderflonium in tow.

Unlike Plato's literary correlates, Whedon neither depicts Horrible as thoroughly evil, nor Hammer as thoroughly virtuous. Each is painted in shades of gray. On the one hand, Horrible is initially hesitant when the E.L.E leader, Bad Horse, requires a murderous deed for admittance. Horrible laments: "Killing is not my style; it's not creative or elegant." This echoes Horrible's response to the irksome Johnny Snow. He refuses to face Johnny in Dooly Park not merely because he's a "poser in a parka," but mostly because the kids who play there might get hurt. Yet Horrible steals and, in a fit of jealous rage, plots to assassinate Hammer. Doing away with the "corporate tool" will definitely gain him entrance to the League. On the other hand, Hammer does manage to keep the city safe from evil villains like Horrible. However, he has very little regard for the citizens he keeps safe and invariably reminds everyone that no one is as heroic as he. Furthermore, he revels in the attention his job provides. He regularly employs his fame (and the "Ham-Jet") to woo women. Moreover, he is dating Penny primarily to hurt Horrible, and not because he cares for her in any genuine way.

Horrible and Hammer are unlike Plato's correlates in another way: neither is portrayed in a very positive light. The end of Whedon's film is a bit confounding. Our last glimpses of Hammer find him in psychotherapy; Horrible, now believed to be the worst villain ever, pitifully sits alone in front of his webcam. So, if the choice is between leading a life like Horrible's or one like Hammer's, Whedon's implicit answer is: neither. It's tempting to offer a Platonic interpretation of why this is so, at least in Hammer's case, whose appetitive element is clearly out of control. He regularly uses his "superhero" status for sexual conquest, calling Penny his "long-time girlfriend" because they might have sex twice ("so he gets to do the 'weird stuff'"). But the Platonic interpretation seems strained regarding Horrible. He is not as shallow or as egotistical as Hammer. Further, he isn't motivated by personal gain. For him, "it's not about making money, but *taking* money—upsetting the status quo—because the status is not . . . quo." So it's not exactly clear how he is Platonically unbalanced. Perhaps this signals a need for a different explanation for why neither Horrible nor Hammer is leading the good life.

Aristotle, Community, and Friendship

Aristotle, although influenced by Plato, often diverges from his teacher. For example, about the good life, Plato stresses the importance of "internal goods" to the near exclusion of "external goods." But Aristotle demurs: "Even excellence [*arête*] proves to be imperfect as an end [on to itself]: for a man might possibly possess it while . . . undergoing the greatest suffering and misfortune. Nobody would call the life of such a man happy, except for the sake of maintaining an argument."[6] The "'maintainer' of the argument" might be Plato, who is invariably interpreted as holding that human excellence—possessing a harmonious soul—is sufficient for true happiness. But if the ultimate end or goal is true happiness, then Aristotle holds that external goods are also required. In fact, he writes: "Happiness . . . needs external goods as well. . . . Many actions can only be performed with the help of instruments, as it were: friends, wealth, and political power. And there are some external goods the absence of which spoils supreme happiness . . . : for a man . . . who lives all by himself and has no children cannot be classified as altogether happy; even less happy perhaps is a man whose children and friends are worthless" (NE 1098b30–1099a10). Aristotle is sometimes criticized for allowing too many external goods to impact happiness, but for the purposes of exploring Whedon's views, we can restrict our attention to the plausible candidates of community and friendship.

The social nature of human beings is a cornerstone to Aristotle's views on the good life. He writes: "For the final and perfect good . . . we do not mean a man who lives his life in isolation . . . since man is by nature a social and political being" (NE 1097b8–10).[7] Even the wisest and most virtuous persons can benefit from community because having colleagues to work with facilitates better contemplation (NE 1177b1). Aristotle implicitly argues that whether a thing's life goes well invariably depends on what kind of thing it is. It's bad for fish to be separated from the water, and likewise bad for oak trees to be kept in a dark closet. If Aristotle is correct that we are naturally social, then it's bad for any human being to live in complete isolation, which explains why solitary confinement is such serious punishment. This also explains why, according to Giles, Marcie has gone "mad." Becoming invisible in the way that she did represents the severest form of solitary confinement.[8]

Having established that the good human life requires living in community, Aristotle further argues that it also requires friendship—living among those who have goodwill toward one another and care about each other's interests. In support of this, Aristotle plausibly contends that friendship is universally valued; regardless of one's current station in life—young or old, wealthy or poor, powerful or disenfranchised—everyone desires friendship. Aristotle further contends that "friends are the greatest of external goods" and "without friends no one would choose to live, though he had all other goods" (NE 1169b9, 1155a5–6). That is, if it's good to live in community with others, it's better to live among those who express mutual goodwill and concern about each other's interests.

In support of this last idea, consider what it would be like to be the last person on Earth. This solitary person, regardless of whatever else she possessed, would exist akin to the fish out of water or the oak tree in the dark. And if one would be harmed by being the last person on Earth, then it is bad to live as if one is all alone. And if it is bad to lead one's life completely separated from others, then one's well-being is improved by entering into meaningful relations with other people, meeting them as equals.[9] Making this sort of connection minimally requires recognizing that the interests of others are no less important than one's own. The value of such connections is enhanced by wishing goodwill to others and conferring benefits simply for their sake. Such connections accomplish profound results when others simultaneously seek one's good, and all involved mutually work for the betterment of the other—simply for its own sake. Fostering this kind of reciprocal relationship requires time, familiarity (participating in common goals, or "sharing the salt," as Aristotle says), and maintaining trust (NE 1156b25–28). Once such a relationship with another is accomplished, one achieves a sort of second self, a true partner, such that one's interests are directly tied into those of the other (NE 1166a30). This is to enjoy the highest and best form of friendship, which is valuable for its own sake and for the benefits it confers (NE 1157b33–36).[10]

Whedon's depictions of Horrible and Hammer become clearer under an Aristotelian lens. Each character, in a very real sense, "lives all by himself." Each lives consciously separate from others, never connecting with anyone in the way, say, Buffy does with Willow (Alyson Hannigan), Mal does with Zoe, or even Angel eventually begins to with Cordelia. Horrible thinks that everyone else is too stupid to recognize that humanity has been devoured by some sort of social plague. Furthermore, with his self-proclaimed "Ph.D. in horribleness," he purposely distances himself from his various partners in crime, most notably "Moist" (Simon Helberg). Hammer smugly believes that his superhero status diametrically sets him apart from everyone else; no one is as important as he, which explains his condescending tone and awkward social skills. Both are alone and friendless, thereby leading undesirable lives.

Across the Whedonverse

Interpreting Whedon through an Aristotelian lens also provides insight into the ways he regularly depicts his other characters and their circumstances. For example, it provides a unifying but rather novel explanation for how and why Whedon's various main characters act wrongfully and subsequently seek redemption. Furthermore, and perhaps more importantly, it persuasively coheres with Whedon's aesthetic choices when portraying these behaviors and circumstances.

Recall in Whedon's screenplay for *Toy Story* (1995) how Andy's toys, each in its distinctive way, work with each other toward the common good of being there for Andy whenever he needs them. They do this simply for Andy's sake; however, they also work toward one another's good, also for its own sake, by ensuring that each gets full and equal chance to receive Andy's attention. But when Andy receives a cool new Buzz Lightyear (Tim Allen voice) for his birthday, Woody (Tom Hanks voice) becomes jealous. Woody, placing his interests selfishly ahead of the common good, schemes to land Buzz behind Andy's desk so the boy cannot find him. In doing so, Woody chooses to distance himself from his friends, Andy's other toys. Whedon aesthetically emphasizes the wrongfulness of Woody's decision, first, by having Buzz fall out of Andy's window, clearly and seriously endangering Buzz, and, second, by Woody being ostracized by the other toys. Whedon reaffirms this by what Woody endures to earn redemption. He bravely rescues Buzz from the misguided Sid and his vicious dog. He also helps Buzz realize that he is indeed a child's plaything, allowing Lightyear to better share in their common good. Their friendship begins to solidify as they help each other relocate Andy. At the very end of the film, Whedon depicts the toys as a harmonious, cohesive group.

Turning to *Angel,* recall that each member of Team Angel agrees to make the world a better place by "helping the helpless."[11] Each plays his or her part to realize this common good, simply for its own sake and not for personal gain. And like worthy team members, they support one another as they seek their goal, with Cordelia's deathbed aid to Angel serving as a particularly striking selfless example ("You're Welcome"). But in season five, we find Gunn (J. August Richards) acting selfishly. Recall that his "brain-boosting" imprint begins to fade, dissipating his rhetorical and legal skills. He becomes desperate for a recharge lest he be relegated to being merely the "muscle" again. A scientist at Wolfram and Hart will perform the procedure only if Gunn agrees to sign a document that frees up an "ancient curio" from customs. The item, an ancient sarcophagus, inexplicably arrives in Fred's (Amy Acker) lab and infects her with the goddess Illyria's essence, which is slowly killing her with a malady that has no known cure. Discovering that his signature resulted in Fred's terminal condition, Gunn is devastated. That Whedon portrays Fred's peril so gravely is evidence that Gunn acted wrongfully. Whedon aesthetically emphasizes this by the extent to which Gunn goes to redeem himself. He willingly sacrifices himself to take Lindsay's (Christian Kane) place in a hell dimension—allowing Team Angel to achieve its immediate goal—even though it means he will have his heart removed daily. That Illyria/Fred later rescues him poetically intimates that Gunn is redeemed (and perhaps forgiven).

Recall that in the *Firefly* episode "Ariel," Jayne (Adam Baldwin) sells out fellow crew members Simon Tam (Sean Maher) and River Tam (Summer Glau) to the Alliance for the reward money. This decision is clearly contrary to their common good. Spaceship *Serenity* is committed to avoiding Alliance involvement at every turn; no matter how far Alliance control extends, they "aim to get a little bit further." When Simon, River, and Jayne get "pinched" by the feds, making the hospital heist messy, Mal "susses out" Jayne's selfish intentions.

Whedon depicts the seriousness of Jayne's wrongful act in a tellingly novel, two-pronged way. First, a fuming Mal threatens to blow Jayne into empty space. Jayne finally confesses, but he remains confused: "Why are you taking this so personal? It's not like I ratted you out to the feds!" Mal barks back: "But you did. You turn on any of my crew, you turn on me." Because the interests of the crew have grown together so tightly, harming one means harming everyone. That Mal is willing to end Jayne speaks to the severity of Jayne's misdeed. Mal relents only after Jayne exhibits genuine remorse, an emotion with which Jayne is unfamiliar. Second, once Simon discovers Jayne's treachery in "Trash," he neither threatens nor seeks retribution. Rather, he seemingly pardons Jayne, invites him to renew their relationship, and surprisingly offers to trust Jayne more. Simon tells Jayne: "No matter how you come down on us, I will never harm you. You're on this table, you're safe. I'm your medic, . . . we're on the same crew. . . . I don't care what you've done. I don't know what you're planning on doing, but I'm trusting you. I think you should do the same." By mercifully reminding Jayne of the importance of trust and friendship, concepts that Jayne has difficulty "wrapping his head around," Simon hopes to accomplish what Mal does: bringing Jayne back into the fold, working for the common good, and strengthening the bonds of friendship.[12]

Whedon further highlights the seriousness of Jayne's misdeed by what he expends to earn redemption. First, Jayne inexplicably spends some of his cut of the hospital heist on the crew in the form of fresh fruit—a rare and prized commodity in the 'verse. Just as inexplicably, he throws the remainder of his hospital bounty into a kitty Zoe collects in the hope of ransoming Mal and Wash (Alan Tudyk) from Niska's vengeful clutches. Second, Jayne is the first crew member to follow Mal in his call to action upon learning the truth about Miranda. This may require each of them to make the ultimate sacrifice. Jayne responds first, seemingly speaking for the crew: "Shepherd Book used to tell me, if you can't do something smart, do something right" (*Serenity*). He then takes a long swig from a whiskey bottle. That Whedon portrays him immediately sliding the bottle directly to Simon, who also drinks, implies that Jayne's character arc is complete; through the efforts of Mal and Simon, Jayne has become a part of the crew, finally "wrapping his head" around the values of community and friendship.[13]

Champs and Tramps

The Aristotelian hypothesis also explains Whedon's portrayal of complex characters like Angel and Saffron. Angel perhaps most closely resembles Plato's conception of the just man. However, it's also pretty clear that Whedon's Champion was not leading the good life until he came to Sunnydale and connected with Buffy and Giles. Angel had been a recluse, at best brooding alone in the hotel, and at worst living in the sewers and feeding off rats. His solitary nights were unbearably complicated by guilt for his past deeds and his misery exacerbated by witnessing the inexplicable violence humans do to each other. But recall Angel's stirring speech to Faith in "Consequences": "Time was, I thought humans existed just to hurt each other. But then I came here. And I found out there are other types of people. People who genuinely wanted to do right. And they make mistakes. And they fall down. You know, but they keep caring. Keep trying. If you can trust us, Faith, this can all change. You don't have to disappear into the darkness." Angel's life has been significantly improved by meeting with people like Buffy and Giles and connecting with them as equals, sharing in a common good. But doing so requires care, trust, and empathy. Surrounded by such support, he was able to leave the darkness behind (inasmuch as an ensouled vampire can). Presumably, Angel would offer this advice to anyone.[14]

Saffron, Whedon's top tramp, fails to lead the good life exactly because she refuses to meaningfully connect with anyone. This perfectly coheres with Whedon's resolution to "Our Mrs. Reynolds." After Saffron hoodwinks the crew, almost getting everyone on board killed, they track her to a remote moon. At gunpoint, she smugly echoes Glaucon, declaring to Mal: "Everybody plays each other. That's all anybody ever does. We play parts." By playing "the part" properly, anyone can selfishly achieve whatever she wants regardless of the consequences. Mal replies: "Yet here I am with a gun to your head. That's 'cause I got people with me, people who trust each other, who do for each other and ain't always looking for the advantage. There's good people in the 'verse. Not many, lord knows, but you only need a few." Whedon thus presents decisive evidence that the bonds of genuine friendship are its own unique reward. Mal doesn't have much, but he has the crew and that is what is ultimately important. Furthermore, Whedon implies that Saffron suffers on both accounts because (like Faith) she is *without* good people who trust and do for each other.[15]

"It's Love, in Point of Fact"

Aristotle holds that genuine friendship is ultimately a form of love (NE 1157b30–35). It's no surprise, then, that the power of love permeates the Whedonverse. It brings a rogue Slayer to her knees. It leads a father to trudge through hell and back to relocate his infant son, only to later give him up to secure the boy's future. It drives a brother to sacrifice his bright future to rescue his sister. It keeps things spinning when they should fall down, and forewarns of another's pain before she keens. It (and a yellow crayon) literally saves the world.

The power of love thus cements an Aristotelian interpretation of Whedon's visions of the good life. It also solidifies Whedon's depiction of both Horrible and Hammer. Each character lives a loveless life and intentionally acts contrary to the values inherent to genuine friendship. Both, in one way or another, benefit by Penny's affections. Both selfishly squander that benefit, realizing it too late (if at all). Hammer, the cowardly "hero," eventually seeks psychotherapy to make sense of his twisted existence. Billy-the-laundry-buddy, the alter ego of Dr. Horrible, perhaps suffers the most; at least he makes strides in meaningfully connecting with "the girl of his dreams." But jealousy gets the better of him and now—"not feeling a thing"—he is utterly and hopelessly lost. And perhaps he is; all that remains is Dr. Horrible.

So, Whedon ultimately advises us to be neither Horrible nor horrible. The former is utterly alone and empty with no hope of redemption. His E.L.E. cohorts are of no consolation, as they will no doubt play him the way Saffron plays her associates, "for bad men do not delight in each other unless some advantage come to the relation" (NE 1157a18–19). Moreover, it is impossible to befriend any horrible person, let alone be loved by him; such people never act for the sake of anyone but themselves. Rather, we should become wise like Giles and Angel, courageous like Buffy and Woody, loyal like Mal and Gunn, honest like Zoe and Cordelia, compassionate like Willow and Kaylee (Jewel Staite), caring like Simon and Fred, intuitive like Wesley and

Inara, and good-humored like Wash and Xander. Following their examples is conducive to becoming the sort of person who forms meaningful, loving connections with others. Although this cannot absolutely guarantee the good human life, perhaps Joss is correct that it cannot begin without it.

Notes

1. Plato, *Republic,* trans. Francis MacDonald Cornford (Oxford: Oxford University Press, 1945). This essay keeps to the standard practice of referring to Platonic passages via the margin page numbers with lettered subsection markers, added by the Stephanus family, early editors of Plato's work. This passage about Gyges can be found at 359d–e. Subsequent references to the *Republic* will be made parenthetically in the main text.

2. For passages that describe, refer to, or allude to the turmoil of the unjust person, see 439e–440b, 444b, 579b–e, 588e–589a.

3. Greg Forster also comes to a similar conclusion (see his "Faith and Plato: 'You're Nothing! Disgusting Murderous Bitch!'" in Buffy the Vampire Slayer *and Philosophy: Fear and Trembling in Sunnydale,* ed. James South [Chicago: Open Court, 2003], 7–19). See also Karl Schudt, "Also Sprach Faith: The Problem of the Happy Rogue Vampire Slayer," ibid., 20–34. The present essay, although containing some affinities with that of Foster and Schudt, takes the relevant Whedonesque connections with Plato in different directions, beginning with the next paragraph.

4. It's worth noting that Whedon arguably agrees with Plato that great wealth invariably interferes with one's ideals and thus with leading the good life. For proof of this claim, see Whedon's graphic novel *Serenity: Better Days* (Milwaukie, Ore.: Dark Horse, 2008).

5. Whedon makes such a claim in the *Firefly* DVD commentary for "Objects in Space" (Beverly Hills, Calif.: Twentieth Century Fox, 2002). But Whedon's humility shouldn't be interpreted as his complete lack of acumen or philosophical insight. Recall his quote in *Show Tracker* (December 12, 2009) about his recent series *Dollhouse:* "We're trying to create something that's more than the sum of its parts. And not just in an 'Oooh, we're heavy with mythology way.' Dare I say we're reaching for something more philosophical?"

6. Quotes from Aristotle's *Nicomachean Ethics* come from either the Martin Oswald translation (New York: Macmillan/Library of the Liberal Arts, 1962) or the W. D. Ross translation (Oxford: Oxford University Press, 1925). This quote is found at 1095b30–1096a5. Hereafter all references to the *Nicomachean Ethics* are given parenthetically in the main text by margin number, signaled by "NE."

7. See also Aristotle's *Politics* 1253a1–5 and 1253a25–30. By the terms "politics" and "political," Aristotle means something more inclusive than how we currently use those terms. Now, we typically use them to refer to "statecraft" or some such, but Aristotle means something closer to "the science of civilized human existence" or perhaps simply "society."

8. Thus Marcie's situation might also allow for the episode to be entitled "Out of

Sight, Out of Mind." Becoming invisible, Marcie is literally "out of sight," which causes her to become "out of her mind." That she becomes "out of her mind" is reason (at least implicitly) to think that Whedon agrees with Aristotle that the good (human) life cannot be led in complete isolation. That Joss agrees with Aristotle's view fits well with his portrayal of Mal from *Firefly*. The only two times that Mal is ever in any serious danger is in "Out of Gas" and "War Stories." In the former, he is fatally wounded and near death; in the latter, he dies, only to be revived by Niska (Michael Fairman) so the crime lord can continue torturing him. On both occasions, Mal is completely alone. He is rescued only upon the return of the crew, and most notably Zoe (Gina Torres).

9. The argument presented here has been influenced by chapters 5 and 6 of Jean Kazez's *The Weight of Things: Philosophy and the Good Life* (Boston: Blackwell, 2007).

10. For an analysis of friendship and erotic love in the Buffyverse, see Melissa M. Milavec and Sharon M. Kaye, "Buffy in the Buff: A Slayer's Solution to the Aristotle's Love Paradox," in Buffy the Vampire Slayer *and Philosophy: Fear and Trembling in Sunnydale,* ed. James South (Chicago: Open Court, 2003), 173–84.

11. The Team's common good is more fully spelled out in "Epiphany" and "Deep Down." In the former, Angel asserts: "People shouldn't suffer as they do. Because if there isn't any bigger meaning, then the smallest act of kindness is the greatest thing in the world." In the latter, and perhaps more poignantly, he instructs his son: "Nothing in the world is the way it ought to be. It's harsh and cruel. But that's why there's us. Champions. It doesn't matter where we come from, what we've done or suffered, or even if we make a difference. We live as though the world was as it *should* be, to show it what it *can* be."

12. That Simon responds mercifully to Jayne's misdeed seems significant given the high regard Whedon places on it. Recall, from "Shindig," Mal's comment that "mercy is the mark of a great man." Furthermore, in "Conviction," Angel tells a Wolfram and Heart subordinate, "There is only one thing more powerful than conviction: mercy." Thus, arguably, Whedon portrays Simon as leading by example in the most powerful or persuasive way possible. Implicitly, if this doesn't work, then River will have no choice but to kill Jayne "with her brain," presumably in some sort of unseemly way.

13. For more on Jayne's moral transformation (and its parallels with Spike's transformation), see Jason Grinnell, "Aristotle, Kant, Spike, and Jayne: Ethics and Character in the Whedonverse," in this volume.

14. Thus Faith fails to lead the good life not merely because she is psychologically conflicted or because her appetitive element is out of control, but because she is horribly (pun intended) alone, as portrayed at the end of "Who Are You?" Rather than embracing Sunnydale and the people Angel found (Buffy, Giles, and the Scoobies), she is traveling away from it, by herself, in an empty train car. Note that she does not redeem herself until after first meaningfully connecting with Angel, and later helping Buffy combat the First in the last season of *Buffy the Vampire Slayer*.

15. Recall that Saffron returns in "Trash." The episode is so titled because Saffron and Mal intend to steal the Lassiter by placing it in the trash chute. Also recall, however, the resolution of the episode. The crew turns the tables on Saffron (more or less success-

fully), playing her for the inside information she possesses about Haymer's floating-island estate. Inara (Morena Baccarin) is waiting for Saffron at the drop point. Inara takes the Lassiter from Saffron and locks her in a trash bin until the authorities arrive. The idea may be that Saffron is where she belongs—in the trash because that is what she is. As trash, she is not fit to be associated with anyone, to her detriment.

Aristotle, Kant, Spike, and Jayne
Ethics and Character in the Whedonverse

Jason D. Grinnell

> Yeah, I could do that, but I'm paralyzed with not caring very much.
> —William the Bloody, *Buffy the Vampire Slayer* ("Triangle")

Imagine you visit a doctor, and the doctor tells you she needs to perform a serious procedure on you. Nervous, you ask her if she is a good doctor. She replies, "Well, I've never been fired or sued for malpractice." I suspect such an answer wouldn't reassure many of us. When you asked the question, you were asking not only about the doctor's skill, but also about her attention to detail, her conscientiousness, and her integrity. You were asking if she seeks to be the best doctor she can be. In effect, you were asking about her *character*. Her answer, on the other hand, addressed her ability to satisfy minimum standards, to "follow the rules." The doctor can be forgiven for thinking this way; after all, life in our litigious society often revolves around identifying what rules must be followed to avoid punishment of one kind or another. We encounter this mind-set in action whenever a politician splits rhetorical hairs to explain how his behavior didn't technically violate the rules, or a student asks herself, "What is the least amount of effort I can put into this class and still earn a passing grade?" We live our lives surrounded by rules, and it's easy to start thinking like the doctor who thinks "good" means "never breaking the rules." Many of us, however, are intuitively convinced that there's more to being a good person than mere rule following. We care about *why* someone performs a particular action, and we're reluctant to give credit without knowing her motivations, her intentions, and her character.

What can *Buffy the Vampire Slayer*'s William the Bloody, a.k.a. "Spike" (James Marsters), and *Firefly*'s Jayne Cobb (Adam Baldwin) teach us about character? A great deal, in fact. Joss Whedon writes intriguing, complex characters, and while the "hero" of each series justifiably attracts a great deal of attention, some of the supporting players are equally fascinating. Spike and Jayne both begin as pretty despicable (but highly entertaining) characters. They develop considerably within their respective series, however, and their character (pun very much intended) arcs illustrate that ethics is about far more than rule following. Through Spike and Jayne, Whedon shows us that however much good one may accomplish, it means little if it's done without good motivations and character, and that developing true moral goodness can be a long and difficult process.

Ancient Greek Views of Character

The idea that character matters as much as consequences is often associated with the ancient Greeks. In Plato's *Republic,* the character Glaucon describes a common view of morality as a sort of bargain.[1] Deep down, Glaucon says, what we really want is to be free of all rules and restraints on our behavior and to be able to do whatever we wish without any fear of punishment. In other words, we each want to be the biggest, toughest kid on the playground. What we most fear, however, is to be completely at the mercy of others, with no power to defend ourselves. In this scenario, we're the smallest, weakest kids on the playground, with no one to turn to for help. As a result of these two elements of human nature, Glaucon argues, each of us agrees to limit his or her freedom in exchange for others limiting theirs. It makes sense to curb my desire to be the playground bully in exchange for not having to worry about what happens when a bigger and stronger bully (or vampire) moves into my neighborhood.

Plato has Glaucon point out, though, that if this is all there is to morality, then the only reason we have to follow *any* moral rules is that we fear being punished if we don't. He illustrates this with a story about a shepherd who discovers a ring that allows him to become invisible at will. The shepherd uses his new power to overthrow a kingdom and set himself up as ruler.[2] The story illustrates that those who do not believe they can be caught or punished have no reason to follow the rules by which the rest of us live. If Glaucon is correct, morality exists to place limits on our freedom. We accept the bargain because it often serves our self-interest, but those of us who value freedom can be expected to resent and resist the demands of morality. Both Spike (a powerful and immortal vampire) and Jayne (a strong and well-armed mercenary on the fringes of society) seem to qualify. Recognizing the problems such persons pose for this view of morality, Plato devotes the rest of *Republic* to arguing that Glaucon is incorrect: that there's more to being a good person than fearing punishment enough to follow rules, and that we have reason to care about our character.

Plato's student Aristotle devotes even more time and care to showing that character matters, and that in order to be a good person one must not only do good things but also do them for good reasons. Aristotle argues that humans have a purpose, a potential that needs to be actualized: to live a life that exercises and develops those distinctive capacities that make us human, a life of good and noble excellence. Persons who don't act or develop according to their purpose fail to actualize that potential and thus fail as persons.

A crucial part of actualizing the life of excellence involves developing character traits such as courage, moderation, and generosity.[3] The truly excellent person doesn't just happen to do things that turn out to be excellent, however; he does them because he strives to *be* excellent. Aristotle tells us that truly excellent things are done by an agent who does them knowingly and voluntarily, and does them for their own sake and because of a "firm and unchanging disposition."[4] He writes: "To be affected when one should, at the things one should, in relation to the people one should, for the reasons one should, and in the way one should; is both intermediate and best, which is what belongs to excellence."[5]

Getting all of that right, however, also requires a type of wisdom. This "practical wisdom" is the ability to identify things that are genuinely valuable, to understand why they are valuable, to determine the best way to pursue them, and to have the proper mental and emotional state while doing so.[6] It encompasses the excellences of character that Aristotle argues are necessary to be a fully actualized, good, and noble person. We develop these excellences by first displaying the potential to do excellent things and then actualizing that potential. He tells us, "We become just by doing just things, moderate by doing moderate things, and courageous by doing courageous things."[7] It is wisdom that fits motivation, emotion, and action together to make up genuinely good character.

While Glaucon attempts to show that being moral is something we do because society demands it, and Plato argues that morality is valuable for its own sake, Aristotle adds that being good is something that is necessary to become fully human.

A Kantian View of Character

The eighteenth-century philosopher Immanuel Kant also offers a theory of ethics that emphasizes the importance of character.[8] Kant argues that much of our reasoning concerning what to do takes the form of a "hypothetical imperative," a combination of some contingent fact with a command. Such imperatives tell us that *if* we have some desire or another, we should follow the command. Take, for example, the standard parent's line, "If you want to grow up to be big and strong, eat your broccoli." It doesn't take long for the vegetable-loathing child to discover the loophole and respond with, "I don't care about growing up to be big and strong." At this point, of course, the child has won the argument. The parent made the mistake of making the command to eat the broccoli conditional upon the desire to be big and strong. Remove the desire, and the command loses its motivational force.[9] Much of our casual moral reasoning fits this pattern and reflects the basic idea Glaucon was describing. When morality is couched only in terms of, "If you don't want to be punished, then follow the rules," we're left with a motivational problem for those who don't fear punishment.

Kant would agree with Plato that this sort of thinking does not reflect truly moral thinking; thus Kant proposes instead a "categorical imperative," a framework for decision making based on reason rather than desire.[10] The categorical imperative takes many forms in Kant's work, but the core idea is that we may only act in ways that would still be rational if they were universal laws, and that we must respect the absolute dignity of all persons by not treating them as mere tools to advance our own goals. We use the categorical imperative to identify our duties, but there is more involved than just *what* we do. Kant also argues that to demonstrate good character, it is crucial that we do the right thing for the right *reason*.

He asks us to consider a merchant who, when given an opportunity to cheat a customer who knows no better, nevertheless deals honestly with him. Of course, this is the right thing to do, but Kant goes on to argue that if the merchant is doing it only because he desires the profit from the customer's future business, we shouldn't praise him for being good.[11] The merchant does what the categorical imperative would tell him is the right thing to do, but only because it serves his self-interest, not because it's the right thing to do. He thus does not demonstrate good character. If we act on the basis of motives other than a sense of moral duty, we are in effect acting on the basis of a hypothetical imperative once again: in this case, "If you want your business to be profitable, behave in such a way that you gain a reputation for honesty." Such desire-based rules are unreliable. The merchant who doesn't take such a long view, instead believing that he would make more money by cheating, won't find himself bound by such a principle, and even the merchant discussed previously may cease following the rules if he should lose the desire to build a reputation for honesty. This is why Kant places so much emphasis on doing the right thing for the right reason, and developing the genuine goodness of a "good will," or a deep commitment to doing one's moral duty regardless of cost. This "good will" is the only thing that "can be regarded as good without qualification."[12]

Self-Interest and Self-Control

Fans of *Buffy the Vampire Slayer* first meet the vampire William the Bloody (Spike) in the season-two episode "School Hard." We learn that Spike is ruthless and somewhat famous for having killed not one but two Slayers. When Spike encounters Angel (David Boreanaz) in Sunnydale, his disdain for human morality is made clear. He denounces Angel for being "housebroken" and is outraged that his "Yoda"—his vampire mentor—is now trying to be "good." Later, Spike kills the leader of the vampires in Sunnydale, proclaiming that there is going to be "less ritual" and "more fun" from now on. Spike's disgust with Angel and refusal to work within the existing vampire hierarchy show his rejection of rules of *any* kind as limitations on his freedom. Spike seems to share Glaucon's view that a person who "has the power to do [injustice] . . . and is a true man would not make an agreement with anyone not to do injustice in order not to suffer it. For him that would be madness."[13]

Firefly's Jayne Cobb also begins as an enemy of his show's protagonist, Malcolm Reynolds (Nathan Fillion). We discover in the episode "Out of Gas" that Mal first met Jayne when Jayne and the men he worked for captured Mal. In a flashback, we learn that Mal offered Jayne a better percentage of the profits, along with his own room on board. Jayne promptly shot his erstwhile boss and turned his gun on another compatriot, asking Mal, "How big a room?" Jayne, like Spike and Glaucon, sees morality as something for those who lack the power to do as they desire. He is motivated by nothing beyond self-interest, and when his desires change, so does his loyalty.

The theme of self-interest as the governing feature of both Spike and Jayne continues to develop in their respective series. In season two of *Buffy*, Angel reverts to Angelus, his evil and soulless pure vampire form, and the form Spike remembered so fondly as his "Yoda." Angelus isn't quite as much fun as Spike remembered, however, since he seems to have his eye on Spike's girlfriend, Drusilla (Juliet Landau), and never tires of mocking the currently injured and wheelchair-bound Spike. Having a taste of the kind of relative weakness Glaucon discusses doesn't please Spike, and when Angelus goes too far in his quest to destroy the world, Spike approaches Buffy (Sarah Michelle Gellar) and proposes an alliance.

SPIKE: I want to stop Angel. I want to save the world. . . .

BUFFY: Ok, fine. You're not down with Angel. Why would you ever come to me?

SPIKE: I want Dru back. I want it like it was before he came back. The way she acts around him . . .

BUFFY: You're pathetic. Earth may be sucked into Hell, and you want help 'cause your girlfriend's a big ho? Well let me take this opportunity to not care.

SPIKE: I can't fight them both alone and neither can you.

BUFFY: All right, talk. What's the deal?

SPIKE: Simple. You let me and Dru skip town, I'll help you kill Angel ("Becoming, Part II")

The deal is struck, and during the final battle scene, Spike carries off an unconscious Drusilla and looks back to see Angelus overpowering Buffy. He says, "God, he's going to kill her," shrugs, and walks away. The consequences of Spike's actions are ultimately "good" since, as a matter of fact, he did give Buffy the help she needed to defeat the thoroughly evil Angelus and save the world. Neither Aristotle nor Kant would judge Spike himself as "good," however: he is missing the crucial aspects of good character and good intent. He doesn't care about Buffy or her prospects for survival; he allied himself with her simply because it was the best way to get what he wanted. Once he's fulfilled his part of the bargain and received what he wanted, he recognizes no independent reason to continue to help her. Glaucon's description of morality has been satisfied. As viewers, however, the scene taps into our intuition that there is still something morally lacking in Spike's actions despite his technical adherence to the terms of the agreement. We, like Aristotle and Kant, want more from Spike.

In the pilot episode of *Firefly,* "Serenity," Jayne also has an opportunity to betray Mal and the crew. A passenger named Dobbs has come aboard, but he turns out to be a mole for the Alliance, the oppressive government of the developed Core planets. When Jayne is sent to interrogate him, Dobbs offers him enough money to "buy his own ship." Dobbs later escapes, seemingly easily, and is shot by Mal. At the episode's close, Mal mentions that he is surprised that Dobbs escaped. Jayne denies any involvement but contends that "it all turned out just fine" anyway. Mal queries: "But he did try to make a deal with you, right? How come you didn't turn on me, Jayne?" Jayne simply replies, "Money wasn't good enough." Mal continues: "What happens when it is?" Jayne: "Well, that'll be an interesting day."

Jayne isn't offended or bothered by Mal's questions or the implication that he *might* turn on Mal; he simply admits and accepts that he *would,* under the right circumstances, and sees no ethical problem with it. He has assessed his goals and believes that for now they are better served by cooperating with the crew of *Serenity.* He is fully aware, however, that one day this may change; when it does, so will his loyalty. Jayne's behavior, like Spike's, has the effect of advancing the protagonist's interests, but here, too, Whedon shows that we should not make the mistake of seeing Jayne as "good." Jayne indicates with his "it all turned out just fine" remark that whether he agreed to betray Mal or not shouldn't really matter since both he and Mal ended up okay; he doesn't see anything beyond this as relevant. Good character requires more than good consequences, though. Jayne lacks the characteristic motivations of a good person, and his commitment to behaviors that have good consequences is thus just as accidental and unreliable as Spike's.

In season four of *Buffy,* Spike is captured by a secret military organization called the Initiative. They implant a chip in his head that makes it impossible for him to cause harm to humans without experiencing intense pain himself. In desperation, he comes to Buffy for help. He explains that he cannot even hit a person, much less bite or feed on one, so she has to help him. When Buffy sarcastically responds that since he has not murdered anyone lately, they should be best friends, she is making the point that it is his (bad) character that matters to her, not his current harmlessness. Bewildered that she doesn't take his forced inability to hurt humans as sufficient to earn her sympathy and trust, Spike offers another bargain, telling Buffy he has information about the Initiative. When Buffy agrees to invite him into her home but insists on tying him up, Spike complains that he is being mistreated. His inability to grasp the idea of character prevents him from understanding that the compassion and care Buffy extends to others is not based on their adherence to the terms of a bargain ("Pangs").[14]

Eventually, Buffy comes to accept that Spike is harmless (at least for the time being) and allows him to go unsupervised. In a later episode, Spike learns that he can hit other vampires and demons without pain and so is able to indulge his love of violence by fighting other evil beings. Of course, this means he often is fighting on the same side as Buffy, and in some cases directly helping her. This is not, however, because of a good will as Kant describes it, or because of an excellence of character as Aristotle describes it. Spike does the right thing in fighting evil creatures, but for the wrong reasons. He's in a situation where he cannot do what he *really* wants to do because of the pain it will cause him, but his desire to kill things *can* be expressed in a way that brings about results that we the viewers (and Buffy the protagonist) find congenial. He doesn't do it because they are evil or because he cares about being a good person. He freely admits this, at one point responding to a request for help by asking if he's supposed to help out of the "evilness of my heart" ("A New Man").

Fighting against demons and in support of Buffy does help Spike make progress, however. Aristotle argues that a process of practice and habituation is necessary to develop good character.[15] Whedon has Spike (and Jayne) follow something very much like the process Aristotle describes, first performing actions that mimic those of good characters, but without the appropriate mental and emotional components, and then developing to the point where they themselves might be said to be "good." By regularly fighting alongside Buffy, Spike is practicing behaving like a good person, and this habituates him to good actions and prepares him to eventually *be* good.

Self-Reflection

Whedon has both Spike and Jayne undergo character shifts as their respective series develop. Each of them seems to begin caring about doing the right thing for the right reasons and about developing those excellences of character Aristotle and Kant identify as the cornerstones of genuine goodness.

Spike displays some subtle changes as season five progresses. In the episode "Family," for example, Spike seems to be genuinely hurt when his contributions to the "Scooby Gang" (i.e., Buffy and her friends) aren't recognized and praised. The episode centers on Tara (Amber Benson), Willow's (Alyson Hannigan) new girlfriend. Believing herself to be a demon and fearing discovery by the gang, Tara casts a spell over the Scoobies to prevent them from seeing demons. Unfortunately, the group is then attacked by minions of Glory (Clare Kramer), the "big bad" of season five. Spike seems to enjoy the show at first, but as he watches the gang struggle against demons they cannot see, he realizes (disgustedly) that he cares too much about Buffy not to help. While wrestling a demon, he mutters, "you're welcome" to a distracted Buffy. Spike later proves that Tara is not a demon and again sarcastically mutters, "you're welcome" in response to the conspicuous absence of thanks.

In a later episode, "Triangle," the gang fights a troll in a bar, causing a balcony to collapse and injure many patrons.[16] In the aftermath of the collapse, Spike ostentatiously places a blanket around a wounded woman and tells her she'll be okay. Buffy confronts him suspiciously:

BUFFY: What are you doing?
SPIKE: Making this woman more comfortable. I'm not sampling, I'll
    have you know. Look at all these lovely blood-covered people. I

could, but not a taste for Spike, not a lick. I knew you wouldn't
like it.
BUFFY: You want credit for not feeding off bleeding disaster victims?
SPIKE: Well . . . yeah.
BUFFY: [Incredulous] You're disgusting.
SPIKE: [Frustrated] What's it take?

In both "Family" and "Triangle," Spike is struggling to overcome his own
character. His previous behavior has made Buffy suspicious of his motives,
and she won't accept him as a true ally despite a number of actions that do,
in fact, help in her battle against evil. Try as he might to understand goodness, though, Spike is still looking for a reward. He wants thanks, praise,
and recognition from Buffy for his deeds. In other words, while he's doing
the right thing and caring about the others after a fashion, he's still acting
on the basis of hypothetical imperatives and a type of self-interest (i.e., If
you want praise, do good deeds). He is performing correct acts, but he
doesn't yet have the correct feelings. His behavior reflects self-control, not
excellence of character. This may be an improvement, but we're still a long
way from true goodness.

Jayne struggles with similar issues. He, like Spike, doesn't seem to grasp
the idea of excellence of character. In the episode "Jaynestown," *Serenity*'s
crew visits Canton, a poor planet of downtrodden and exploited laborers
("mudders"). They discover that the mudders have erected a statue of Jayne.
Jayne, confused, insists he's only been to the planet once, when he robbed the
local magistrate and fled. Later, when the crew is in a local tavern, a musi-
cian sings about Jayne as the "hero of Canton," who "robbed from the rich
and gave to the poor." We learn that Jayne was forced to dump the loot out
of his ship in order to escape. It fell to the mudders below, who attributed
great heroism and benevolence to Jayne. Jayne is eventually recognized,
and the mudders, assuming that he has returned to save them, offer him
the best whiskey in the house. Jayne embraces his role and celebrates with
the adoring mudders.

We learn that the mudders united to resist the magistrate's attempts to
reclaim the money, and to defend the statue of Jayne. We also discover that
Jayne pushed his partner, Stitch, out of the ship when it was necessary to
save himself, and the magistrate has had Stitch imprisoned ever since. Once
again, we see evidence of Jayne's ruthless pursuit of his self-interest and his
disregard for all other considerations.

The next morning, Jayne learns of Mal's plan to use a "Jayne Day" celebration to distract everyone long enough for *Serenity* to take on her cargo

and get away. Uncharacteristically, Jayne seems genuinely troubled by this and asks: "I don't know. You think we should be using my fame to hood-wink folks? . . . No, really, Mal. I mean, maybe there's something to this. The mudders . . . I think I really made a difference in their lives. You know . . . Me. Jayne Cobb." To see Jayne caring about others and being troubled by the thought of using them to advance his own interests suggests that Jayne's ethical outlook is beginning to shift. Perhaps, for example, he is beginning to see others as valuable in themselves.

At the Jayne Day gathering, Jayne makes a short speech to the cheer-ing mudders, but then an armed Stitch disrupts the festivities and tells the crowd what really caused their windfall. He denounces Jayne for pushing him out of the ship, contending that *everybody* except "the Hero of Canton" has the decency to look out for a partner. When he takes aim and attempts to kill Jayne, a young mudder jumps in front of the shot and is killed. Jayne then beats Stitch to death in front of the crowd. Jayne, now visibly upset, shouts at the lifeless body of the boy who saved him and then denounces the crowd, shouting: "You think there's someone just gonna drop money on ya? . . . Money they could use? . . . Well there ain't people like that. There's just people like me."

As we noted earlier, Jayne's worldview is based on the idea that there is nothing more to morality than self-interest. He seems to believe some version of Glaucon's view, that morality is an arrangement of rules we fol-low only to avoid punishment and advance our own interests. The crucial part in this episode for our purposes, however, is in his grappling with the possibility that there could be others who genuinely believe differently. If he can be mistaken for one, perhaps he has the potential to actually *be* one.

As *Serenity* departs, Jayne is clearly troubled. He tells Mal: "Don't make no sense. What—Why the hell did that mudder have to go and do that for, Mal—jumpin' in front of the shotgun blast? . . . Hell, there weren't a one of 'em understood what happened out there. They're probably sticking that statue right back up. . . . I don't know why that eats at me so." The self-sacrifice of a person who viewed him as a role model rattles Jayne, as does the mudders' belief that genuinely altruistic people actually exist. He seems prepared to change further, and in the next episode he does so.

Serenity next visits Ariel, one of the Core planets, in the episode "Ariel." Here Jayne acts on his better-established character traits and contacts an Alliance agent to turn in River and Simon for a reward. When Jayne hands them over to the authorities, however, he, too, is arrested. Eventually they all get free, and back aboard the ship, Simon praises a seemingly embar-rassed Jayne and tells everyone that they only survived because of his help.

Mal, however, later knocks Jayne out and traps him in the ship's airlock. When Jayne regains consciousness, Mal confronts him with his suspicion that Jayne called the authorities. Jayne swears he did nothing of the sort, but Mal is unmoved. As they get closer to space and Jayne's imminent death in the open airlock, Jayne apologizes, and Mal demands to know why he is apologizing. Jayne declares that the "money was too good. I got stupid." Mal is unmoved, and Jayne demands to know why Mal is taking things so personally, when it was not Mal that Jayne betrayed. Mal, of genuinely heroic character, declares: "But you did! You turn on any of my crew, you turn on me! If it's such a concept you can't seem to wrap your head around . . . then you got no place here. You did it to me, Jayne, and that's a fact." We see something like comprehension on Jayne's face, and as Mal walks away and leaves him to die, Jayne stops begging and arguing.

> JAYNE: What are you gonna tell the others?
> MAL: About what?
> JAYNE: About why I'm dead.
> MAL: I hadn't thought about it.
> JAYNE: Make something up. . . . Don't tell them what I did. ("Ariel")

At this change in tone and focus, Mal relents, and lets Jayne in.

Jayne's character has changed. While he once nonchalantly admitted that he would have betrayed Mal had the reward been better, he now seems deeply troubled about what others would think of his treachery. Jayne feels the shame and guilt over his behavior that was hinted at in the previous episode. He's beginning to *care* about his behavior and what it reveals about him as a person to himself and to others. The kind of character excellence emphasized by Aristotle and Kant is starting to take root in Jayne. Mal seems to recognize change, and Whedon leads us to believe that this is what causes him to spare Jayne.

In the case of *Buffy*, Whedon has more time to develop Spike's character. In the season-five episode "Intervention," for example, the fallen god Glory captures Spike and tortures him to find out the identity of the "key," whom we know to be Buffy's sister, Dawn. The once thoroughly self-interested and mercenary Spike refuses to tell her and even tries to provoke Glory into killing him to avoid revealing the secret. He succeeds in making her angry enough to kick him through a wall, allowing him to escape. Spike explains that he kept the secret because Dawn's death would destroy Buffy, and he "couldn't live [with] her being in that much pain. I'd let Glory kill me first. Nearly bloody did."

Spike has come a long way. He demonstrates great courage, refuses to act to advance his own narrow interests, and is willing to die to prevent harm to Dawn and Buffy. He is beginning to display the results of his habituation at Buffy's side. He has gained practice in doing the right thing and is getting closer to doing it for the right reasons. We may admire his willingness to sacrifice himself for those to whom he has an emotional tie, but what true excellence requires is that he do these things because they are the good and noble things to do. Acting out of love for Buffy is still operating on the basis of a hypothetical imperative, and the most we should say of Spike is that his behavior is in accordance with excellence. While we are likely to find this a much less troubling motivation than his earlier ones, he does not yet demonstrate the good and noble character Aristotle suggests all humans should cultivate or act from a good will as described by Kant.

The Right Things for the Right Reasons

In the final televised season of *Buffy*, Spike's soul has been restored ("Grave").[17] In the *Buffy* universe, this means he must also carry the guilt and shame for all the things he did as a vampire without a soul. He struggles to cope, and Buffy comes to rely on him more and more as the season unfolds and the ultimate battle with "the First," the primeval source of all evil, draws closer. Near the end, Buffy receives a mystical amulet that can be worn only by a truly good champion. No one is sure what it will do, but Spike is the one who comes forward to bear it.

In the final episode, the First unleashes a vast army of supervampires on the Hellmouth. Buffy and the Scooby gang fight valiantly, but there are too many vampires, and they're clearly losing. As the ground caves in around them, however, sunlight strikes Spike's amulet, and he begins to glow and project light all around the cavern, killing every vampire it hits. Unfortunately, Spike himself isn't immune to the effects. Buffy tries to pull him out, but he refuses, telling her that he has to stay and do the "cleanup" (i.e., finish off the vampire army). Buffy tells him that she loves him, and Spike replies: "No you don't. But thanks for sayin' it" ("Chosen"). As the flames consume him, he laughs with the joy of being genuinely good.[18] Spike is no longer a calculating self-interest pursuer, and he knows Buffy won't love him no matter what he does. He has become, in Aristotle's language, a person who is affected when he should be, at the things he should be, in relation to the people he should be, for the reasons he should be, and in the way he should be.[19] In other words, he is now acting nobly as a result of excellences of character. Kant, too, would approve for Spike is not acting out of selfishness or treating others as tools to reach his own goals. Nor is he acting to save Buffy in particular, or for her praise and rewards. He is acting on the basis of a good will for its own sake and performing good acts for the sake of goodness.[20]

Jayne fares better, but he, too, abandons his selfishness and acts out of genuine goodness. In the motion picture *Serenity*, Mal, Jayne, and the rest of the crew discover that the Alliance has attempted to modify human beings to behave as more docile and productive citizens. This modification went horribly wrong and wiped out most of an entire planet's population. The few who survived were transformed into "Reavers"—humans whose basest instincts are magnified beyond all self-control, who travel the galaxy killing, raping, and cannibalizing wherever and whenever they can. Horrified, the crew of *Serenity* realizes this information needs to be publicized. To do so, however, will likely result in their deaths. There's no prospect of any reward beyond getting the word out, and there's little chance of survival. Realizing this, the erstwhile amoral mercenary Jayne Cobb declares, "If you can't do something smart, do something right." It's a bit of a laugh-line in the movie, but it echoes his earlier attitude toward morality and rule following as something for suckers and the weak. Now, though, Jayne has become the sort of man who'll risk his life for the sake of doing what's right. When he's confronted with knowledge of the Reavers—humans who demonstrate what an amoral life of pure self-interest really looks like—Jayne realizes that both they and the forces that created them must be stopped. He cares about getting the word out more than he cares about his reward or even his life because he knows it's the right thing to do. Like Spike, when he does the right thing now, it's for the right reasons. In other words, he, like Spike, is finally demonstrating both Aristotelian wisdom and a Kantian good will.

The development of both Spike and Jayne teaches us a great deal about character, in that both are initially classic cases of persons who don't concern themselves with ethics. For that matter, it might be more accurate to suggest that at first they just don't *get* ethics. They may follow certain rules and in some situations act very much like the heroes with whom they interact, but, at least initially, they aren't *good* characters. Whedon shows us that ethics isn't about merely producing good consequences or following the rules to meet some minimum threshold of good-enough behavior. It is, rather, about developing the wisdom and excellence of character that will allow us to be genuinely good. Spike and Jayne reveal the many layers of ethics and the important differences between the moral correctness of acts and the moral goodness of persons.

Notes

I would like to thank John Draeger and John Burnight for their many helpful comments (and, in the case of Burnight, for introducing me to Whedon's work many years ago). Thank you also to Evan Kreider and Dean Kowalski for their hard work organizing and editing this volume.

1. Plato, *Republic,* trans. G. M. A. Grube and C. D. C. Reeve (Indianapolis: Hackett, 1992).

2. Ibid., 33–43.

3. The Greek term I am translating as "excellence" is *arête.* It is also sometimes translated as "virtue."

4. Aristotle, *Nicomachean Ethics,* trans. Sarah Broadie and Christopher Rowe (New York: Oxford University Press, 2002), 115.

5. Ibid., 117.

6. The Greek term I am translating as "practical wisdom" is *phronesis.*

7. Aristotle, *Nicomachean Ethics,* 111.

8. Immanuel Kant lived from 1724 to 1804.

9. Consider, "If you can't do the time, don't do the crime." How persuasive is this if I *can* do the time?

10. Immanuel Kant, *Grounding for the Metaphysics of Morals,* trans. James W. Ellington, 3rd ed. (Indianapolis: Hackett, 1993).

11. Ibid., 10.

12. Ibid., 7.

13. Plato, *Republic,* 35.

14. In light of his own minimalistic interpretation of their last bargain, Spike's expectation that Buffy will go beyond the narrow terms of the agreement further indicates his selfishness and deep confusion about ethics.

15. Aristotle, *Nicomachean Ethics,* 115.

16. Spike, however, has a chance to fight the troll by himself but declares, "Yeah, I could do that, but I'm paralyzed with not caring very much" ("Triangle"). It is only when Buffy arrives and Spike has the opportunity to be seen fighting the troll that he gets involved.

17. Spike passes a grueling test administered by a powerful demon in order to be able to "give Buffy what she deserves." By the time of the test, things have gone badly wrong between Spike and Buffy, and Spike tells himself he is doing this so the demon will remove his chip and allow him to kill Buffy. The demon seems to understand Spike better than he understands himself and, upon the successful completion of Spike's test, gives him what he desires and restores Spike's soul. Much like Spike's early denial and rationalization of his feelings for Buffy, Spike's self-knowledge (or lack thereof) makes for a fascinating set of ethics discussions as well.

18. One of the last things Spike tells Buffy is that he can really, finally, "feel" his soul. Aristotle argues that ethics is about excellent activity of the soul.

19. Aristotle, *Nicomachean Ethics,* 117.

20. In a happy coincidence, in section 394 of the *Grounding,* Kant tells us that a good will would "like a jewel, still shine by its own light as something that has full value in itself." The amulet that Spike is wearing is a large jewel, and it is his goodness of character that allows it to sparkle and save the world (Kant, *Grounding for the Metaphysics of Morals,* 8).

Companions, Dolls, and Whores

Joss Whedon on Sex and Prostitution

Tait Szabo

The fantasy worlds of Joss Whedon serve as a lens through which we may view our own conventions about sex and sexual morality, especially by looking at the way Whedon presents prostitution. In *Firefly* and *Serenity*, Inara Serra (Morena Baccarin) makes a living as a "Companion." Companionship in the world of *Firefly/Serenity* differs from prostitution as we know it. Inara's work represents what prostitution could look like if it were transformed into a respectable profession, and it shows us that this transformation is at least conceptually possible. Inara helps to expose the fact that much of our own sexual morality has less to do with necessary features of sex and more to do with contingent social conventions. In *Dollhouse*, Echo (Eliza Dushku) is a "doll," or an "active"—a body whose original mind has been wiped away so that it is ready to be imprinted with any number of temporary personas in order to satisfy the fantasies of the rich clients of the Dollhouse, fantasies that sometimes involve sexual activity. While it is easy to see the positive portrayal of prostitution in *Firefly/Serenity*, Whedon's view of prostitution seems to be different in *Dollhouse*. By the end of *Dollhouse*, Echo is a sympathetic hero, presented as someone wrongfully treated. Nevertheless, as we shall see, Whedon's treatment of prostitution in *Dollhouse* complements rather than undermines his treatment of prostitution in *Firefly/Serenity*. Thus, through *Firefly/Serenity* and *Dollhouse* together, Whedon demonstrates what morally unobjectionable prostitution could look like.

Sex in the Twenty-sixth Century

Throughout their history, humans have demonstrated a variety of attitudes and legal approaches to sex and prostitution. The changing history of sexual norms gives the appearance that these norms are merely culturally dependent. While cultural and historical variation does not entail moral relativism with respect to sex and prostitution, such variation nevertheless does give us reason to pause and consider whether our own attitudes toward sex and prostitution reflect eternal moral truths or are merely the result of contingent cultural influences.

According to the lore of Joss Whedon's world of *Firefly* and *Serenity*, as humankind colonized the galaxy, attitudes toward sex and prostitution changed, as did the institution and practice of prostitution.[1] By the twenty-sixth century, prostitution was legal, strictly regulated, and quite different in form from earlier practices. In the episode "Out of Gas," in which we see flashbacks of how several members of *Serenity*'s crew came aboard *Serenity*, we first meet Kaylee Frye (Jewel Staite) in a moment of sexual activity. Although Captain Malcolm "Mal" Reynolds (Nathan Fillion) averts his eyes, the fact that his first meeting with Kaylee occurs while she is engaged in sexual activity in *Serenity*'s engine room with Mal's recently hired and soon to be fired engineer, Bester (Dax Griffin), does not matter to him. Nor does it matter to Kaylee. Neither is the audience given the impression that either Mal or Kaylee is in any way defective in character due to this. Embarrassment about sex in a situation like this barely occurs to either of them. Mal's turning away of his eyes seems to be more about respecting others' privacy than anything else. In "Heart of Gold," when Kaylee notices the male prostitutes in a brothel, she is asked whether she "could really lie with someone being paid for it," to which she responds, "Well it's not like anyone else is lining up to, you know, examine me." Far from being embarrassed or ashamed of having sex with a prostitute, it seems to her to be a potentially worthwhile idea.

Also in "Heart of Gold," Mal has passionate sex with Nandi (Melinda Clarke), the madam of a bordello. He is not being serviced, however, and he certainly isn't paying. Mal and Nandi share genuine attraction. On his way out of Nandi's room, Mal bumps into Inara and awkwardly tries to pretend he hasn't just slept with Nandi. "One of the virtues of not being puritanical about sex," Inara says, "is not feeling embarrassed afterwards. You should look into it." After Nandi is shot and killed, Inara genuinely tells Mal that she was glad he had been with Nandi the previous night.

Attitudes toward sex in the world of *Firefly/Serenity* differ from our own, but the most striking dissimilarity is shown in the difference between contemporary prostitution and twenty-sixth-century companionship. Although the word "prostitution" can be used in a variety of ways, in this context it is used to refer to the exchange of some tangible good (usually money) from one person (usually a man) to another person (usually a woman) for sexual services. Contemporary prostitution in the United States is also character-ized by certain additional tendencies: women of color are overrepresented in prostitution; about 55 percent have been victims of sexual assault (48 percent have been victims of sexual assault at least five times); at least 51 percent have been victims of domestic violence; about 35 percent have some disability; about 27 percent have a mental illness (particularly bipolar disorder); at least 20 percent have been victims of incest; the mean initia-tion age is twenty-three years old; and the average time in the profession is eight years.[2] Prostitution is currently illegal everywhere in the United States except in some counties of Nevada, where it is legal, but highly regulated. The illegality of prostitution typically includes prohibitions on selling and purchasing sexual services, on pimping, and on running a business where this is known to occur. Companionship in *Firefly/Serenity* differs from con-temporary prostitution in just about every way. In fact, companionship is highly regarded. In the following sections, we will see what companionship looks like and how it differs from contemporary prostitution.

Companionship

The common picture of a contemporary prostitute is of a poor, unhealthy, victimized streetwalker. This could not be more different from the Compan-ions of *Firefly/Serenity*. In "Bushwhacked," an Alliance captain says to Inara, "It's a curiosity—a woman of stature such as yourself falling in with these types." Inara explains: "Not in the least. It's a mutually beneficial business arrangement. I rent the shuttle from Captain Reynolds, which allows me to expand my client base. And the Captain finds that having a Companion on board opens certain doors that might otherwise be closed to him." In "Out of Gas," we learn how Inara initially came aboard *Serenity* and the nature of her business arrangement with Mal. In a flashback, we see Mal showing Inara the shuttle that she would eventually rent. Inara makes it clear what their arrangement would be: "Were we to enter into this arrangement, Captain Reynolds, there are a few things I would require from you, the foremost be-ing complete autonomy. This shuttle would be my home. No crew member, including yourself, would be allowed entrance without my express invita-tion. . . . And just so we're clear, under no circumstances will I be servicing you or anyone who is under your employ. . . . The other thing I would insist upon is some measure of assurance that when I make an appointment with a client I'm in a position to keep that appointment, so far as assurances are possible in a vessel of this type." Inara then explains to Mal that he will rent the shuttle to her without considering her application and at one-quarter of his asking price because "You want me. You want me on your ship . . . because I can bring something that your surveyor or any of the other fish you have on line can't: a certain respectability. With what little I've seen of your operation, I suspect that's something you could use."

In the first episode of *Firefly*, "Serenity," about eight months after Inara joins *Serenity*, the crew makes a stop to pick up Inara, who has been with a client. Mal is tense before the arrival of the "ambassador," as he refers to Inara. He says, "Someone on this boat has to make an honest living," and someone has to lend some "respectability" to the crew, as he puts it. He later refers to her as "a legitimate businesswoman." Another passenger on *Serenity*, Derrial Book (Ron Glass), the shepherd (which is similar to a priest or pastor), gladly greets the "ambassador" only to become the target of laughter from Mal, who then explains: "She is pretty much our ambassador. There's plenty planets that wouldn't let you dock without a decent Companion on board." In "The Message," Mal is having trouble fencing a stolen artifact. Inara tries to offer her help, but Mal refuses, saying: "I ain't listening. Look, just because you helped out on the job don't make you a crook. I will not have you jeopardizing your career over this." To call a contemporary prostitute a respectable, legitimate businessperson could only be done with tongue firmly planted in cheek. In *Firefly/Serenity*, on the other hand, it is reality.

Companions are more than businesspersons, however. In "The Train Job," we find out a little more about the life of a Companion. It doesn't take long for the shepherd to understand Inara's status. "I'm surprised a respectable Companion would sail with this crew," he notes. Kaylee asks Inara, "Have you ever had to service a really hideous client with boils and the like?" Inara answers: "A Companion chooses her own clients. That's Guild law. But physical appearance doesn't matter so terribly. You look for compatibility of spirit. There's an energy about a person that's difficult to hide. You try to feel that and—" She is interrupted by Mal, who informs them a job has come up. "Congratulations," replies Inara. "This job wouldn't be on a decently civilized planet where I could screen some respectable clients perhaps?" When Mal and Zoe Alleyne (Gina Torres), pretending to be married partners, get caught on the job in the mining town Paradiso, the crew needs to rescue them but faces difficulty in doing so. Book suggests that someone respectable might be able to get to them, so they send Inara. She tells the local authority figure, Sheriff Bourne (Gregg Henry), that Mal is her "indentured man." The people of the town are excited to see a "registered Companion," probably for the first time, and the sheriff respects and trusts her. Mal and Zoe are relinquished to Inara without any difficulty. As a Companion, Inara is more than a respectable, legitimate businesswoman. She holds a very high social status, more like that of a celebrity or a member of the nobility.

Companionship is about more than the Companion, of course. "Jaynestown" offers further insight into companionship. As Inara leaves for a job, Kaylee, without irony, says, "Hey Inara, going off for some glamorous romance?" "Let's hope so," says Inara. Kaylee sends her off with, "Have good sex." This particular job involves a father, Magistrate Higgins (Gregory Itzen), who has hired Inara to deal with the "particular problem" of his twenty-six-year-old son's virginity. When he sees Inara's room, he complains, "I brought you here to bed my son, not throw him a tea party." Inara explains, "Sir, the Companion greeting ceremony is a ritual with centuries of tradition," and as he continues to complain, Inara shows him to the door and makes it clear who was in charge: "Mr. Higgins, you're not allowed here. . . . As I said, this room is a consecrated place of union. Only your son belongs here. Now why don't you go on and let us begin our work. Good night, Mr. Higgins." Once the father is gone, Inara sits with his son, Fess Higgins (Zachary Kranzler). "This whole thing, it is embarrassing," says Fess, sheepishly. "My father's right again, I guess. We have to bring you here," but Inara doesn't let him finish. "Your father isn't right, Fess. It's not embarrassing to be a virgin. It's simply one state of being. As far as bringing me here, Companions choose the people they're to be with very carefully. For example, if your father had asked me to come here for him, I wouldn't have. . . . You're different from him. The more you accept that, the stronger you'll become." She takes off his glasses and kisses him. Later, when they're together in bed, Inara explains: "Our time together, it's a ritual, a symbol, it means something to your father. I hope it was not entirely forgettable for you. But it doesn't make you a man. You do that yourself." It is clear from this episode and others that companionship is not merely about sexual pleasure. Inara is the young man's therapist or counselor. She empowers Fess and aids his development into a confident, independent adult.

The structure, quality, and status of companionship are guarded by the Guild. Companions are governed by Guild law. In "Ariel," Inara is getting dropped off at a Core planet when *Serenity*'s pilot, Hoban "Wash" Washburne (Alan Tudyk), remarks: "Big stop just to renew your license to companion. Can you use 'companion' as a verb?" "It's Guild law," explains Inara; "All Companions are required to undergo physical examination once a year." Later in the same episode, Kaylee asks, "What's the Companion policy on dating?" "It's complicated," answers Inara. "Well that figures," Kaylee responds. This is in stark contrast to criminal, unregulated contemporary prostitution. This difference is actually present in *Firefly/Serenity* itself. Not all providers of sexual services choose to operate under Guild law. The result looks much more like contemporary prostitution, thus highlighting how different companionship is. The next section juxtaposes Companions with the other kind of sexual service providers in *Firefly/Serenity*.

Companions and Whores

Companions in *Firefly/Serenity* are contrasted with "whores," who find themselves operating under conditions much closer to those of contemporary prostitution. In the Inara flashback of "Out of Gas," when Inara responds to Mal's query whether she has trouble with the Alliance by stating that she supported Unification, Mal replies, "Well, I don't suppose you're the only whore that did." Without missing a beat, Inara adds, "Oh, one further addendum: that's the last time you get to call me whore." "Absolutely. Never again," Mal says, which, by this episode, we all know is a lie. Later in the same episode, as Inara is approached by Book, she asks, "Would you like to lecture me on the wickedness of my ways?" "I brought you some supper, but if you'd prefer a lecture, I have a few very catchy ones prepped. Sin and hellfire, and one has lepers," says Book with a smile. Book then tells Inara that it was unjust of Mal to call her a whore. "Believe me, I've called him worse." In "Trash," short on work, Inara implies to Mal that he may be deliberately keeping them in territories where she cannot find work. Mal responds, "How about I stay out of your whoring"—he is interrupted by Inara, who says, "Well that didn't take long—" She is cut off, too: "And you keep out of my thieving," says Mal. A whore in *Firefly/Serenity* is clearly contrasted with a Companion, and not favorably. When Mal uses the word "whore," it is not because he fails to acknowledge the distinction. Book also knows it is inaccurate and "unjust," as he says, to refer to a Companion as a whore, and any discomfort or disapproval he has of companionship is due to his outdated and personal religious beliefs rather than to any common societal attitude.

As we saw in the previous section, Companions are legitimate businesspersons with high social standing and social power. Although they provide sexual services, they are not to be confused with mere whores. In "Shindig," we see Inara in the process of selecting her clients, who apply for the "honor" of her company. She implies to Mal that it can be more difficult for a man to "attract" a Companion than a woman who is not a Companion. On the planet Persephone, during the titular party or shindig, her current chosen client, Atherton Wing, offers her a "life," if she wants it: she could live on Persephone as his personal Companion. Mal, chasing a job, crashes the party. Inara asks him what he is doing there. Mal, more interested in Inara's business, says: "Maybe I just want to see a professional work. Is this the hardest part would you say, or does that come later?" "You have no call trying to make me ashamed of my work," she replies. "What I do is legal. And how's that smuggling coming?" "My work's illegal," answers Mal, "but at least it's honest." Mal's complaint regarding Inara's work has nothing to do with sex, but rather with a dishonesty that he sees in it. He explains: "All this, the lie of it. That man parading you around on his arm as if he actually won you. As if he loves you. And everyone here going along with it." Inara disagreed: "These people like me, and I like them. I like Atherton, too, by the way. . . . And he likes me, whether you see it or not. . . . He's made me an offer. You may think he doesn't honor me, but he wants me to live here. I'd be his personal Companion. I could live well here. Call me pretentious, but there is some appeal in that." "You're right," said Mal. "I don't have the call to stop you. You've got the right to a decent life."

Atherton grows displeased as Mal and Inara dance and talk. He goes to them and roughly draws Inara away from Mal. "Whoah now," Mal says to Atherton, "Watch yourself. No need for hands on." "Excuse me, she's not here with you, Captain. She's mine," responds Atherton. Mal doesn't like this response at all: "Yours? She don't belong to nobody." Atherton sees it differently: "Money changed hands, which makes her mine tonight. No matter how you dress her up she's still a—" Mal punches him, knocking him down. He cannot allow Atherton to refer to Inara as a whore. Mal appears to be correct about the dishonesty of Inara's arrangement with Atherton, but it isn't companionship that gives rise to the problem, but rather Atherton's poor attitude and behavior. In fact, specifically, it was Atherton's failure to recognize the distinction between Companions and whores that was the problem.

After he knocks Atherton down, it is then explained to a surprised Mal that, according to local custom, Atherton and Mal are expected to duel to the death with swords the following morning. Before the duel, Inara visits Mal. "So, how come you're still attached to him. . . . Thought he made it pretty clear he's got no regard for you," says Mal. Inara replies: "You did manage to push him into saying something, yes. Made a nice justification for the punch." "He insulted you," says Mal. "I hit him. Seemed like the thing to do. Why'd this get so complicated?" Inara explains how he can flee, but Mal won't: "I didn't do this to prove a point to you. I actually thought I was defending your honor. I never back down from a fight." As he won't flee, Inara, being an "educated woman and all," gives Mal a sword-fighting lesson. "They teach you that in whore academy?" asks Mal. Inara, appearing stung, replies: "You have a strange sense of nobility, Captain. You'll lay a man out for implying I'm a whore, but you keep calling me one to my face." Mal explains: "I might not show respect to your job, but he didn't respect you. That's the difference. Inara, he doesn't even see you." They then have an exchange about following the rules of society, after which Mal says: "You think following the rules will buy you a nice life, even if the rules make you a slave. Don't take his offer." The way Mal sees it, remaining a Companion as she is means freedom, but becoming Atherton's personal Companion would be the end of her freedom.

The next morning, Mal and Atherton duel. It looks at first as if Atherton is toying with Mal, letting him think he is doing well, and then Mal is injured. Just when it looks like Atherton is going to finish Mal, Inara calls out: "Atherton, wait! I'll stay here, exclusive to you. Just let him live." This distracts Atherton, who is then surprised and beaten by Mal. Mal is informed that he is expected to "finish" his opponent; otherwise it would be humiliating for Atherton. Mal pokes him a few times, but lets him live. Humiliated, but not done yet, Atherton yells to Inara: "You set this up, whore, after I bought and paid for you." It is clear that by calling her "whore," he is only showing his own low character. None of the bystanders seem to share his opinion of Inara. He threatens her: "Get ready to starve," he says; "I'll see to it you never work again." It is not Mal who truly defeats Atherton; Inara provides the final blow: "Actually, that's not how it works. You see, you've earned yourself a black mark in the client registry. No Companion is going to contract with you ever again." A bystander quips to Atherton: "You'll have to rely on your winning personality to get women. God help you." "Mighty fine shindig," says Mal, as he leaves with Inara holding him up.

In "Heart of Gold," the *Serenity* crew aids an independent bordello after its madam, Nandi, contacts Inara for help. A dangerous gunslinger who impregnated a prostitute intends to collect the child against her will. When asking the *Serenity* crew for help, Inara explains: "They're not Companions. They're whores." When Mal notes that Inara never cared for that word herself, she answers: "It applies. They're not registered with the Guild." They are independent, she explains. Inara used the word "whore" in a technical way, without any value judgment. Nandi was trained as a Companion, but found a Companion's life to be too "restricting." While Companions have to follow Guild law, as we've seen, Nandi's greater freedom comes at a price. As she explains: "Half the girls are strung out on drugs. There's no Guild out here, they let men run the houses, and they don't ask for references." The prostitutes in Nandi's bordello, and presumably at other bordellos not governed by the Guild, are treated in a degrading way. Nandi's bordello provides us a glimpse at what prostitution looks like outside of legal regulation and Guild law. It isn't pretty, and it is much closer to contemporary prostitution.

The Dollhouse

Firefly/Serenity and Inara show prostitution in a respectable form. Companionship is devoid of the features often pointed to in order to demonstrate the wrongness of prostitution as an institution. The institution of prostitution today, however, cannot adequately be evaluated without addressing sexual trafficking and nonconsensual sex. We need not defend here the recognition of nonconsensual sex as seriously morally wrong. In the *Firefly* episode "Our Mrs. Reynolds," Jayne Cobb (Adam Baldwin) offers his most beloved gun, a "Callahan full-bore autolock with customized trigger," which he calls Vera, to Mal in exchange for Mal's new "wife," Saffron (Christina Hendricks). "She's not to be bought. Nor bartered, nor borrowed or lent. She's a human woman," says Mal, sternly. Prostitution or any other institution that involves nonconsensual sex is morally objectionable specifically due to the nonconsensual nature of the sex. We must consider whether all prostitution involves nonconsensual sex, and, if so, how we should ultimately view it, even if, as in the case of Companions like Inara, it is devoid of other objectionable features.

In order to do this, let us now consider Whedon's more recent show *Dollhouse*. Before we can determine whether *Dollhouse* involves prostitution with nonconsensual sex, we should first see whether it involves prostitution at all. In return for hefty sums of money, actives of the Dollhouse are imprinted to satisfy a client's desires, and those desires often include sexual activity. Echo's risky engagement in "The Target" involves sexual activity. Her engagement in "Man on the Street" is a repeat engagement that involves sexual activity. In "A Spy in the House of Love," Echo is imprinted as a dominatrix. Another active, Victor (Enver Gjokaj), is frequently imprinted for a love affair with "Mrs. Lonely Hearts," who turned out to be Dollhouse leader Adelle DeWitt (Olivia Williams) herself. Some people on the street, as shown in testimonials in the episode "A Man on the Street," certainly view the Dollhouse as engaged in prostitution. "They got people programmed to do whatever. Could be for sex or, you know, kill a guy," says one man. "If they'd had it in my day," says an older man, "I'd have had Betty Grable every night. Or Ida Lupino. Every man that fought for his country should have the right to an Ida Lupino." Another man, standing next to his wife, who chuckles awkwardly at his response for the camera, says: "Hey, everyone's got their fantasies, right? A guy wants to know what it's like, you know, to be with another man. Just once, nothing queeny. Two guys checking it out, and then the other one forgets. That could be sweet for some guys."

Not all of Echo's engagements involve sexual activity, and they sometimes involve activities that are recognizably virtuous. In the second engagement we see in "Ghosts," Echo rescues a kidnapped girl. In "Stage Fright," Echo saves a well-known singer from a murderous fan (and from herself). In "Haunted," she is imprinted with the memories of a recently deceased friend of DeWitt so that she can solve her own murder and reconcile with her family in the form of a new will. In "Briar Rose," Echo begins the process of helping a severely troubled young child.

The engagements of actives might not always involve sex, but they do sometimes, and that is enough to charge the Dollhouse with prostitution. Furthermore, it is more similar to contemporary prostitution than the companionship of *Firefly/Serenity*. Instead of an independent woman choosing her clients, for example, Caroline signs a contract to allow herself to be used as an active according to the arrangements made by the Dollhouse. The Dollhouse is paid per arrangement, and Caroline will be paid once her contract expires. In the meantime, however, Caroline seems more like a prostitute working under the orders of a pimp. In fact, in "A Spy in the House of Love," Boyd Langton (Harry Lennix), Echo's handler and eventual head of security at the Dollhouse, refers to the employees of the Dollhouse precisely as pimps. The question now, then, is whether the sexual activities of the dolls are consensual.

Caroline Farrell is the original persona that inhabited Echo's body. At the beginning of the first episode, "Ghost," we see Caroline in discussion with DeWitt. We learn that Caroline was given a choice to volunteer to become an active for the Dollhouse. In "Echoes," we see DeWitt present Caroline with the choice. "My offer is this: Your life . . . for your life," she says. "I get five years, you get the rest. You'll be free." Caroline does not seem to think of this as a real choice; rather, she feels compelled to "volunteer" due to circumstances. On the other hand, according to Adelle, the circumstances are a result of Caroline's previous choices. "Actions have consequences," she says. In "Omega," Caroline, in the body of another person named Wendy (Ashley Johnson), is asked by Echo why she became an active in the Dollhouse. "It's complicated," is the answer. The complicated circumstances that led Caroline to accept DeWitt's offer are pieced together over the course of the two seasons of *Dollhouse*. A college student idealist, Caroline broke into a Rossum Corporation building on her campus to expose their immoral experiments. Her boyfriend, Leo Carpenter (Josh Cooke), was shot and killed by security during the break-in, and he died in Caroline's arms. About a year later, during a second infiltration, Bennett Halverson (Summer Glau), who helped Caroline to infiltrate Rossum, was injured and left behind. Caroline refers to herself as a "terrorist" by this point. In "Getting Closer," Echo tells DeWitt that she made Caroline sound evil. DeWitt replies: "She's not evil. She's worse. She's an idealist." Caroline leaves a trail of destruction, injury, and even death in the wake of her crusade against Rossum. Those are the actions that had the consequence that she must either become an active for the Dollhouse or face the legal ramifications of her actions. While we can understand that it does not seem to Caroline to be a real choice, we can also understand why DeWitt insists that it is.

Caroline's own history is unique, but being a volunteer active was not. In "Gray Hour," Topher Brink (Fran Kranz), the genius programmer of the Dollhouse, says, regarding all of the actives, "They volunteered for this." "So we're told," is Boyd's reply. Boyd's doubts aside, we see that other actives desire to make this choice. In "Echoes," Sam Jennings (Mechad Brooks) is given an offer similar to Caroline's. DeWitt makes the option more attractive to Sam by telling him: "Once you sign these papers, your mother will begin receiving a monthly stipend large enough to solve her financial problems. It will continue for five years, and at the end of that time, you will be quite capable of supporting her all on your own." In "Needs," DeWitt tells Caroline about the other actives: "I made the same promise to them to protect them from the unbearable truths that brought them here." For example, Madeline Costley, who becomes the active named November (Miracle Laurie), became an active in order to escape the painful loss of her infant child. In "Omega," DeWitt explains to Boyd that the Dollhouse initially used prisoners as actives. "We offered an opportunity to trade lengthy prison sentences for a five year term of service with us," she explains. In "Man on the Street," some of the people on the street giving their testimonials describe becoming an active in the Dollhouse as a potentially choice-worthy option. One woman says: "So being a Doll, you do whatever. And you don't got to remember nothing. Or study. Or pay rent. And you just party with rich people all the time? Where's the dotted line?" Another woman adds: "If you could have somebody be the perfect person, the moment you wish for that you know you're never going to get, and someone signed on to do that, to help you . . . I think that could be okay. I think that could be maybe beautiful."

Early on, however, Paul Ballard (Tahmoh Penikett) believes that the

Dollhouse is engaged in human trafficking and that the process of making a person into a doll is akin to murder. "If the only way to imprint a human being with a new personality is to remove their own completely, we're talking about people walking around who may as well have been murdered," he says. Ballard learns later, however, that the original personas are saved and restored at the expiration of an active's contract. But is such a contract legitimate? In "Briar Rose," Ballard says to DeWitt; "I don't even care that these people signed themselves over to you. There is no provision for consensual slavery. It is wrong." In "Omega," Echo asks Caroline, who is in the body of Wendy, why she won't return to her body. Caroline replies, "I did sign a contract." Echo, however, recently imprinted with all of her previous personas by Alpha (Alan Tudyk), replies: "I have thirty-eight brains. Not one of them thinks you can sign a contract to be a slave." In another testimonial from "Man on the Street," a woman notes, "There's one thing people will always need is slaves." When the reporter replies that "some of the versions of the story say the Dolls themselves are volunteers," the woman responds: "There's only one reason someone would volunteer to be a slave is if they is one already. Volunteer. You must be out of your (bleep) mind."

Are the employees of the Dollhouse out of their minds to believe that the actives are (highly paid) volunteers? Are potential actives out of their minds if they believe they make a voluntary choice to become an active? Would we be out of our own minds to believe it? Employees of the Dollhouse certainly did seem to believe that actives were volunteers. In "Belonging," when DeWitt learns that the active Sierra (Dichen Lachman) may not have voluntarily become an active, contrary to their previous understanding of the situation, she becomes irate. Being an active might not seem all that bad, either. We have already learned the reasons for at least some of the actives volunteering for the Dollhouse. Furthermore, in "Omega," after Caroline accepts DeWitt's offer, she is shown around the Dollhouse, and DeWitt informs her: "You'll be served five-star cuisine here. You'll never want for anything. This isn't the end of your life," adding, "It's five years, and to you, it will feel like an instant." Later in "Omega," we also learn that the terms of the contracts are indeed honored. Madeline Costley, or the active November, is excused from her contract early in an arrangement with Ballard. She leaves the Dollhouse as a free and wealthy woman.

Comparing Inara and Caroline/Echo

Caroline is presented with a choice and chooses to have her persona temporarily wiped in order to become an active. Whatever subsequent actions she is compelled to do, she voluntarily put herself in the position to be so compelled. Nevertheless, toward the end of *Dollhouse,* Whedon takes the position that Caroline and Echo are treated wrongly. Whedon seems to hold the position stated by Ballard that "there is no provision for consensual slavery. It is wrong." Even if, in some sense, Caroline voluntarily became an active, her subsequent choices as Echo are not voluntary. Any sexual activity in which she engages is nonconsensual. To the extent that the Dollhouse is engaged in prostitution, then, it is engaged in morally objectionable activity. This conclusion gives rise to an apparent difficulty in understanding Whedon's views because he did not treat prostitution, or at least companionship, as wrong in *Firefly/Serenity.* Did he change his mind?

Not necessarily. As we saw above, in the case of *Firefly/Serenity,* other than the voluntary choice to obey Guild law, Inara enjoys complete autonomy. In contrast, Echo, at least early on in *Dollhouse,* is under the complete control of her programmer. Although Caroline voluntarily submits to becoming an active, her—or Echo's—subsequent situation is one of complete servitude (at least until Echo's own persona develops and she begins calling the shots). Inara's situation is importantly different. She not only voluntarily chooses to become a Companion, but she maintains her autonomy throughout her work as one. The contrasting cases illuminate the centrally important feature that, for Whedon, makes prostitution either objectionable or acceptable (if not respectable)—namely, continuous autonomy. Mal makes this clear to Inara when he tells her that becoming Atherton's personal Companion would be slavery, while continuing to work as she has, namely as an independent Companion, means continued freedom. Even if Caroline/Echo were well-treated by clients, faced no risks, and volunteered to be an active, her situation would differ from Inara's with respect to continuing autonomy, and that difference makes the case of Caroline/Echo morally objectionable—and as such, to be prevented—but allows the case of Inara to be recognized as morally permissible and even respectable.

What matters morally to Whedon is continuous autonomy. As we see him show in *Dollhouse,* the absence of autonomy is objectionable, and therefore Caroline/Echo, or any active, no matter how voluntarily they give up control over themselves initially, are wrongly treated. Inara, on the other hand, maintains her autonomy continuously throughout her work as a Companion. She is engaged in activity that should only be regulated, as it was by the Guild, rather than prohibited and criminalized. Furthermore, to the extent that companionship is good for her and for her clients, her profession is not only permissible, but respectable and worthy of high regard. It is a long way to go from contemporary prostitution to something resembling companionship, but Whedon illustrates the possibility, and even the desirability, of such a change.

Notes

1. Whedon, Joss. *Serenity: The Official Visual Companion* (London: Titan Books, 2005), 12–15.

2. Information from the Chrysalis Project, the Empowerment Program, www .empowermentprogram.org/.

Fashioning Feminism

Whedon, Women, and Wardrobe

Patricia Brace

A common contention among scholars is that the Western ideal of beauty has acted as a social guard for the patriarchal culture—keeping women in their places through a series of constraining concepts of body shape, cosmetics, and clothing.[1] To seek the societal idea of beauty is to conform to the limits men want to place upon women. However, Camille Paglia, a self-proclaimed "equity feminist," argues that women can seek equality without giving up beauty.[2] Joss Whedon agrees, or so I argue here. That Buffy Summers (Sarah Michelle Gellar) has a silly name and is blond and beautiful doesn't mean she cannot also be intelligent and physically powerful. Whedon sees his show as a way of teaching boys about competent girls: "If I can make teenage boys comfortable with a girl who takes charge of a situation without their knowing that's what's happening, it's better than sitting down and selling them on feminism."[3] Joss Whedon turns this beauty myth on its head by his use of clothing as female empowerment. This essay examines how Whedon's characters use fashion as a reflection of their intelligence and physical skills, and sometimes as emblematic of their inner conflicts that invariably lead to important catharses.

Waves of Feminism and the "Sex or Sorcery" of Fashion

Fashion, including clothing, ornamentation, and cosmetics has been viewed by scholars as either detracting from or contributing to the feminist movement and its goals. Linda M. Scott states: "American feminism takes a dim view of beauty. Across the spectrum of academic and popular literature, feminist writers have consistently argued that a woman's attempt to cultivate her appearance makes her the dupe of fashion, the plaything of men, and thus a collaborator in her own oppression."[4] Scott, however, makes a convincing argument that our standards of beauty are not merely a patriarchal conspiracy to debase women, but an important historical point of conflict between different schools and generations of feminism itself. Scott traces the historical evolution of feminism. The first wave began in the late nineteenth century with the suffrage movement. Second-wave feminists gained prominence in the later part of the twentieth century, only to give way to the third wave, with its offshoot nouveau "girlie" culture. Throughout her work, Scott gives a detailed analysis on the seeming dichotomy between those who believe any attempt to alter their appearance to conform to some societal standard of "beauty" contravenes feminist ideals and those who believe that the fight for equal rights means they should be allowed to act and dress in a way that pleases, fulfills, and even empowers them.

The primary goal of early first-wave feminism, known as the "woman movement," was gaining rights equivalent to those enjoyed by men, such as the vote, legal and property equality, and freedom of movement. Parallel to this call for equal rights was what became known as the "dress reform movement," which, as Scott states, "pretended to [be] a clear-cut choice between 'nature' and 'artifice.' . . . The risks of 'artifice' were cast in moral and magical terms—*sex* or *sorcery* was never far behind a fashionable look."[5] Some founding mothers of the movement, such as Susan B. Anthony, followed the Anglo-Protestant tradition of Puritan dress, believing that simplicity and lack of adornment were reflective of moral virtues such as modesty, chastity, and piety. The idea was that by becoming free of the literal and figurative constraints of fashion—restrictive corsets and layers of hot, heavy petticoats—women could better contemplate other forms of liberation as well. This became a staple of our traditional understanding of dress reform.

The myth of a singular "feminist" standard of dress to which all women should aspire, however, ignores important factors of ethnicity, social and economic status, and even physical practicality. That some "feminist elite" could dictate this mode of dress is even more problematic; if these women objected to men telling them how to dress, why should they be allowed to do the same? The "new woman" look of a white, bloomer-clad, bicycle-riding, college-educated, single career gal risked ignoring the very real contributions made to the movement by women of any different race or different social, economic, or marital status. Even after women's suffrage was passed in 1920, the issue of control over dress continued to influence how feminists viewed the "problem" of fashion throughout the twentieth and into the twenty-first century. Traditionally, whoever decides what someone else wears has power over them and control over their social status. Think of the Cinderella story, in which three *women* kept orphaned Cinderella living in the ashes, wearing dirty rags, worked to exhaustion, and humiliated at every turn.

Second-wave feminism focused on the passage of the Equal Rights Amendment (ERA), reproductive rights, and workplace reform such as equal pay for equal work. It, too, was marked by inner conflict over leadership, this time between the campus-centered, distinctly anticapitalist "New Feminists" and the more corporate professional National Organization for Women (NOW). Part of the conflict was, again, the desire to control the appearance of others. Scott characterizes the debate as being between the "young radicals" and the "accomplished professionals."[6] The New Feminists argued that the "dress for success," or "power dressing," of the professional women of the 1970s and 1980s was actually antifeminist because raising one's status in the corporate world was inherently capitalistic. The exciting fact that the NOW feminists were actually breaking through the glass ceiling into careers previously closed off to women was ignored by the New Feminists in favor of yet more focus on dress reform. For example, Helen Gurley Brown, the accomplished author and founder of *Cosmopolitan* magazine, "was prominent among the first ranks of the Second Wave. Yet her interest in sex, her commercial success, and her personal appearance have made her an outsider in contemporary feminism."[7] The audience for Brown's work tended to be representative of the group from which she herself had come: single working-class women seeking to get ahead on their own terms in both work and love.

Personal appearance in terms of (alleged) sexual provocation was another source of contention. If men are the oppressors of women, anything specifically designed to attract them must be bad. Of course, this reduces fashion to a single, impossibly narrow, issue and refuses to recognize that women can dress to please themselves and that women can (and do) also oppress each other. Brown's "Cosmo Girl" approaches sexuality with deliberation, making her own choices among the men she meets, and usually (aided by the pill) without the goal of marriage. In Brown's publications, women's dress, sexuality, health, and career achievement are all given an important and valued place. The women in the Buffyverse are almost all focused on achieving this same type of personal and economic autonomy. It isn't that they don't seek exclusive love relationships, but rather that they don't rely on them for total financial and sexual fulfillment.[8]

The final type of feminism important to an analysis of fashion in the Buffyverse is the so-called third wave, with its offshoot modern "girlie" culture. Rachel Fudge identifies the third wave with multiple trends in the movement since the early 1990s, including political activism on issues like voting and abortion rights, while recognizing that "from its first utterance, the notion of a third wave has generated controversy and concern that both the media and young women were (and are), in their own ways, flattening the powerful complexities and nuances of second-wave feminism into a man-hating, anti-lipstick stereotype, and setting up a generational antagonism."[9] This concern parallels the struggles for leadership and control in both the first and second waves of the feminist movement, including the debate over dress. This plays out in the so-called "girlie" movement, with its decidedly "profemininity" style of feminism. Some critics even label it "postfeminism" because its practitioners seem to have little interest in the traditional issues of the first and second waves and are even seen as regressive. As Fudge describes them, the girlie tenets include "the reclamation of makeup and other girly accoutrements, and the validation of traditionally female activities like cooking, crafting, and talking about sex, [as] . . . a valid way to express the desire for equality—valuing the inherently female aspects of life, rather than trying to erase them."[10] The first episode of *Buffy the Vampire Slayer* aired in 1997, and the series featured powerful young women who liked makeup, fashion, and talking about sex, and a young witch or two who did "cooking and crafting" of spells. The Buffyverse, like much of Whedon's work, was cutting-edge.

Writers such as Scott and Fudge challenge the reader to recognize the fact that women's fashion choices are affected by a complex series of historical-cultural factors, including economic and social status, education level, and employment. How we dress and adorn ourselves is as much a freedom of expression as any written or spoken discourse. Expecting individuals to conform to any fashion standard, whether Birkenstocks or Manolos, and whether imposed by a patriarchy or a matriarchy limits that freedom. So-called girlie-culture feminism emphasizes a woman's personal freedom to autonomously adorn herself *for herself* and not merely to attain fulfillment via the male gaze. This position may be a bit tenuous—Just how autonomous are girlie-culture choices in a still male-dominated society?—but not implausible. This balancing act is also reflected in Whedon's corpus.

Witness Willow

"Buffy Studies" are replete with Whedon's feminism.[11] But when fashion is discussed in these articles, the focus is often on what is seen as the problematic sexualization of the female characters through their dress. According to Heather Olsen: "Whedon concedes that feminism and TV writing isn't an easy match. The many women who think the violence on *Buffy* is over the top (and who find the title character's skimpy outfits a bit of a contradiction) would agree."[12] But perhaps the contradiction is more apparent than real.

The thesis that Whedon empowers rather than objectifies his characters through fashion (broadly conceived) is first grounded in noting how much care is taken to use wardrobe to differentiate between them, establish personality traits, and reflect their physical, emotional, and psychological states. A prime example of this is the episode "Halloween," where several characters are transformed into the personae of their chosen costumes. Willow (Alyson Hannigan) rather uncharacteristically dons a sexy miniskirted outfit; however, she covers it up with a sheet and goes as a ghost, reflecting her feelings of invisibility and inadequacy. Such a marked wardrobe change for a Whedon character either reflects a change in her moral or psychological state, or shows a deliberate attempt to alter those states. In other words, clothing may reveal as much as it hides, and when that clothing is specifically chosen by a director and costume designer to fit the writer's idea of that character, it is important to recognize its power within the narrative.[13] In *Buffy*, one of the best examples of this is indeed Willow, who makes several psychological and sexual transformations throughout the seven-year run of the series, each of them reflected in her wardrobe.

Early in season one, Willow wears jumpers and tights, has long straight red hair, and wears little to no makeup; per Cordelia, Willow models "the softer side of Sears."[14] Willow appears very much unlike wealthy, stylishly dressed and coifed Cordelia (Charisma Carpenter), and the trendy, miniskirted, belly-baring Buffy. She thus represents an almost presexual state of innocence. Willow's power is her innate goodness and her keen intelligence, including cyber-geek and language skills, which she uses in service of Buffy's mission to fight evil as one of the "Slayerettes" (or "Scoobies").

Two seasons later, in "The Wish," the viewer glimpses a different side to Willow via a parallel-universe vampire Willow. Dressed in a cleavage-baring, tight, black-leather corset and pants and with a new shorter haircut and makeup, this version of the character is a vicious, voracious monster, who gets sexually excited by torturing Angel (David Boreanaz) and is also sexually involved with her erstwhile crush Xander (who has also been vamped). When Vamp Willow reappears in the episode "Doppelgangland," original-recipe Willow is called on to impersonate her vampire twin. As Lorna Jowett aptly points out, "Where Willow is at this stage still timid and retiring, Vamp Willow is confident, powerful, and successful in establishing what she wants and getting it—characteristics that might be identified as 'feminist.'"[15] She is also identified as bisexual; we see that in addition to her relationship with Vamp Xander, she is also "outed" by regular Willow, who says, "I think I'm kinda gay," foreshadowing her later lesbian relationships.

Season three seems to be an important turning point for Willow's character. She asserts her (this-worldly) sexuality through her first romantic relationship with werewolf Daniel "Oz" Osbourne (Seth Green) and plays a vital role in thwarting the demon-ascension of Mayor Wilkins (Harry Groener). When Willow is a college student in season four, her clothing choices move beyond the androgynous and adolescent as she cultivates a more adult, albeit quirky, fashion sense reflecting her more adult life circumstances. This season finds her unsuccessfully looking for community with the campus Wiccan group and struggling to find a balance in her relationship with Oz, eventually resulting in his departure, giving her the opportunity to explore her romantic feelings for the gentle Wiccan Tara Maclay (Amber Benson).[16]

Season four contains a particularly poignant example of Willow's transformation. In the season finale, "Restless," Willow's insecurities about her approaching adulthood are manifested in the dream she shares with Buffy, Xander, and Giles after they have combined their strengths to defeat the Initiative-created creature Adam (George Hertzberg). The common dream uses the trope of appearing in a play for which one is unprepared, in this case on the first day of class. As others in the class see her fashionable clothes, they congratulate her on already being in character. When Buffy tells her she needs to remove her costume, and Willow reiterates how it is "just my outfit," Buffy responds by literally ripping the clothes off her back, revealing the first-season-style long hair, white blouse, tights, and muddy brown jumper. Willow seems to have a case of "imposter syndrome," fearing that the truth of her sexuality and growing Wiccan powers will shock her friends, who expect her to remain the innocent girl they know and love. Her willingness to delve further than ever before into her new sexuality and possibly dangerous magicks are symbolized by the Greek letters Willow paints on Tara's back before she goes to the drama class. Her obvious familiarity with Tara's nude body underlines her gay sexuality, and the foreign letters are like those in the arcane books used for casting spells.[17]

If one watches Willow's dress choices in the next two seasons, more and more often her color palette moves toward black. The shift is of course symbolic of her giving in to evil, which that color traditionally symbolizes in Western culture, but also indicates that she is gaining mystical power.[18] By season six, Willow is addicted to the power, and after Tara is murdered by the evil nerd Warren Meers (Adam Busch), she goes full "Dark Willow." As she drains the spells from the most arcane books in the Magic Shop ("Seeing Red"), the letters slide up her arms and face to become part of her, which was foreshadowed by the spell she painted on Tara in "Restless." This time not only her eyes but also her hair, and perhaps even her blood, turn black, which gives her pale face a distinctly veined look. Empowered by her rage and despair, Dark Willow's black Goth wardrobe is reminiscent of Vamp Willow in season three, reflecting her descent into evil.

Throughout season seven, Willow is afraid of reawakening her dark side and initially limits her magic use, returning to some of the original areas of power for her: research, computers, and science. Willow slowly reembraces her identity as a lesbian and as a witch, though not without some trepidation. In the *Buffy* series finale, "Chosen," while she chants the spell to save Sunnydale from the First, she appears to become light—her hair turns white, flowing, and billowing around her face—indicating that despite her fears that she would revert to Dark Willow, she is in fact the total opposite, a fully empowered White Witch. The viewer thus beholds Willow's true power; drawing on the divine feminine, she empowers a whole new generation of Slayers. As Willow moves from mousy high school science-nerd to "the most powerful Wiccan in North America," from introverted girl tongue-tied around boys to a confident adult in consensual lesbian relationships, and from the blackness of evil to the blinding forces of light, Whedon mirrors Willow's transformations in her wardrobe.

Buffy's "Keen Fashion Sense"

This interpretation of Willow sheds light on Buffy's costumes, including Whedon's earliest depictions of the blond Slayer in the 1992 original motion picture. Confronting Lothos (Rutger Hauer), the master vampire, Buffy (Kristi Swanson) pulls a cross out of her black leather jacket (worn over her white poufy mini and tights), to which the master reacts: "This is your defense? Pu-lease! Your puny faith?" He grabs the cross and it bursts into flame. Buffy replies, "No"—then she whips out a can of hair spray, archly says, "My keen fashion sense!" and uses the spray as a blow torch. This is a powerful young woman who makes use of everything at her disposal to fight evil, including cosmetics. A can of Aqua-Net, that which no man would carry, serves Buffy as a powerful weapon. Whedon's characters are complex people constructed within complex narratives; just as in real life, their style makes important statements about who they are. Thus, fashion freedom often equates to personal freedom in the Whedonverse.

Returning to the television series, consider the season-one episode "The Harvest." Buffy, still new to Sunnydale, hesitates over what to wear to the Bronze. She's narrowed her choices to two outfits: "slutty" versus "Hi, would you like a copy of the Watchtower?" She muses, "I used to be so good at this," and ends up picking neither, settling instead for a more casual look: black pants and baby blue blouse. Giles meets up with her at the Bronze, chides her for not being attuned to her surroundings, and challenges her to spot a vampire. She subsequently draws his attention to a certain man because of the clothes he is wearing, saying: "Trust me, only someone living underground for the last ten years would think that was still the look." This recognition allows her to save Willow, who will become her best friend and an important ally. Buffy's laudable fashion choices often lead to success in her Slayer-related activities.

Buffy's penchant for chic casual clothing did not go unnoticed. Recall an exchange with the distinctly second-wave feminist professor—and Initiative project leader—Maggie Walsh (Lindsay Crouse) regarding an upcoming demon hunt:

> WALSH: They do have keen eyesight, however. You might want to be suited up for this.
> BUFFY: Oh. (Glancing at the military green around her) You mean the camo and stuff? I thought about it, but on me it's gonna look all "Private Benjamin." . . . Don't worry I've patrolled in this halter many times. ("The I in Team")

Walsh, true to her second-wave NOW moorings, implies that Buffy is inappropriately dressed for the task at hand. This will impede Buffy's success. Furthermore, Buffy's power, represented by her girlie style and sexual relationship with Riley, is a threat to Walsh's own. How much so is revealed later in the episode, when the professor unsuccessfully plots to have Buffy killed.

But Buffy also suffered through inner conflicts, of course. Some represent her personal difficulties associated with being the teenage Chosen One. For example, in "Prophecy Girl," as a symbol of both her innocence and her refusal to give up teenage dating rituals, like an important dance, for her slaying duties, Buffy wears a stylish, long, white, flowing dress and high heels. Although she momentarily dies, she nevertheless defeats the terrifying, powerful, all-black-leather-clad ancient vampire the Master (who opines, "By the way, I like the dress"). Some represent conflicts created by adult responsibilities. In "Flooded," she dons a traditional NOW-feminist red power-color jacket and a tightly fitted black "professional" woman skirt when applying for a bank loan. When a demon appears, Buffy is unable to do her roundhouse kicks or other ninja moves; she pouts, "Stupid skirt!" and rips it up the seams. She is trying to reconcile being both a responsible adult, caring for her home and sister, and a Slayer; the skirt symbolizes that struggle.

Buffy also struggles with intimate relationships in season six. In "Gone," Buffy's personally troubling romantic liaisons with Spike result in her decision to cut the long blond locks he adores. Her new short haircut represents an assertion of her independence, mirroring the "New Girls," or "flappers," who bobbed their hair in the 1920s. Their new style was also emblematic of their new independence—along with their lipstick, rolled stockings, and uncorseted straight silhouette. Moreover, in Willow's drama class dream from "Restless," recall that Buffy appears as a flapper, wearing a bobbed black wig, heavy eye makeup, and a sequined black dress. In her soliloquy in the dream play, she rails against men, disgusted with their "one urge." Her haircut in season six seems to be an echo of that sentiment. It is important to note, however, that in that same episode, after she is turned invisible by the evil Nerds, Buffy returns to Spike's bed, but on her own terms, as the one in control. His male gaze is negated by her invisibility, putting her back in the power position.[19]

The Higher (Fashion) Power of Cordelia Chase

That Willow and Buffy can be interpreted as expressing feminist ideals probably won't surprise too many people. But what about Cordelia? She seems to be an iconic vision of patriarchal beauty: tall, shapely, thin, and striking. She cultivates male gaze and subsequent female envy by dressing in an expensive, form-fitting, and revealing wardrobe. In "Welcome to the Hellmouth," she quizzes new Sunnydale High student Buffy Summers on the two most important subjects, boys and fashion. She expresses envy at Buffy having lived in Los Angeles simply because of the shopping opportunities: "Oh, I would *kill* to live in L.A. That close to that many shoes?" She is head cheerleader, most popular girl, and self-proclaimed "nastiest girl" in the high school, but still acts as the shrieking damsel in distress (especially early in the series), requiring Buffy to save her (for example, in "Out of Sight, Out of Mind").

However, a closer examination of Cordelia reveals that she is not merely eye candy for Whedon's male viewers; she, too, is representative of girlie-culture feminine power. She has her own minions, known as the "Cordettes," who reflect and reinforce her power. She's highly intelligent (acing her SATs), but deliberately chooses to play this down, instead emphasizing her looks.[20] Moreover, Jennifer Crusie contends that Cordelia is also extremely practical.[21] She knows how to play the social game and negotiates it with a clear-minded, steely determination, secure in her status and power as "Queen

C" of Sunnydale. But living on the Hellmouth leads her to recognize the existence of factors that could impinge on her rule. She begins to take action. Cordy fights back in "Prophecy Girl." She uses whatever she has, driving her fancy car through the school corridors to rescue Willow and a teacher and, with her own perfect orthodontia, bites a vamp trying to break into the library, defiantly yelling, "See how you like it!" From that point she becomes an unofficial member of the Slayerettes (Scoobies), and even risks her social position by dating Xander Harris, telling the Cordettes, "I do what I want to do and I wear what I want to wear and you know what, I'll date whoever the hell I want to date, no matter how lame he is" ("Bewitched, Bothered, and Bewildered").

Like Willow and Buffy, Cordy has faced adversity. Outwardly, she had to deal with her father's unfortunate business decisions, which drained the family's wealth. After graduation, Cordy moves to Los Angeles, where she is destitute, living in a vermin-infested apartment and trying to eke out a living as an actress ("City of . . ."). A peek in her closet shows that she has only one nice dress, and for Cordy, that is rock bottom. Just as Buffy prefers casual chic, Cordy prefers higher fashion. Thus, a lack of fashionable clothes symbolizes Cordy's lack of power. But a chance encounter with Angel signals a turning point. She pushes him to open a paranormal detective agency in which she takes part. Their motto of "helping the helpless" is closely followed by her insistence on finding paying clients. Her intelligence, tenacity, and practicality serve her well. She begins to raise her economic and social status. She finds better (though haunted) living space.[22] She upgrades her wardrobe, slowly reestablishing herself and regaining her power. When half-demon Doyle (Glenn Quinn) passes on to her the prophetic visions from the Powers That Be meant to guide Angel, Cordelia's evolution from shallow high school prom queen to responsible empathetic adult picks up speed. Though her love of fashion continues unabated (hardly an episode in the first three seasons of *Angel* goes by without her mentioning some famous designer, shopping, or beauty products), Cordelia's own wardrobe is limited by her lowered economic status. But it is now *her* wardrobe, the by-product of her efforts as an individual. Furthermore, she often decides against the "prom queen" look. While at work, she dresses for the most part in practical but still stylish form-fitting slacks and skirts, casual short-sleeve and halter tops with splashes of color. This change in style parallels her decision to become more involved in Team Angel's mission to "help the helpless."[23]

Cordelia's greater involvement in the Team's mission has two additional noteworthy fashion connections. First, she cuts her hair, initially to shoulder length, then into more of a bob at chin length, quite similar to Buffy's hairstyle in season six. In an intriguing example of life imitating art, Charisma Carpenter informs viewers that she asked to lose her long chestnut locks because they "weighed down her head."[24] This fact no doubt impinged on her abilities to be faithful to her character. Arguably, then, the shorter (and blonder) style corresponds with her greater responsibilities at the agency; it may also reflect her maturity during the period when Angel fired the entire group. The Team nevertheless continues to "help the helpless" without their Champion. Angel's eventual return and attempts at reconciliation occasion the second connection. Cordy remains resentful, not merely because Angel abandoned them, but also because he gave away the clothes she had left at the hotel without her permission. Thus Angel disrespects Cordy both professionally and personally. In "Disharmony," Angel tries to make amends but is successful only at the end of the episode, when he buys her what looks to be a whole new wardrobe, one that fits her new style choices. Her giddy reaction is thus neither merely a materialistic, prom-queen relapse, nor evidence of a bribe, but is indicative of Angel's wherewithal. This is Angel showing that he understands how deeply he wounded her by giving away her few prized, *earned* possessions.

Another notable example of Cordelia using fashion as empowerment is in the season-three episode "Billy." A very confident and adult Cordelia confronts the dangerous Wolfram and Hart lawyer Lila Morgan (Stephanie Romanov) on a fact-finding mission. Cordy, recognizing Lila's bruises as the result of being horribly beaten by one of the firm's clients, reaches out to her. Cordy informs Lila that she was just like her, a "vicious bitch, but with better shoes." Lila scoffs that she is wearing Boracchi. As they continue to discuss shoes, they continue to bond, doing so in what show writer Tim Minear labels "deadpan Dragnet style."[25] This tenuous bond allows two powerful women, one good and one evil, to unite in a feminist cause—to destroy the misogynist demon responsible for many women's deaths and Lila's injuries—by sharing an understanding that, as Cordelia puts it, "No woman should ever have to go through that, and no woman strong enough to wear the mantle of 'vicious bitch' would ever put up with it." Thus misogynist violence is the true enemy, and Whedon implies that fashion empowerment can be an effective tool in addressing it.

The Pylea-Princess Arc (and Other Feminist Affronts)

In the season-two episode "Belonging," Cordelia, still aspiring to be an actress, lands a part in a national commercial. However, the advertisement "requires" her to wear a very revealing bikini and suffer through being treated like a piece of meat. The commercial director's ill-treatment of Cordelia, symbolized by his sarcastic reference to her as "Princess," angers Angel, but she recognizes that it is the price she must pay to have a Hollywood career. If the fashion-empowerment interpretation of Whedon's female characters holds up, it must seemingly do so even in episodes that appear to be exploitive of them. Therefore, it must be argued that Whedon costumes Cordelia in such revealing ways in the Pylea-Princess arc to convey some deeper positive message about female empowerment. But how?

The viewer recognizes that Cordelia has a beautiful, toned body, which facilitates her landing the commercial spot. However, this sort of success isn't exactly the kind of power feminists covet. After all, Cordy's "power" is quickly usurped by the misogynist director because he determines whether or not she keeps the job, and to him it matters not that she is a smart, heroic woman with mystical visions empowering her to "help the helpless" as a member of Team Angel. All he really cares about is most effectively exploiting her cleavage to sell a product. This gets right to the crux of second-wave feminist issues with body display in advertising, in mainstream film and television, and especially in pornography. Who controls, who chooses, who has the power? In a still male-dominated society, can girlie culture allow women to achieve a sufficient level of autonomy to assert themselves as individuals?

Finding herself sucked into the demon universe of Pylea, Cordy tries to save herself with the power of shoes, clicking her high heels together three times, but alas, she is not Dorothy in Oz, and the fashion rules are different in Pylea. The twisty irony of Cordelia's trip to Pylea is that humans are considered ugly cattle, and the once bikini-clad Cordy is quickly sold into slavery, dressed in baggy burlap, and forced to shovel manure. Her visions, not her beauty, are what get her noticed and elevated to what at first appears to be the highest status in the land, when she is proclaimed princess. This surprises both the audience and Angel and company, who have come to rescue her. That she is wearing an outfit just as revealing as the earlier bikini is not lost on her, but this time it comes with a crown and a throne and real princess power, or so she believes. Arguably, Whedon's statement is that although denizens of Earth see Cordy as voluptuous and desirable, the Pyleans do not. To them, Cordy's princess garb is presumably analogous to humans dressing up their pets. In fact, Cordelia is just a puppet for the evil Covenant of Trombli, which tries to steal the only thing of worth to them, her visions, by forcing her to "com-shuck" with the part-human Groosalug (the handsome—for a human—Mark Lutz). This command to have sex is, in effect, a proxy rape intended to steal her only power in this dimension, which will pass to Groo during the act. With Angel and her other friends' help, the Covenant is defeated before she loses her visions, and Cordelia even beheads the chief priest all by herself, reasserting her power and symbolically castrating the all-male order.

Perhaps the impetus of the Pylea-Princess arc is to remind the viewer that just as beauty cannot define a person, clothes cannot "make the man (or woman)." That is, fashion empowerment can be an effective tool for expressing personhood, and external agencies that suppress this freedom invariably act impermissibly, but it cannot do all the work of defining an individual. This coheres well with a noteworthy *Buffy* example involving Cordelia. After Xander's betrayal of her with Willow in "Lover's Walk" (after which her humiliation is represented by her donning—shudder—sweat pants), Cordy girds her loins for battle, and in "The Wish," she returns to school dressed in what looks to be an insanely expensive dried-blood-color leather miniskirt, matching jacket, d'Orsay pumps, and a Prada bag. It is at this point, however, that the power of fashion fails her; the Cordettes readily see that both the outfit and air of confidence is just a veneer and cruelly mock and shun her for daring to defy the infamously rigid social pecking order of high school life by dating a nerd. Thus, fashion empowerment, like any power, has its limits and can only accomplish so much. But the fact that it accomplishes as much as it does in the Whedonverse is testament to its creator.

Seen another way, however, perhaps Whedon's implicit message is that what a character consciously decides *not* to wear is just as important as how she decides to adorn herself. This was certainly true of Willow, who consciously decided to avoid the black accoutrements of dark magicks. In Cordy's case, note that, once rescued from Pylea, she gives up the scanty costumes of the stage, screen, and throne. She is no longer willing to pay the price of admission for such roles. That this was a conscious decision is supported by her rejection of the Groosalug even though he followed her through the portal to her world. The fact that he continued to refer to her as "princess" further evinces her rejection of that life and its costumes. Of course, this doesn't mean that she completely gives up the empowerment of higher fashion—recall her striking dress in "Waiting in the Wings"—but it is to say that she has made an important turn. Consequently, the Pylea-Princess arc can be interpreted as an important lynchpin in Cordelia's transformation from Homecoming beauty queen to responsible, heroic figure committed to "helping the helpless."[26]

Whedon on the High Wire

So, if nothing else, the balancing act Whedon attempts with empowered individuality reflective of third-wave girlie feminism is intriguing. Rachel Fudge concurs: "Caught between demands that initially appear to be in conflict—be pretty, be smart; be homecoming queen, be savior of the world—Buffy finds a balance, a middle ground that may be lonely but is undeniably empowering. Femininity—girlness—is a slippery slope, and at least *Buffy* honors our intelligence enough to allow us these contradictions and even occasionally poke fun at them."[27] What Fudge claims of Buffy arguably applies to Willow and, perhaps, even Cordelia. Whether the fashion empowerment thesis argued for here also applies to Whedon's other strong female characters—Zoe (Gina Torres), Inara (Morena Baccarin), Kaylee (Jewel Staite), and Echo/Caroline (Eliza Dushku)—and if so, to what extent, remains to be seen. That will require following Joss's (high wire) act just a bit further, but would be certainly worthwhile.

Notes

This essay is dedicated to my fashion maven sister, Diane, who, like Cordelia, understands the power of shoes.

1. For example, see Naomi Wolfe, *The Beauty Myth* (New York: Harper Perennial, 1991, 2002).

2. Ben Wattenberg, "Has Feminism Gone Too Far?" Guests: Camille Paglia and Christina Hoff Sommers, ThinkTank,'" November 4, 1994, www.menweb.org/paglsomm .htm.

3. Bryan Appleyard, "Buffy the Vampire Slayer," *Sunday Times,* December 10, 2000.

4. Linda M. Scott, *Fresh Lipstick: Redressing Fashion and Feminism* (New York: Palgrave MacMillan, 2005), 1.

5. Ibid., 14, emphasis added.

6. Ibid., 320.

7. Ibid., 48.

8. For example, though her age places her in the second wave of feminism, Joyce Summers (Kristine Sutherland) is a single, divorced mother raising one and then two daughters, running her own successful art gallery, and, like her daughters, negotiating the trials and tribulations of dating on the Hellmouth. She seems fully capable of supporting her family and is also admired for her style and beauty by fashion maven Cordelia Chase, who, in season two's "School Hard," says of Joyce, "Now that's a woman who knows how to moisturize"; by Buffy's Watcher, Rupert Giles (Anthony Head), who has sex with her while in his season-three "Band Candy" chocolate-induced teenage Ripper persona; and by Buffy's friend Xander Harris (Nicholas Brendan), who fantasizes about her as she stands in her bedroom doorway wearing a negligee in the season-four finale, "Restless."

9. Rachel Fudge, "Everything You Always Wanted to Know about Feminism, But

Were Afraid to Ask," in *bitchmedia*, 2005, www.bitchmagazine.org/article/everything-about-feminism.

10. Ibid.

11. For a list of relevant articles, see Darin Givens, "Buffy the Patriarchy Slayer," http://daringivens.home.mindspring.com/btps.html; see also Lorna Jowett, *Sex and the Slayer: A Gender Studies Primer for the Buffy Fan* (Middletown, Ct.: Wesleyan University Press, 2005); Jessica Prata Miller, "'The I in Team': Buffy and Feminist Ethics," Thomas Hibbs, "*Buffy the Vampire Slayer* as Feminist Noir," and Mimi Marinucci, "Feminism and the Ethics of Violence: Why Buffy Kicks Ass," in *Buffy the Vampire Slayer and Philosophy*, ed. James B. South (Chicago: Open Court Press, 2003); and Frances Early, "The Female Just Warrior Reimagined: From Boudicca to Buffy," in *Athena's Daughters: Television's New Women Warriors*, ed. Frances Early and Kathleen Kennedy (Syracuse, N.Y.: Syracuse University Press, 2003) .

12. Heather Olsen, "He Gives Us the Creeps," *Ms* magazine, August/September, 1999.

13. This accords with the thought of Anne Hollander: "Clothes make the man, not because they make up or invent what the man is or dress him up for show but because they actually create his conscious self" (*Seeing through Clothes* [New York: Viking, 1978], 444).

14. A careful inspection of Willow's jumper in the first episode reveals that she is wearing a pin shaped like a bowling pin on her dress. Yes, bowling may signify nerdiness, but it's an elegant visual pun as well: it's a bowling-pin *pin,* and it shows her smart, quirky sense of humor.

15. Jowett, *Sex and the Slayer*, 81. It is a testament to Alyson Hannigan's acting that even when both characters appear on screen at the same time, we have no trouble differentiating between them regardless of the costume.

16. For a great discussion of the young witch Tara Maclay and her fashion sense, see Peg Aloi, "Skin Pale as Apple Blossom," in *Seven Seasons of Buffy: Science Fiction and Fantasy Writers Discuss Their Favorite Television Show,* ed. Glenn Yeffeth (Dallas: BenBella, 2003).

17. Xander's view of Willow in the dream is also telling. He envisions her as half of a stereotypical "girl on girl" fantasy—she and Tara appear as almost caricature "lipstick lesbians," wearing heavy red lipstick and midriff-baring miniskirted outfits, inviting Xander to participate in a threesome with them. Their costuming shows how Xander has objectified them, something he wouldn't consciously do, but parodies the male television viewers' titillation at the lesbian couple.

18. Hollander eloquently expresses this sentiment: "There is one steady current in the course of fashion that always gains power, whenever it comes to the surface, from the ancient flavor of antifashion. This is the habit of wearing black. The symbolism of black as a color for clothing seems stronger and longer lasting than that of any other color except white—and black maintains its edge because of its standard connotations of the sinister. Black conjures fear of the blind darkness of night and the eternal darkness of death " (*Seeing through Clothes*, 365).

19. Spike loves how Buffy looks—she is an attractive, slender, blue-eyed blonde—and he is, after all, the one who had Warren Meers make the "Buffybot" an exact physical duplicate of the Slayer in "Intervention." Yet he soon grows tired of his toy and in the course of the series seems to learn that Buffy's power of attraction for him is not just how she looks, but who she is, as a person, which he so eloquently expresses in "Touched."

20. For a more thorough discussion of this aspect of Cordelia's character, see Jowett, "Girl Power," 30–33.

21. Jennifer Crusie, "The Assassination of Cordelia Chase," in *Five Seasons of Angel: Science Fiction and Fantasy Authors Discuss Their Favorite Vampire*, ed. Glenn Yeffeth (Dallas: BenBella, 2004), 189.

22. Recall, in "RM W/A VU," that when a ghost tries to convince her to commit suicide, it makes the mistake of calling her a "little bitch," which rouses Cordy from her fear: "I'm not a sniveling whiny little 'Cry-Buffy.' I'm the nastiest girl in Sunnydale history. I take crap from no one."

23. Interestingly enough, the few times we see the Los Angeles Cordy dressed to the nines for a date or party invariably end badly, such as when she attracts a vampire's interest in "City of . . . ," when she is impregnated with demon spawn ("Expecting"), or when her date abandons her during a vampire attack ("The Bachelor Party"). Arguably, this reversion to the Sunnydale Cordelia can be interpreted as Cordelia not being faithful to who she currently is.

24. "Hi, I'm Cordelia," *Angel: Season 2*, DVD commentary (Hollywood, Calif.: Twentieth Century Fox, 2000).

25. "Billy," *Angel: Season 3*, DVD commentary (Hollywood, Calif.: Twentieth Century Fox, 2001).

26. For a dissenting (and sometimes disparaging) view of Cordelia's character transformation and fashion choices in the later seasons of *Angel*, see Crusie, "The Assassination of Cordelia Chase."

27. Rachel Fudge, "The Buffy Effect, or a Tale of Cleavage and Marketing," *Bitch: Feminist Response to Popular Culture*, no. 10 (1999): 18–21, 58.

Heroes and Villains

Morality, the Will to Power, and the Overman in the Work of Joss Whedon

Gary Heba with Robin Murphy

> He who fights with monsters should look to it that he himself does not become a monster.
> —Nietzsche, *Beyond Good and Evil,* Aphorism 146.

Whether looking at *Buffy, Angel, Firefly, Serenity, Dollhouse,* or even *Dr. Horrible's Sing-Along Blog,* all of Joss Whedon's projects can be viewed as treatises on the struggle between good and evil that occurs on both supernatural (including technologically created supernature as in *Firefly* and *Dollhouse*) and natural planes of existence. What makes Whedon's work interesting philosophically is his interest in exploring the dimensions of power relationships—natural, supernatural, and sexual—and the morality of those who wield that power in a way that inextricably binds power to morality. The Whedonverse is populated by characters pursuing and/or possessing superhuman, even godlike, power, and in this respect, Whedon's work reflects an interesting moral perspective on the Nietzschean concepts of the overman and the will to power.

But the overman doesn't just suddenly emerge, fully formed—it is something that must evolve, and the argument presented here is that the major characters in *Buffy the Vampire Slayer* and Whedon's other series work through several stages of moral development that correspond very closely to the moral development described in the three essays in *On the Genealogy of Morality.* Because of their superpowers, however, characters like Buffy, River, and Echo can all be said to represent, in one shape or form, a version of Nietzsche's overman, who must both confront and determine their morality, such that the morality of the overman, as represented by the actions these characters display, constitutes, in essence, a fourth "essay" in Nietzsche's *Genealogy.*

Published in 1888, Nietzsche's *On the Genealogy of Morality* is "prized by commentators as his most important and systematic work."[1] In three essays, Nietzsche outlines both a lineage and a critique of how Judeo-Christian morality developed in discrete stages to influence not only the historical development of religious organizations, but also the moral codes of conduct developed by these same organizations that dictate rules of behavior. Thus, since religions tend to be the secular arbiters of divine providence and will, they also become the de facto custodians of social values and morality. Nietzsche was not antimoral, but, as his *On the Genealogy of Morality* demonstrates, he was definitely not a proponent of *religious* morality. Walter Kaufmann writes that "if one considers the history of modern philosophy from Descartes, it is surely, for good or ill, the story of an emancipation from religion. . . . Nietzsche is one of the first thinkers with a comprehensive philosophy that completes the break with religion."[2] This makes Nietzsche an ideal candidate to announce that "God is dead" and also to outline the path that leads from the death of God to the birth of the overman.[3]

"First Essay—'Good and Evil,' 'Good and Bad,'" Masters and Slaves

Nietzsche here establishes the basic concept that drives the formation of Judeo-Christian morality—the master/slave relationship. Nietzsche posits that basic concepts of Good, Evil, and Bad all grow out of a two-part society whereby "a militarily and politically dominant group of 'masters' exercises absolute control over a completely subordinate group of 'slaves.'"[4] The inevitable conflict in this one-sided power structure breeds what Nietzsche calls *"ressentiment,"* or resentment, in the slaves toward their masters. The master/slave relationship generated inverted systems of value for both groups in terms of what is good and what is evil. For the masters, what is good is themselves and the general air of "nobility" they exude; conversely, all that is not noble is "evil." However, for the slaves, "when the eye of *ressentiment* looks at the nobles, it does not see . . . courage, truthfulness and the like that the nobles had themselves perceived; it sees instead only cruelty, tyranny, lustfulness, insatiability and godlessness."[5] With this reversal of values between master and slave is born the foundation for all moral and class warfare.

While the master/slave dynamic in *Buffy* does not derive from a power held by a god or religious institution, there are other forces (natural and supernatural) and organizations at work capable of breeding the same kind of *ressentiment.* For example, Buffy (Sarah Michelle Gellar) resents being chosen as the Slayer, and several times she rebels against the Council of

Watchers. In season one, when the Master (Mark Metcalf) is preparing to ascend, Buffy learns of the prophecy that he will kill her, making her decide to quit as the Slayer: "I'm only sixteen. I don't want to die." And who could blame her? Being chosen is a primal violation of Buffy's identity—an identity-jacking, if you will. All of Buffy Summers's hopes and aspirations are subordinate to "In every generation, a Slayer is born," and so she is enslaved to her role as the Chosen. She questions not only the sacrifices she has to make in her life (dating, family, career), but what her role as Slayer is doing to her: "Being a perfect Slayer means being too hard to love at all" ("Intervention"). Her decision to quit as Slayer in season one is short-lived, but her *ressentiment* remains throughout the series, as we also learn in season seven that there are additional layers of hierarchy above the council she must confront.

The character of Faith (Eliza Dushku), the Slayer who was chosen when Buffy's first replacement was killed, does not seem burdened with any *ressentiment* toward being chosen—on the contrary, she only seems to revel in that role. Her credo, "Want, take, have, forget," is a good indication that, as Slayer, she sees herself as above it all ("Bad Girls"). It also indicates that she enjoys slaying, as Buffy says, "a little too much" ("Faith, Hope, and Trick"). In a commentary feature for season three, Joss Whedon says that "Faith is Buffy's evil twin," and throughout the series she is portrayed as Buffy's reflection in reverse, a representation of what the Slayer could be without a conscience.

What Faith does resent is playing second Slayer to Buffy. The difference between these two Slayers is made dramatically clear in a conversation between Buffy and Faith after Faith has accidentally killed the Deputy Mayor (Jack Plotnick) and shows no remorse:

> FAITH: Something made us different, B. We're warriors. We're built to kill.
> BUFFY: To kill demons, but it does not mean that we get to pass judgment on people like we're better than everybody.
> FAITH: We *are* better. People need us to survive. In the balance, nobody's going to cry over some random bystander who got caught in the crossfire.
> BUFFY: I am.
> FAITH: That's your loss. ("Consequences")

This exchange illustrates the moral chasm between the two Slayers, and at the root of this divide is the master/slave distinction: Faith essentially adopts the moral code of the masters where slaves (or bystanders, in this case) are expendable and of lesser value than the Chosen. In contrast, Buffy, in her *ressentiment* at being the Chosen, sees her Slayer role more as that of servant, and the differences between the Slayers forms a dialectic that is explored through the remainder of the series.

Finally, though in a very subliminal way, the specter of the master/slave equation derived from Christianity permeates the series. God is mentioned, Buffy wears a large crucifix through most of season one; vampires invade churches; holy water is used. Although in the background, not the foreground, the presence of Christianity is felt through these and other signifiers throughout *Buffy*. While Christianity is not assailed outright, its occasional presence is enough to remind us that the possibility of God exists in *Buffy*.

"Second Essay—'Guilt,' 'Bad Conscience' and Related Matters"

Nietzsche's second essay, "'Guilt,' 'Bad Conscience' and Related Matters," describes the psychological mechanisms of guilt in the master/slave equation. The idea of a "bad conscience" arises when the "instinct of freedom [is] pushed back, repressed, incarcerated within itself and finally able to discharge and unleash itself only against itself."[6] When the slaves' instinct for freedom (his/her "will to power") is driven back, the "bad conscience" "for no longer being able to live an expansive and instinctual life . . . [becomes] . . . a feeling of guilt and shame at being alive."[7] Further, denied freedom, and with no power to retaliate, the slaves find that "all instincts that do not discharge themselves outwardly (like guilt), *turn inward*—this is what I call the *internalization* of man; thus it was that man first developed what was later called his 'soul.'"[8]

This is an entirely apt description of Angel's (David Boreanaz) moral situation throughout the *Buffy* series. In the history of television, Angel ranks high on the list of tragic characters: a vampire with a soul so that he cannot feed without guilt, considerably dampening his vampiric will to power, and a curse that will transform him into his darker half, Angelus, if he feels one moment of true happiness, as he does in season two, forcing Buffy to kill him just at the moment he regains his soul. In Nietzsche's conception, the "soul" for Angel manifests itself in an endless trail of present and future suffering for actions he had taken in the past. Later in the series, Spike (James Marsters) also develops a soul, and just as the dialectic of the Slayer nature is explored through the pairing of Buffy/Faith, the pairing of Angel/Spike represents the duality of vampire nature in *Buffy*. Both vampires suffer not only for their past misdeeds, but also to prove themselves worthy of Buffy's affections. Spike's moral development is especially interesting here since he is able to repress his vampire instinct; at first, he accomplishes this through the use of a chip, but later, he does so through his guilt over his past, but *before* he has a soul. Unlike Angel, Spike uses his guilt, as Nietzsche suggests, to manufacture his soul through an act of will.

While guilt is the motivation that drives two of the major vampires in the series, Buffy herself has only a few, though major, confrontations with it. The first two are in season three, when she initially covers up for Faith's murder, and later in the season after she has beaten/stabbed Faith into a coma. Buffy seems genuinely remorseful about putting Faith into this state, but she does not then devote herself to making the wrong right. This is because Buffy is, up to a point, an unwilling, but still dutiful slave, and has no reason to feel guilt for these actions since she only carried out her Slayerly duties. Buffy's third, more serious confrontation with her guilt occurs near the end of season seven, after Glory kidnaps Dawn, and Buffy enters a catatonic state, not because she failed in her duties as a Slayer, but because she failed in her duties as a sister and was unable to keep her "childhood" promise to take care of Dawn (Michelle Trachtenberg). Ultimately, Willow (Alyson Hannigan) persuades Buffy to come out of her state by appealing to Buffy's role as Slayer/slave and letting her know that she can save the world, and her sister, too.

These illustrations show how Nietzsche's views on the development of guilt can be seen as major driving forces for a number of characters in the series discussed here. But an endless life of guilt leaves the slave class in a state of abject despair, and in his third essay, Nietzsche examines how guilt is historically "treated" with an ascetic approach.

"Third Essay"—The Ascetic Ideal and Atonement/Redemption

Asceticism can be described as a turning away from the world around us that, like the development of guilt, results in a turning inward. Like Zarathustra, the popular conception of the ascetic individual is that of a hermit, a solitary person who chooses to be so because of a cultural (to clean the body) or spiritual (to clean the soul) imperative. In either sense, there is the idea that the body/soul is unclean/sick, and that this is the true source of the slaves' suffering. *Ressentiment* breeds the initial "bad conscience" in the slaves, a sickness from which they must be healed. The ascetic priest, one of the ruling class of "masters" Nietzsche described in the first essay, now is capable of transforming the slaves' feelings of "bad conscience," or guilt, into a tangible commodity—sin—and the priest's power has value because it succeeds in changing the direction of the slaves' *ressentiment*. The *ressentiment* that was directed at the masters is now turned by the slaves upon themselves. The slaves are sick, unclean, but through the moral trick performed by the priest, it becomes clear that their only cure is "to engage in a progressive spiral of forms of self-abnegation and self-denial . . . life operating against life."[9]

As discussed earlier, the guilt that Spike and Angel feel leads them on a quest to seek healing through redemption by denying their instinct to hunt and feed—it is a sacrifice they make so the guilt from their sins can be kept at bay. This type of self-denial is key to understanding the ascetic ideal. Healing or redemption can be achieved only through sacrifice. While Angel and Spike seek redemption in order to save their souls, it is unclear exactly from what their souls are being saved. Without a God to appease, it seems that the moral goal for both is to simply find a way to exist in their unlife that allows them to exist without the wracking torture of guilt, so that, even though they are monsters, they are able to feel like men.

Of the various forms of self-denial available—abstinence, silence, fasting, poverty, humility—perhaps the most ascetic of all is self-sacrifice, and we also have an example of that in *Buffy*. While on her Slayer Quest, the First Slayer (Sharon Ferguson) tells Buffy that "death is her gift" ("Intervention"). At first, Buffy is unsure how to interpret this: "Guess I'm just a killer after all," and it's not until she realizes that the blood that Glory (Clare Kramer) needs from Dawn is the same as hers that Buffy understands that the gift is her death. Buffy's goal in her sacrifice is neither redemption nor salvation, though. Buffy matter-of-factly says to Dawn just before her final leap, "This is the work I do" ("The Gift"). Buffy's act is completely selfless—the pinnacle of the ascetic ideal—and it can be viewed as an *imitatio Christi*—her life is given in exchange so that others can be saved. Though salvation in the Buffyverse is not spiritual, the analogy to the dominant metaphor of sacrifice in the Christian mythos is difficult to ignore, though it does come with a twist. Whereas Jesus' sacrifice and resurrection opened the doors of Heaven, Buffy's second resurrection in season six weakens the force of the Slayer line and sets in motion events that lead to a reopening of the gates of Hell in season seven. Thus, it may follow that Buffy represents, in terms of the Slayer mythology, a kind of anti-Christ (or, at least, anti-Slayer).

As we have seen throughout Nietzsche's three essays, the master/slave binary breeds *ressentiment* in the slaves, leading them to develop guilt and bad feelings that can be healed through the self-denial of asceticism. Nietzsche's formal discussion of morality ends here, but the cultural score is still masters 1, slaves 0. Left in a limbo of ascetic self-denial, slaves have a method for healing, but they remain slaves. Through the concept of the overman, however, Nietzsche begins to outline a path to the slaves' freedom.

Fourth Essay—The Overman, the Will to Power, and Transformation

The idea of the overman is perhaps one of the most widely misunderstood of Nietzsche's concepts. It is introduced in *Also Sprach Zarathustra* as the titular prophet declares: "*I teach you the overman.* Man is something that shall be overcome. What have you done to overcome him?"[10]

Nietzsche's concept of the overman, or superman, has been read by many as a desire for physical human power and perfection, and in the case of Hitler, racial perfection.[11] But the twisted, megalomaniacal overman that came to be associated with Nazi interpretations of it does not overcome what is worst in man—it celebrates it—and as such, has served, through the second half of the twentieth century and into the present day, as a kind of template for the representation of villains. For example, characters in the television series *Andromeda*, who have used genetic nanotechnologies to create a race of overmen, are called Nietzscheans. Obviously, through political manipulations and misappropriation of Nietzsche's ideas, the overman has developed a very negative reputation in popular culture, one that has been impossible to dislodge from the collective consciousness.

This popular interpretation imagines the overman lacking any sense of moral responsibility except inasmuch as the "Big Bads" in *Buffy*, like the Master, Glorificus, and the First, are responsible for seeking the means and ends to realize their will to power. But that is more a reflection of the fascist interpretation of the overman, and we argue that Nietzsche had something far different in mind with origins in the idea of the will to power, and his ideas of a "higher type."

According to Nietzsche, the will to power is composed of three parts: First, "the whole of life is a single field of forces created by an inhuman will to power which produces human consciousness as one of its effects. . . . Second, the aim of life is neither self-preservation nor moral and spiritual enlightenment, but the *increase* of power, and . . . the third element is . . . that the will to power . . . is a way of becoming *master* of something."[12] This "something" is a knowledge of power hierarchies and how to "work" them in order to gain power over them. Thus, "the will to power is not just power or force, but Will to Power: always will for more power."[13]

But toward what end is the will to power to be used? For Nietzsche, the overman embodies the will to power that enables a person to live outside societal conventions and can be considered as a revolutionary figure. As such, the overman is a threat to the status quo and its institutions because it is his goal to undo them. In the final television season of *Buffy*, Buffy Summers becomes just that in relation to the structures that created and maintained the Slayer lineage. Part of her revolution is to overthrow the patriarchal rules and power structures that gave rise to Slayers as they now are. The other part of her revolution is empowerment—it diminishes Buffy's absolute will to power, but it is the ultimate act of it as well—to make many chosen instead of only one. Up against the armies of the First, Buffy seems to realize that the old way—one Slayer, thousands of Über-vampires—is not going to work this time, and that there is a need for a paradigm shift, a revolution, a new Slayerdom that does not involve the patriarchal violation of a single Chosen. Instead, by offering a choice to any who are willing, Buffy enables each of the Potentials to have a share of her power, thereby decentralizing and democratizing it. One can argue that Buffy's decision here, as a general, is simply utilitarian—there is strength in numbers. However, her impassioned speech about allowing each girl with potential to choose her power suggests otherwise. Like Spartacus or Lincoln, Buffy has the power to free the slaves with her actions, which demonstrate how an "ascending" or active interpretation of life celebrates the power of a strong will to create and affirm its own values, what Nietzsche referred to as "a higher self." We argue that this is a better approximation of what Nietzsche had in mind for the overman than the fascist misinterpretation of the concept so deeply rooted in popular culture narratives. Buffy's action is transformational and nihilistic because it completely overturns the master/slave dynamic: the Shadow Men, the Watchers—the former masters are irrelevant now.

We can gain further insight into what the overman's qualities might be by examining what Nietzsche refers to as a "higher type." In *Ecce Homo*, Nietzsche discusses the five qualities that make creative geniuses like Goethe and Beethoven (and himself) stand apart:

1. The higher type is solitary and deals with others only instrumentally.
2. The higher type seeks burdens and responsibilities, as he is driven toward the completion of a unifying project.
3. The higher type is essentially healthy and resilient.
4. The higher type affirms life.
5. The higher type has a distinctive bearing toward others; and toward himself he has self-reverence.[14]

While all of these qualities can be seen in Whedon's heroes, the most relevant for our discussion are numbers two and four. In the case of the second quality, the burdens and responsibilities are all too obvious for the heroes, but they are all steps toward some final goal in each of Whedon's series. The fourth quality may be the most important of all because the Dionysian or life-affirming attitude of the higher being "affirms his life unconditionally; insofar as he affirms it *including* the 'suffering' or other hardships it has involved."[15] These two qualities are related, as the burdens and responsibilities each character takes on always cause suffering and hardship in the Whedonverse, but he/she accepts this suffering as another step toward the overall goal.

The Overman as Choice and Dialectic in the Whedonverse

Whedon's explorations of power, especially of superpowered individuals, acknowledges a popular interpretation of Nietzsche's overman as a soulless, megalomaniacal instrument driven by the will to individual power (the bad guys, like the Master and Glory, and some of the good guys at times, like Spike and Faith). Whedon, in fact, seems to parody this interpretation of the overman through his villains who, with their snarky asides, tend to be cartoonish and campy in a Freddy Krueger kind of way. But viewers also observe a dialectical counterpart to this version of the overman, and what we find in *Buffy* is a critique and transformation of the concept such that the overman can also aspire to a more life-affirming and constructive will to power.

Along with the "master race" version of the overman, Nietzsche is also, unfairly, associated with nihilism in the popular collective unconscious, most likely because of his name being mentioned in *Time* magazine's 1966 cover story, "Is God Dead?"[16] A common belief about nihilism is that since there is no final "truth," life is necessarily rendered meaningless, and that is one logical consequence of nihilistic belief. Nihilism does not deny "truth," per se, but rather our ability to know it. Nietzsche says that man "will rather will nothingness than not will," and in the absence of a unifying truth, the will to nothingness is especially evident in existential and postmodern thought as well as Hot Topic stores.[17] But if it is man's instinct *to will*, a nihilistic orientation does not preclude that, in the absence of an ultimate "truth," man (or overman) can also will something more life-affirming, like a socially constructed set of values that, although arbitrary, can still function to improve the quality of life through change or revolution. Through Zarathustra, Nietzsche says: "Human existence is uncanny, and still without meaning. . . . I will teach men the meaning of their existence—the overman."[18] Unlike the existentialists, from this declaration it follows that Nietzsche saw existence as having at least the potential for meaning, although not the meaning ascribed to it by the church or the masters, and "the experience of nihilism as a moral crisis remains the indispensable point of transition" that makes it possible for a new meaning to form.[19] Thus, any sense of nihilism in Nietzsche is not the end goal, but a necessary transitional step in the process of constructing new social and moral meaning that is seen in Buffy's decision to destroy the system of values the Masters set in place, but *in order to replace those systems with better ones*—call it constructive nihilism—and the overman will lead the way. Far from being nihilistic, Nietzsche's overman offers an antidote to the very meaninglessness and pessimism he found in Schopenhauer.[20]

Angel is an interesting case of the overman because he came to his function through a curse. Because of his past as the nasty Angelus, the will to be something more life-affirming comes from his fate as a vampire with a soul. He feels the moral need to make up for the wrongs he's done and tries to live by his own constructed values of improving the lives of others. He, like Buffy, understands the true meaning of his existence—a will to help the underdog. He suffers through the constant memory of what he did to his victims, accepts this as his burden, and sees his responsibility in making the lives of those around him safer—as the Champion. Ultimately, Angel is alone in his quest for atonement from the community, a slave to his spiritual soul.

In many ways, Angel is a true superman because of his supernatural powers. He's strong, fast, and hard to kill. But he's also more than both his human and vampire counterparts—he has surpassed the physical limitations of the human and the moral limitations of the vampire. Because of Angelus's history of mayhem, Angel wants to cause an upheaval of the system of values fostered by Wolfram and Hart that plagues his city and replace that system with something more moral, civic, and meaningful by helping the helpless. A major plot of Angel is to bend the will to power of Wolfram and Hart, who won't kill him because they believe that he plays a major role in the coming apocalypse, as the prophesy throughout the series promises. However, for Angel, his life is meaningless without his will to help people.

In *Firefly* (2002), the character of River (Summer Glau) provides a problematic case of the overman. Essentially, River is a prodigy recruited by the Alliance, who experiment on her, leaving her delusional and apparently insane. Her status as an overman is more complicated because of this, and her journey of self-recognition throughout the series positions her more as an overman "in progress" who is at first more controlled by her powers than she is in control of them—a result of the Alliance's experiments—and later begins her evolution as she begins to understand and control them.

River's battle with the master/slave dynamic is both internal (the demons she struggles against) and external (the Alliance), something we also see in *Buffy* and *Angel.*

By the end of *Serenity* (2005), she has started to transcend the Alliance's alterations, as well as the limitations of humanity, and is on her way to becoming something more because of a need to save the ship's crew from the Reavers, a community of bestial, murderous people who were altered through a compound the Alliance put into the air on their planet, Miranda. River "embraces the will to power" by locking herself into the ship's hold with the Reavers and destroying them to save her crew. Before she goes in, she says to her brother, "you've always taken care of me. . . . my turn." In this, true to the nature of a higher type, she shows a willingness to take on a burden, and perhaps because she realizes how much of a burden she has been to the crew thus far, she can control the power she gained through the Alliance's experiments so that "no power in the 'verse can stop me" ("War Stories"). If the true nature of the overman is to "surpass," be a "bridge," and offer "deliverance," then by the end of *Serenity,* River begins to recognize that she has *bent the will* of the Alliance to her own, leading to a truce with the Alliance and altering the power structure of the master/slave binary.[21]

It should be emphasized that by the end of the film, River is only beginning to see her potential in a way she can control; she cannot claim full overman status. Given the early cancellation of the series, we can only speculate about what River may have become. To be fair, it would be similarly hard to imagine Buffy becoming a revolutionary general if all we had to go on was the first season.

One of Whedon's more unusual megalomaniacal instruments is the character Dr. Horrible (Neil Patrick Harris) from the short film *Dr. Horrible's Sing-Along Blog* (2008). Dr. Horrible's primary goal is to become a member of the Evil League of Evil led by Bad Horse. After several failed attempts at evil to support his application, Bad Horse gives an ultimatum for membership: assassination. The audience also knows Dr. Horrible is in love with Penny (Felicia Day), and when his arch nemesis, Captain Hammer (Nathan Fillion), wins Penny's love through an act of kindness, Dr. Horrible finally decides Captain Hammer must die. He sings in "It's a Brand New Day" that he finally reached a point of no remorse because Captain Hammer, ironically, has "shown him the light." He once wanted to rid the world of the "plague that devoured humanity," but now he sees the path and it's to "the evil in me." His plan to kill Captain Hammer goes horribly wrong, however, and Penny is killed instead.

Though he initially wants to bend the will of the world and control everything for his life with Penny, unrequited love pushes him to the more fascist will to power; he feels that the "evil inside is on the rise." In the end, his accidental sacrifice of Penny does not help him overcome the worst in man or mankind and only helps him finally gain membership into the Evil League of Evil. The victory is hollow, though, and the very last frame of him shows what he's become: alone, a nightmare, and unable to feel "a thing." *Dr. Horrible* offers almost a parody of the overman concept—Dr. Horrible isn't competent enough to be convincingly evil, and Captain Hammer, as revealed in the cringe-inducing song, "Everyone's a Hero in Their Own Way," is too narcissistic and socially unconcerned to really be considered good. Both seek their respective titles of "villain" and "hero," but neither truly deserves these titles, much less that of "overman."

Whedon's latest series, *Dollhouse,* offers a dystopian view of the world where mind-wipes and personality implants are possible. In the series, the Rossum Corporation is clearly the master, in control of the actives, who have signed five-year contracts for their services. Many of the actives have signed with Rossum as a way to avoid jail or punishment for other offenses, in what is a kind of identity-relocation project. Being under contract, the actives are willing slaves, but slaves nonetheless. The Dollhouse, itself, is an underground panopticon designed so that the actives can always be observed and monitored. The central character, Echo (Eliza Dushku), is an active who begins to remember parts of her personality that have been wiped, gradually becoming aware that something isn't quite right.

The most overtly Nietzschean moment in Whedon occurs in the "Omega" episode of *Dollhouse.* Alpha (Alan Tudyk), one of the first actives programmed by the Rossum Corporation's mind-jacking technology, has gone rogue after an accidental "composite event" left him imprinted with the personalities, memories, and skills of forty-eight people. Alpha escapes the Dollhouse, killing and mutilating many of the staff and actives. He later returns to kidnap Echo in an attempt to make her "a superior creature; an ascended being":

ALPHA: We're not just humans anymore, not just multiple personalities.
ECHO: We're not gods.
ALPHA: All right. Übermensch. Nietzsche predicted our rise—perfected, objective, something new.
ECHO: New superior people with a little German thrown in—what

could possibly go wrong? . . . Don't tell me you're some superior, ascended being. To ascend to anything, you don't cut up women. ("Omega")

Echo's reference to Hitler and the concept of the master race, taken in context with the recurring line from the show, "Are you your best today?" clearly links Alpha to the fascist version of the overman who has not really ascended to anything. Like all of Whedon's villains, Alpha is at once a formidable foe and also a pathetic, power-hungry fool. While he succeeds in overthrowing the Dollhouse and unleashes the mind-wiping technology, the result is a world thrown into chaos with 90 percent of the world's population turned into mind-wiped, violent zombies ("Epitaph One"). In all the Whedonverse, Alpha represents the nihilist supreme for his role in creating a world without order, identity, or meaning.

As a counterforce to Alpha, Echo eventually regains her original personality of Caroline, and after the Dollhouse is attacked, she and the remaining restored actives set out to shut down Rossum's main servers in Arizona. Like all of Whedon's heroes, Echo/Caroline struggles internally, but emerges from the struggle as leader of the actives. While the actives are successful in shutting down Rossum's servers, civilization is literally in ruins and must be rebuilt, and we are led to believe that Echo/Caroline will emerge as one of the principal leaders, earning her the role of the life-affirming overman of the series.

Whedon contra Nietzsche?

So just how Nietzschean is Whedon? It depends on which Nietzsche one is looking at. On the one hand, there is the Nietzsche who was alleged to have given a philosophical backbone to the politics of the Nazi Party, and whose nihilism has been interpreted to conclude that all values are meaningless. We have argued that although this is the conception most deeply held in the collective consciousness, it is, in fact, a counterfeit Nietzsche. On the other hand, then, is the reclaimed Nietzsche whose concept of the overman can be seen as a life-affirming agent of positive social and cultural change as shown in the previous discussion of Whedon's series. Whedon offers both to reveal a dialectic of power and morality, and as we have argued, he sides more closely with the latter Nietzsche than the former.

Although Whedon, like Nietzsche, critiques contemporary Judeo-Christian morality, especially in terms of its views on sexuality, his critique only goes so far. Ultimately, he rejects the fascistic interpretation of the overman as having no place in a society that values love of family and community, without which there is no basis for society at all. Characters like Buffy, Angel, River, and Echo, while all possessing superpowers, have also evolved morally, as members of a community. Their actions and sacrifices more truly overcome what is worst in man (and demon, and God) and are more deserving of the title "overman." Finally, it is a fulfillment of their own wills to power that allows Angel, River, Echo, and Buffy to become supermen and superwomen. Nietzsche argued that religious systems of value needed to die out before the overman could appear. Because there is no explicitly religious system of values in *Buffy*, placing a value system in a purely secular context does achieve a nihilistic goal. It transplants the source of morality to one's community, even though it does not essentially change the basic moral code.

Greg Forster writes that Whedon forcefully rejects the Christian worldview in favor of a "nihilistic outlook."[22] The answer is both yes and no. The Christian worldview is never assailed directly in any of Whedon's series, but the basic tenets of Christian morality—love, forgiveness, sacrifice, good deeds, redemption—are hard at work in the Whedonverse, and they seem very much to be the direction in which the moral compass of the shows is strongly bent. Although Whedon may show nihilistic tendencies, they are like Nietzsche's, and are intended to destroy a value system in order to replace it with a better one. That being said, however, the moral precepts guiding the actions of Whedon's heroes are still familiarly Christian. Maybe in this way, Whedon is preserving what is life-affirming from Christian values but placing these values within a new structure. Perhaps this is the most subversive kind of revolution, one in which enough remains morally familiar so that we don't even notice that the revolution has already been televised.

Notes

1. Friedrich Nietzsche, *On the Genealogy of Morality*, revised student edition, trans. Carol Diethe, ed. Keith Ansell-Pearson (Cambridge: Cambridge University Press, 2007), xiii.

2. Friedrich Nietzsche, *The Portable Nietzsche*, trans. and ed. Walter Kaufmann (New York: Penguin, 1980), 17.

3. Nietzsche writes on the death of God in several places in his work. In *The Gay Science*, the phrase "God is dead" is found in sections 108, 125 and 343. It also appears in *Thus Spoke Zarathustra* in the prologue, sec. 2; and pt. 1, sec. 22, passage 3. It is widely regarded by critics that Nietzsche was not referring to the literal death of God, but the death of religious systems of value and morality.

4. Nietzsche, *Genealogy,* xxl.

5. Ibid., 17.

6. Lee Spinks, *Friedrich Nietzsche* (New York: Routledge, 2003), 70.

7. Nietzsche, *Genealogy,* 57.

8. Ibid., 57.

9. Ibid., xxvi.

10. Friedrich Nietzsche, *Thus Spoke Zarathustra: A Book for All and None,* trans. Walter Kaufmann (New York: Penguin, 1978), 12.

11. To say the least, Nietzsche was not concerned with the values of what was later to become the Nazi Party in Germany, and in a draft for the *Preface* to *Beyond Good and Evil,* Nietzsche writes: "I wish I had written it (*The Will To Power*) in French, so it might not appear to be a confirmation of the aspirations of the German *Reich.* The Germans of today are not thinkers any more: something else delights and impresses them. The will to power as a principle might be intelligible to them" (Nietzsche, *The Portable Nietzsche,* 442). Even before Hitler was born, Nietzsche already observed a tendency in the German people toward a type of totalitarian nationalism that did not sit well with his views on the individual and the state. However, after Nietzsche's death, his sister, Elizabeth became the executor of her brother's literary estate. With her husband, "Elizabeth 'edited' and tampered with Nietzsche's writings, interpreting his 'will to power' and his war rhetoric in such a manner as to make of him a proto-Nazi theorist" (Irving M. Zeitlin, *Nietzsche: A Re-Examination* [Cambridge, Mass.: Polity Press, 1994], 15).

12. Spinks, *Nietzsche,* 137–39.

13. Alphonso Lingis, "The Will to Power," in *The New Nietzsche,* ed. David B. Allison (New York: Delta, 1977), 38.

14. Brian Leiter, *Nietzsche: On Morality* (New York: Routledge, 2002), 116–20.

15. Diethe, *Genealogy,* 68.

16. "Is God Dead?" *Time,* April 8, 1966, cover story.

17. Nietzsche, *Genealogy,* 68.

18. Nietzsche, *Zarathustra,* 7.

19. Spinks, *Nietzsche,* 109.

20. Although once an admirer of Schopenhauer, Nietzsche grew to disagree with Schopenhauer's view of morality, which posits a "world of continual, senseless suffering . . . and all to no end except to restart the painful cycle anew. . . . Would we not, in fact, be better off dead?" (Leiter, *On Morality,* 56). Nietzsche found this view to be overly pessimistic and challenged it in his later work, seeking to reevaluate the values that lead to the conclusion that life is meaningless to "establish a viable alternative verdict" (Richard Schacht, ed., *Nietzsche, Genealogy, Morality: Essays on Nietzsche's Genealogy of Morals* (Berkeley and Los Angeles: University of California Press, 1994), 478.

21. Martin Heidegger in *The New Nietzsche,* ed. David B. Allison (New York: Delta, 1977), 68–78.

22. Greg Forster, "Faith and Plato: 'You're Nothing! Disgusting, Murderous Bitch!'" in *Buffy the Vampire Slayer and Philosophy: Fear and Loathing in Sunnydale,* ed. James B. South (Chicago: Open Court, 2003), 25.

Part 3

"I'm All of Them, but None of Them
Is Me": The Human Condition

Seeking Authenticity in the Whedonverse

Joseph J. Foy and Dean A. Kowalski

> No one asks for their life to change, not really. But it does. . . . So what are we, helpless? Puppets? No. The big moments are gonna come. You can't help that. It's what you do afterwards that counts. That's when you find out who you are.
> —Whistler, *Buffy the Vampire Slayer*, "Becoming, Part I"

Willow Rosenberg (Alyson Hannigan) has her choice of any university in the United States—and five in Europe, including Oxford—although she is unsure about going to school in a foreign country. For Xander Harris (Nicholas Brendon), everything in life is foreign territory. Jack Kerouac will be his next teacher; the open road will be his school. Buffy Summers (Sarah Michelle Gellar) has the opportunity and inclination to attend Northwestern University in Illinois, but must weigh this against her responsibilities in California as the Slayer-on-the-Hellmouth, to say nothing of her committed relationship with Angel (David Boreanaz). The *Buffy the Vampire Slayer* episode "Choices" is thus fully immersed in the discomfort of maturation, when young people begin to see that their lives are about to be radically altered by circumstance. Each of us must juggle the conflicts between self and other, what is expected of us, and what we want for ourselves. Art thereby reflects life, which attests to the allure of the Whedonverse.

Joss Whedon regularly crafts narratives that vividly enable the viewer to reflect on the questions: Who am I? Who do I want to be? It is in this struggle for personal identity that Whedon seems to be imparting a lesson that is woven throughout his entire corpus. But part of the lesson is an enriched understanding of various forces and social institutions that tend to displace individual identity and autonomy. In the Whedonverse, such forces are often depicted as obstacles the heroes must overcome. When successful,

Whedon's heroes thereby gain an enriched sense of their authentic self. This essay, accordingly, explores the importance of autonomy and authenticity in the Whedonverse in the hope of better understanding Whedon's art and what it says about our lives. We argue that Whedon's tales of the personal struggles of sympathetic and relatable characters are ultimately designed to prompt us—his audience—to reexamine the choices each of us makes and thus the kind of person each of us is becoming.

Angst and Horribleness

In *Being and Time,* Martin Heidegger describes how personal identities are shaped and influenced by the world. Identity, he argues, is largely acquired from relationships with families, friends, and communities.[1] Heidegger asserts that most people will uncritically accept the social and cultural values imparted to them and will allow themselves to be defined by externally established life goals. So, we invariably accept that we ought to go to school, get a nine-to-five career, find a spouse, mortgage a house, and have 2.5 children who will do us proud by going to school, getting a nine-to-five career, finding a spouse, and mortgaging a house. But why do we desire these things? Is it because we have chosen them as goals we truly value? Or is it merely living out the social narrative of what we are told to value and seek with our lives? Heidegger suggests that few will begin to ask such questions, most being content instead to lead the life society has defined for them without critically reflecting on what is being imposed or why. It is this state of being that Heidegger asserts is "inauthentic."

Heidegger suggests that in order for a person to begin to see through the banal aspects of the everyday, she must be somehow moved to a state of reflection. Most people, however, are content with an unexamined life, which offers them the comfort of social acceptance and a predefined sense of identity. It is only when a person begins to experience a form of angst, a type of anxiety in which the individual becomes discomforted by how her life and sense of self are both organized and arranged in relation to the world, that she begins to critically evaluate who she is and what is meaningful. This examination of identity will develop within her a sense of agency and autonomy, a desire to authentically define value and meaning for herself rather than merely accepting social conventions.

Dr. Horrible's Sing-Along Blog (2008) provides a poignant critique of a society defined by inauthentic living. Through the character of Billy (Neil Patrick Harris), Whedon derides a consumerist culture in which people seem to mindlessly wander through life, comfortably willing to overlook a reality that "any dolt with half a brain" can clearly see is "insane." Billy's own sense of angst that arises from his loathing of the illusionary veneer of modern society leads him to become "Dr. Horrible," a supervillain described by Billy as the real him ("not a joke, not a dork, not a failure"). Dr. Horrible is determined to destroy the status quo because, as evinced by the countless atrocities going unaddressed throughout the world, "the status is *not* quo." He becomes set on spurring social awareness of the all-pervasive "filth and lies" that inhibit authentic existence. Billy is awakened to his true self by his own discomfort and what he describes as the sound of human hearts breaking all around him, which no one else—including those whose hopes and dreams have shattered apart—seems to notice. This angst causes him to critically reflect on the structure of his own life in relation to the rest of society.

In contrast, Dr. Horrible's nemesis, Captain Hammer (Nathan Fillion), is an embodiment of the inauthentic. His shallow self-absorption prevents him from making any kind of genuine connection with those around him, and his actions and rhetoric seem entirely contradictory to what might be expected from a heroic figure and purported role model. He is summed up best by Billy. When Penny (Felicia Day)—the girl of Billy's dreams—begins dating Hammer, Billy is dismayed. Penny tries to convince Billy that under Hammer's cheesy exterior there is a layer that is "totally sweet." Billy slyly replies, "And sometimes there's a third, even deeper level and that one is the same as the top one—like pie." Billy's sarcastic assessment of Hammer may be tinged by jealousy, but it ultimately rings true. Hammer simply promulgates the status quo narrative that "everyone's a hero in their way," even when they are not doing anything to improve society in a meaningful manner. And, while Hammer demeans his audience with quips about their hygiene, intelligence, and other inadequacies (especially given his obvious superiorities), his groupies still parrot back: "We're heroes too. We're just like you."

The literary critic and scholar Lionel Trilling would explain Hammer's lack of authenticity via his lack of sincerity. Sincerity is expressed artistically through genuine action, characters behaving in a manner that they intend without outward or self-deception.[2] Clearly Hammer falls short of this standard. He has contrived a persona to project a heroic facade. He performs what society considers "good acts" not because he believes them to be right but because it feeds his ego through the accolades he receives. He begins a relationship with Penny not because he cares for her, but because he can use her sexually and finds it another way to exasperate Dr. Horrible. Trilling cites a famous passage from *Hamlet:* "To thine own self be true. And it dost follow, as the night the day, thou canst not then be false to any man."

The authentic character is one who engages in critical self-reflection and presents his considered self to society without dishonesty.[3]

The contented ignorance and blind acceptance of the public in *Dr. Horrible* is apparent. They cannot, for example, be bothered to sign a petition to help establish a homeless shelter in an abandoned building—though they would later praise Hammer for doing just that—because they are glued to the news to find out "who's gay." Their lives are rather comfortable, giving them no reason to critically evaluate who they really are, or what they truly desire. Perhaps this explains why, despite their discomfort during the final showdown at the press conference, Hammer's groupies are so quick to begin consumption of Dr. Horrible paraphernalia after their erstwhile superhero's downfall. They are not committed to professed principles of heroism or villainy. They are consumers living within a bourgeois society whose inert values and lives remain critically unshaken even if superficially they undergo some type of change.

Therefore, perhaps the message behind Dr. Horrible's death ray actually targets the assembled press conference audience. He sings:

> Look at these people, amazing how sheep will
> Show up for the slaughter
> No one condemning, you lined up like lemmings
> You lead to the water
> Why can't they see what I see? Why can't they hear the lies?
> Maybe the fee's too pricey for them to realize.[4]

Horrible's actions (per the lyrics of "Slipping") represent his attempt to move society toward self-reflection. He implicitly reasons that this will occur only upon an angst-generating experience. This, in turn, requires an uncomfortable awareness of one's actual place with respect to operative social realities. Dr. Horrible thus decides that he must take it upon himself to shake people out of their unexamined existence. He sings: "I bring you pain, the kind you can't suffer quietly / Fire up your brain, remind you inside you're rioting." The best way to do this, he reasons, is to show Hammer for the fraud that he really is.

Pylean Beasts and Parliament Monsters

Angst experiences are occasioned by the realization that there exist factors working against authenticity. These factors are varied in the Whedonverse. As the Dr. Horrible example shows, they are not always recognized. Again, art reflects life. Whedon's characters that do recognize them are invariably portrayed positively; those that don't are often portrayed negatively, proving who the real monsters of the Whedonverse are.

In *Buffy the Vampire Slayer* and *Angel,* a vampire is created when the essence of the original demon is passed from one human host to the next, banishing (or extinguishing) a person's soul. The vampire retains various basic characteristics of its original human host, but his or her authentic humanity and the future prospects for such have been displaced, dispelling a person's conscience and drawing him or her toward vile, predatory acts. Consider the example of Liam (David Boreanaz) from eighteenth-century Ireland. He was far from perfectly virtuous, but, upon being seduced and turned into the vampire "Angelus" by Darla (Julie Benz), he mercilessly tortures and utterly destroys his victims. When a gypsy curse results in his reensoulment, transforming him from Angelus to Angel, he is thereby psychologically tortured by his past misdeeds—the century of crimes he committed as the soulless Angelus. His new "un-life" is originally spent lurking in the shadows, feeding on alley rats and shunning everyone. He so reviles himself that he de facto removes himself from humanity so as to suffer in silence. In 1996, a strange demon named Whistler (Max Perlich) abruptly introduces himself: "I mean, I'm not a bad guy. Not all demons are dedicated to the destruction of all life" ("Becoming, Part I"). Confused, Angel responds: "Whadaya mean, I can go either way?" Whistler smiles: "I mean that you can become an even more useless rodent than you already are, or you can become someone. A person. Someone to be counted." Whistler's thinly veiled challenge arguably represents a kind of angst-generating experience. Already filled with angst via his inerrant memories of Angelus, Angel takes advantage of it; he immediately begins seeking redemption for Angelus's evil acts. The remorse he endured and the redemption he seeks are evidence that Angel would not have performed such malevolent deeds autonomously (despite his Irish father's low opinion of his son).

Whedon's ingenious twist on the vampire tale, then, is his implicit interpretation of the tragedy of vampiric existence. Apart from the suffering inflicted on Angelus's victims, the process of becoming a vampire itself seems to be tragic; this is so because the demonic presence displaces the soul, thereby removing the possibility of the full actualization of an individual's identity and authentic existence. Lacking a soul—the seat of moral conscience in the Whedonverse—one loses the ability to autonomously choose between right and wrong. At the very least, the presence of the demonic essence asserts such a force over the individual that for all practical purposes, he or she no longer possesses the freedom required to be fully in control of his or her body. As Whedon once noted, "soulless creatures can do good and souled creatures can do evil, but . . . the soul-free are instinctually drawn toward doing evil while those with souls tend to instinctually want to do good."[5]

In the Whedonverse, then, the soulless face obstacles that the souled do not. Invariably, such obstacles are insurmountable, resulting in the tragedy of an inauthentic life. Angel's case, the vampire with a soul, again proves rather instructive. When he and the team travel to the Pylea dimension, his vampiric essence manifests differently. He is able to walk in the sun, and he makes a reflection. However, when the demon surfaces, it transforms him into a monstrous beast. He has green skin, horns, claws for hands, and an utterly ferocious blood-thirst. Unable to speak, he savagely tears his victims limb from limb. Once back in Fred's (Amy Acker) cave, the Angel-beast sees its reflection and is seemingly alarmed. Angel morphs back into his human form and confides to Fred: "The monster . . . They—they [Wes and Gunn] saw what I really am. I can't go back. Not now. I can never go back [to face them]" ("Through the Looking Glass"). But Angel soon reconsiders because his friends need his help and he desires to help them. He chooses to fight the monster inside. He sincerely apologizes to Gunn (J. August Richards) for his shameful behavior. Wesley (Alexis Denisof) reminds Angel: "We know you. We know you're a man with a demon inside—not the other way around. *We* know you have the strength to do what needs to be done, and you will come back to us" ("There's No Place Like Plrtz Glrb"). In fact, when Angel battles the Groosalug (Mark Lutz) later in the episode, his vampiric nature morphs into the Angel-beast, but he somehow controls it and returns to human form, telling Groo: "We're not gonna do this. We're gonna find another way." Angel's strength of will allows him to overcome the obstacle presented by his vampiric essence, even though it manifests much more virulently in Pylea. This was a difficult but autonomous choice. Angel's success (in part) explains why he is a hero, a Champion.

Of course, not all of Whedon's characters heroically succeed. In *Firefly* and *Serenity* (2005), identities have not been stripped by some demonic force, but are merely surrendered by those who uncritically accept the dominant political and economic paradigms that the Alliance and its governing body, the Parliament, promulgate.[6] The Operative (Chiwetel Ejiofor) serves as an embodiment of such uncritical acceptance. As an agent of the state, he is completely invisible, possessing neither name nor rank. As he puts it in *Serenity*, "Like this facility [Mathias's top-secret lab], I don't exist." He is unaware and unconcerned about why the Alliance sends him on his missions; secrets are not his concern, keeping them is. He has been ordered to assassinate

River Tam and Simon Tam (Summer Glau and Sean Maher)—and those who would harbor them. When Mal (Nathan Fillion) later asks, "Do you know why they sent you?" the Operative simply replies: "It's not my place to ask. I believe in something greater than myself. A better world. A world without sin." Mal subsequently queries: "So me and mine gotta lay down and die . . . so you can live in your better world?" In response, the Operative freely admits the moral dubiousness of his actions: "I'm not going to live there. There's no place for me there . . . any more than there is for you, Malcolm. . . . I'm a monster. What I do is evil. I have no illusions about it, but it must be done." The Operative is merely following orders and playing a role in the bureaucratic machine. There is no room for him as an individual to question the system, even when he would otherwise judge his personal acts as being "evil." He has fully bought into the idea that—if allowed to take full, totalitarian control of the system—the world the Alliance promises is one that can properly meet the needs and interests of all.

In some ways, the character known simply as "the Operative" is the most disturbing of all of Whedon's "monsters" because his identity has not been fancifully displaced demonically or corrupted by dark magic. He has willingly accepted the subordination of his own sense of right and wrong via an unquestioned loyalty to the state. Abandoning his personal freedom, he is no longer responsible for the acts he labels as evil. He thus lives an inauthentic, manufactured life and seeks to force the same on everyone else. He calls to mind the "good Nazi"—one who commits the greatest atrocities in the name of following orders.

Whedon's aesthetic portrayal of the Operative provides evidence that this character represents something undesirable. Upon learning from Mal what the Parliament wanted him to keep secret, the Operative tells his men to stand down. He facilitates the repairs to spaceship *Serenity* and allows its crew to go free. But prior to takeoff, the Operative approaches Mal. The Operative, notably framed by the rainstorm behind him, assures Mal they won't meet again; of himself, the Operative explains, "there is nothing left to see." Unlike Mal, who owns his beliefs—the few that he does have—the Operative is owned by his belief in the Alliance, a belief that completely displaces his identity. With his belief in the Alliance shattered, the Operative becomes invisible; he has indeed ceased to exist in every sense that matters.[7] Therefore, perhaps Whedon's overarching message in *Firefly/Serenity* is this: Displacement of individual identity need not result from supernatural forces or fictional technology; it can also occur in response to the real-world threats of a life overly administered by social and political forces. In this, Whedon speaks to all of us.

"Big Damn Heroes . . . Ain't We Just?"

The authentic individual, therefore, is one who makes autonomous choices despite operant sources of displacement, develops a form of personal agency, and thereby, in a very genuine sense, shapes her own identity. Such individuals enjoy positive portrayals in the Whedonverse. Some examples are obvious and well known. In *Buffy the Vampire Slayer,* Buffy's antagonistic relationship with the overly regimented and depersonalized Watchers' Council and their expectations for a Slayer stands in stark contrast with the almost familial bond she develops with Giles (Anthony Stewart Head) and the friendships that help define her.[8] Buffy somehow manages to laudably navigate her Slayer duties with her various personal relationships.[9] Other examples, just as interesting, are not as renowned. Their pervasiveness is perhaps most surprising.

In *Toy Story* (1995), Buzz Lightyear (voiced by Tim Allen) newly "out of the box" sees himself as the ultimate hero, destined to save the world from the evil Emperor Zurg. In an early confrontation with Woody (voiced by Tom Hanks), Buzz scoffs at the ridiculous notion that he is a child's plaything, a manufactured action figure among countless others. He is a "space ranger," not a toy, and there is nothing Woody can say to convince him otherwise. But then Buzz spies a television commercial for Buzz Lightyear action figures, complete with the alarming disclaimer: "Not a flying toy." The reality of that message thunders upon him when he is unable to fly out of a window in the attempt to save himself and Woody; Buzz falls, breaking his arm off in the process. The angst that results from his discovery causes Buzz to question who he really is. He also begins to question his purpose in life. Depressed, he quickly concludes that he is nobody. Worse than that, he's no different than thousands of other manufactured nobodies just like him. But Buzz's angst experience, with some further encouragement from Woody, soon leads him to a new revelation. The prospects of an authentic life remain. Rather than the delusional acceptance of the programmed narrative of "To Infinity and Beyond," he redefines himself according to those things that he autonomously comes to value—his friendship with Woody and the love of his boy, Andy. Buzz's angst, born of personal tragedy, drives him to leave his artificial life behind, putting him on the path to an authentic one.

Firefly's Simon Tam graduated in the top 3 percent from the best medical academy on Osiris. He finished his internship in eight months. A gifted surgeon, he looked forward to a lengthy, rewarding, and lucrative career. He was to become a brilliant doctor—his father spoke of little else—and with his installation among the prestigious Medical Elect looming, he was about to realize all of his parents' dreams. He is the product of all the Alliance has to offer; he and his family have only benefited from Unification.

Simon's sister, River, is evidently the true prodigy of the family. (Simon admits that he feels like a bit of "an idiot child" in comparison.) She attends the Academy, a school for the gifted. The Tams receive a few letters at first, but then there is no contact for months. Finally a letter arrives that makes no sense—until Simon realizes it is actually in code. With the help of his university professors, he finally deciphers it: "They're hurting us. Get me out." Against his father's explicit instruction, Simon quickly eschews all that his life has been. He contacts underground, anti-establishment factions. They offer him a deal: If he funds their operations, they will help him smuggle River out of the Academy. He drains his entire fortune. His father disowns him. With false credentials, he infiltrates the Academy posing as a Parliament member. The siblings narrowly escape to Boros, book passage on a transport ship, Firefly-class, and now associate with other brigands—naughty men hoping to slip about free of Alliance involvement. His life is now protecting River, one day making her well again. Some would echo Dr. Mathias's (Michael Hitchcock) assessment in *Serenity*: Simon "turned his back on his whole life. Madness." But in many respects, Simon isn't mad; he is the quintessential picture of authenticity in the Whedonverse.[10]

Spike (James Marsters) is an interesting and rare example of a soulless creature seeking authenticity. The vampire Spike was once William, a helpless romantic and "bloody bad" poet who was mocked and ridiculed. This weakens him, impeding his transformation into a more authentic existence. After being rejected by the woman he loves, William meets the vampire Drusilla (Juliet Landau). Dru sires him, creating Spike, who comes to rival Angelus as one of the most powerful and wicked vampires who has ever walked the Earth. In Sunnydale, Spike immediately positions himself as Buffy's unyielding antagonist. But this begins to change after Buffy's resurrection; they fall into a twisted intimate relationship. Spike comes to love Buffy, but she does not, and cannot, love him in return. Rather, she simply uses him to try to feel something, anything. Spike is so consumed by his obsession for Buffy that he, on one occasion, attempts to rape her, and is afterwards horrified by what he has done. It is this anguish that impels him on a quest to do something that no other vampire, not even Angel, has done—*earn* back his soul. The result is an authentically chosen combination of William, his romantically poetic human-self, and Spike, his powerful vampire-self. His love for Buffy arouses a need within him to overcome the demonic displacement of his soul; he thereby reclaims himself and defines his sense of identity autonomously and authentically. It is from that self-empowerment that Spike becomes a

Champion: he sacrifices himself to save the world—and forever closes the Sunnydale Hellmouth.

In *Dollhouse,* Echo (Eliza Dushku) is the name given to Caroline Farrell upon her decision to have her complete psychological profile removed, only to be reimprinted with various other temporary profiles. But Echo is unique among the other actives in that she slowly grows into, or perhaps reclaims, an awareness of her authentic self. In a manner that bears a striking similarity to the cloned Ripley (Sigourney Weaver) in Whedon's *Alien: Resurrection,* Echo's consciousness evolves in a manner that causes her to retain flashes of life before the Dollhouse. She also manages physical and mental characteristics that transcend her numerous imprints. Her seeming ability to go beyond her temporary imprints places Echo in incredibly high demand among Rossum's customers. However, as she becomes increasingly aware of who she truly is, Echo also becomes more immune to the imprinting. As she grows into an awareness of her true, authentic self, Echo becomes resistant to the imposition of lives and personalities that she did not choose (her successive imprints). Thus, what empowers her to go beyond the personality currently imprinted upon her seems to be her capacity to autonomously control those imprinted characteristics. This control signals Caroline's reemergence; regaining her pre-Dollhouse psyche enables her uniqueness as a doll. It also signals her uniqueness as a person (leaving one to wonder what Joss might be implying about human psychology).

In each of his narratives, Whedon presents individuals struggling to understand and define a sense of self apart from the depersonalized and inauthentic life embraced by systems of authority and the mass populace. That is what makes them atypical and heroic figures. After all, just because we might become discomfited occasionally does not mean that we will stop uncritically adopting socially defined values. Indeed, philosophers like Heidegger suggest that our taking responsibility for authentically determining our own values and goals is rare. So, characters like Angel, Buzz, Simon, and Echo are heroic exactly because they choose an authentic life of personal responsibility. For audiences, then, Whedon poses an interesting philosophical question: Which life would you rather embrace? The easy life of imposed values and standards, which may include oppressing and displacing the identity of others? Or the authentic life of the heroic figure?

"Muldering Out" Jossian Authenticity

Another philosophical question quickly emerges: To what extent do Whedon's heroes, and his corpus generally, affirm existentialist principles?

Is Whedon an existentialist? There is some prima facie evidence that suggests such questions should be answered in the affirmative—beginning with Joss's DVD commentary for "Objects in Space."[11]

Existentialism is nothing if not an affirmation of authentic existence. Consider that the noted existentialist Jean-Paul Sartre would undoubtedly concur with Whedon's portrayals of Captain Hammer and the Operative as characters leading inauthentic lives. According to Sartre, "Man first of all exists, encounters himself, surges up in the world and defines himself afterwards."[12] This captures Sartre's slogan, "Existence precedes essence." We human beings encounter ourselves as completely free beings; this radical freedom allows us to define ourselves in any way we choose. This leads Sartre to affirm, "Man is nothing else but that which he makes of himself."[13] As completely free, there are absolutely no limits on an individual. True, there exist facts outside of our control—what Sartre calls "facticity"—but we remain free to respond to them as we will. Thus, who we become in life is completely up to us. This is indeed an awesome, frightening burden because we have no one to blame but ourselves for our station. Some cannot bear the weight of this responsibility and allow themselves to be defined by external circumstances. We allow such forces to de facto choose for us. But this is to live in Sartrean "bad faith." It is to make an object of yourself, which belies your experiences as a (radically free) subject. On this interpretation, the Operative lives an inauthentic life because he identifies himself as a mere cog in the Alliance machine; Hammer uncritically accepts current social mores of "heroism."

It's true that the quest for authenticity is prominent in the Whedonverse. However, ascribing a thoroughgoing existentialism to Whedon and his characters seems implausible. The sticking point has to do with the locus of value. Existentialists, and Sartre in particular, are clear that value is subjectively placed on the world *only* by the choices we make. Sartre writes: "We have neither behind us, nor before us a luminous realm of values, any means of justification or excuse. We are left alone, without excuse."[14] Thus, something is good, for you, only because you (autonomously) choose it. On this account, Simon's autonomous decision to rescue his sister would be morally equivalent to his decision to eschew everything to learn how to juggle baby geese. Existentialists acknowledge no intrinsic value difference between these autonomous choices. But it's clear that Whedon intends Simon's choice to be seen as commendable; it is indeed heroic and importantly set apart from other choices he could have autonomously made. Similar evaluations might be made of Mal's choice to broadcast the Miranda file, Buffy's decision to sacrifice her life for Dawn's (Michelle Trachtenberg), and Doyle's (Glenn Quinn) analogous sacrifice for the immigrants and Angel's greater mission.

That existentialism is ill-fitted to the Whedonverse is further supported by a reanalysis of *Dr. Horrible.* On a Sartrean analysis, apart, perhaps, from Horrible's decision to acquiesce to Bad Horse's demand for an assassination, Horrible leads an authentic life. He refuses to be defined by a consumerist society. On a thoroughgoing existentialist interpretation, Billy/Horrible should be commended simply for making autonomous decisions.[15] However, the song "My Eyes" seems to be a microcosm of the Whedonverse in that it speaks to the objective existence of good and evil. Penny stresses the "good in everyone's heart" and by keeping "it safe and sound," you can "turn a life around." She advocates living your life in ways that turn the lives of others around—for the better. Analogous messages can be found in Angel's mentoring relationship with Faith (Eliza Dushku), Simon's relationship with River, and, arguably, Paul Ballard's (Tahmoh Penikett) attempts to rescue Caroline. Thus, this *kind* of choice is morally commendable, which implies that some choices, even if freely made, are not. Furthermore, the fact that Horrible did not keep Penny safe and sound explains why he is portrayed so negatively at the end of the film. He realizes only too late how life with Penny could have turned things around for him. Dr. Horrible is, therefore, not a heroic figure simply because he seeks the authentic life; he is a tragic one.[16]

Finally, the most worrisome difficulty for interpreting Whedon as a thoroughgoing existentialist is the "Paradiso Problem." In "The Train Job," Whedon posits that individuals—when they are fully conscious of all relevant facts—incur objectively binding moral obligations. Upon Mal's returning of the medical supplies to Paradiso, Sheriff Bourne (Gregg Henry) says to him: "These are tough times. A man can get a job. He might not look too close at what that job is. But a man learns all the details of a situation like ours . . . well . . . then he has a choice." Mal solemnly responds, "I don't believe he does." Because Mal implies that no other choice is morally acceptable, Whedon implicitly affirms that returning the medical supplies is what any individual ought to do. This is evidence that Whedon affirms the existence of goodness—moral value—apart from the autonomous choices we make. Some autonomous choices are good and others are bad, all of which is inconsistent with a thoroughgoing existentialism.

What, then, of authenticity in the Whedonverse? Perhaps Joss's message about the unexamined life is more Socratic than Sartrean. Socrates was adamant about thinking our choices over carefully and not simply acting out of unreflective habit or kowtowing to current arbitrary mores. Through careful reflection, we are better able to determine our obligations and how best to fulfill them. Recall Socrates' famous words: "It is the greatest good for a man to discuss virtue every day . . . for the unexamined life is not worth living."[17] Virtue can only be discussed and thus sought if it exists in its own right. Furthermore, consider how Whedon's heroes—Buffy, Angel, Mal, Simon, and, arguably, Paul Ballard—are reflected in the following Socratic rebuke: "You are wrong sir, if you think that a man who is any good at all should take into account the risk of life or death; he should look to this only in his actions, whether what he does is right or wrong, whether he is acting like a good or bad man."[18] For Socrates, personal autonomy is tantamount to moral autonomy; being true to yourself and doing the right thing are synonymous. Whedon's heroes invariably do the right thing in Whistler's "big moments" despite overwhelming psychological and social forces acting against them, resulting in them becoming more authentic individuals. Perhaps all of us could become "big damn heroes" with the Socratic project of being truer to ourselves.

More "Choices"

Accordingly, the significance and nobility of Willow's choice to forego Oxford is easier to see. In her words: "The other night, you know, being captured and all, facing off with Faith. Things just, kind of, got clear. I mean, you've [Buffy] been fighting evil here for three years, and I've helped some, and now we're supposed to decide what we want to do with our lives. And I just realized that that's what I want to do. Fight evil, help people. I mean, I—I think it's worth doing. And I don't think you do it because you have to. It's a good fight, Buffy, and I want in" ("Choices"). The fact that there is evil to be fought and that it is good to help people in need reaffirms a nonexistential interpretation of the Whedonverse. The fact that Willow, like Simon, has autonomously decided to give up a bright future for a worthy cause reaffirms a Socratic interpretation of the examined life.

But Joss might also be teaching us something else (or additional) about the examined life. We ought not to "deem weird" or otherwise disparage the Xanders of the world, those "Bohemian anti-establishment" types who don't seem to fit any obvious, prefabricated mold, nor do they wish to. There are many conceptions of the good life, and none of them should be discouraged without just cause. But how might we reconcile the subjectivist understanding of the good offered by Sartre with the more objective schema of what is right presented by Socrates, both of which emerge throughout Whedon's corpus?

One such possibility is offered by John Rawls, who attempts to merge the subjectively determined values of individuals in a pluralistic society with a more objective understanding of the social and political conditions that must exist to enable individuals to pursue those values to the utmost. Rawls suggests that a single doctrine that would comprehensively guide all affairs of life (a suggestion that Socrates might embrace) is not viable given the multiplicity of people holding different religious, philosophical, and moral perspectives.[19] Instead of one universal doctrine for life, "a person's good is determined by what is for him the most rational long-term plan of life given reasonably favorable circumstances. A man is happy when he is more or less successfully in the way of carrying out this plan."[20]

Similarly, Whedon offers a Rawlsian framework for understanding justice by presenting subjective understandings of the good while recognizing and defending an objective set of external goods that must be present to allow individuals the ability to autonomously choose and freely pursue their version of the good life. Individuals must be provided the basic political, social, and economic goods necessary for autonomously choosing the life they have authentically chosen. Such a perspective calls for a commitment to the securing of primary goods for all, while recognizing and respecting the differences that arise from a plurality of life plans. In this regard, nothing obviously prevents Xander from leading the examined life on the open road. Forces that would prevent him from autonomously seeking the good are to be condemned. Should Xander simply kowtow to these forces, he tragically leads an inauthentic life. That the world loses unique individuals like Xander, Oz (Seth Green), and Lorne (Andy Hallett) is the deeper tragedy. So if, upon Xander's careful examination, going his own way will "help him find himself," then perhaps it will help him find others as they are, sincerely, and everyone's life is enriched. In this, Joss again speaks to us all.

Notes

1. Martin Heidegger, *Being and Time*, trans. Joan Stambaugh (Albany: University of New York Press, 1996).

2. Lionel Trilling, *Sincerity and Authenticity* (Cambridge: Harvard University Press, 1972).

3. It is worth noting that the lesbian relationship between Tara and Willow experiences its own form of displacement because of social norms and imposed values. Whedon has commented to fans on occasion that the reason why Willow and Tara's relationship was relegated to subtext was because of network concerns over social reactions to open portrayals of homosexuality (see Sarah Warn, "'Buffy' to Show First Lesbian Sex Scene on Broadcast TV," *After Ellen*, April 3, 2003, www.afterellen.com/TV/buffy-sex.html). The sexual aspects of their relationship remain implied and metaphorical until Tara's

death, even after the show moved from the WB to UPN. It wasn't until "Touched," the twentieth episode of the seventh and final televised season, that Willow and Kennedy (Iyari Limon) were actually allowed to engage in sexual activity, something that Buffy and Angel performed on-screen early in season two.

4. *Dr. Horrible's Sing-Along Blog,* DVD (Los Angeles: Mutant Enemy Productions, 2008).

5. Whedon's comments were made at the Museum of Television and Radio's Eighteenth Annual William S. Paley Television Festival at the Director's Guild Theatre in Los Angeles, as recounted in "HERC Spent Last Night with Team Whedon," *Ain't It Cool News,* March 4, 2001, www.aintitcool.com/display.cgi?id=8315.

6. For those interested in a crash-course reminder of how the Alliance came to be, see Joss Whedon, "Brief History of the Universe circa 2507 A.D.," *Serenity: The Official Visual Companion* (London: Titan, 2005), 12–15.

7. Whedon's portrayal of the Operative, especially with respect to how the character differs from his heroes, is incredibly rich. Consider that Mal also lost perhaps his most cherished belief at the Battle of Serenity Valley. However, the fact that Mal perseveres is evidence that he owns his belief in God; it doesn't own him. (Whedon explores this a bit in a scene cut from the theatrical release; the Operative asks Mal: "You lost everything in that battle. Everything you had, everything you were . . . how did you go on?") Mal is analogous to Buffy at the end of season two of *Buffy.* Buffy has lost everything: her mother has disowned her; she has been expelled from school; she has cast a reensouled Angel into hell. But Buffy perseveres; she refuses to be completely defined by the forces impinging upon her identity. It seems, then, that characters like Mal and Buffy are to be commended for their authenticity and those like the Operative disparaged for their lack of it. This idea is further explored in the next section.

8. Similar themes about the struggle for personal identity are present in *Firefly,* where Mal (Nathan Fillion) and the crew of *Serenity* seek to carve out a sphere of personal space for themselves apart from the expanding influence of the state. For more on this, see Joseph Foy, "The State of Nature and Social Contracts on Spaceship *Serenity,*" in this volume.

9. Not that this was always easily accomplished. The episode "Once More with Feeling"—Whedon's first attempt at a "dramedy-musical"—serves as a microcosm of the constant struggles for authenticity among the Scoobies, Buffy, and Giles. For example, although the lyrics to "I've Got a Theory/The Bunny Song" ("What can't we face if we're together? / What's in this place that we can't weather? / Apocalypse? We've all been there. / The same old trips. Why should we care? / We have to try. We'll pay the price. / It's do or die. [Buffy] *Hey, I've died twice!*") affirm their commitment to authenticity, a careful viewing—including how those lyrics get acted out—uncovers potential sources of inauthentic choices.

10. For a stimulating discussion of whether Mal or Simon is the true hero of *Firefly/Serenity,* see Shanna Swendson, "A Tale of Two Heroes," in *Serenity Found: More Unauthorized Essays on Joss Whedon's* Firefly *Universe,* ed. Jane Espenson (Dallas: BenBella, 2007), 67–78.

11. For more on existential themes related to Whedon and "Objects in Space," see David Baggett, "*Firefly* and Freedom," in this volume. See also Lyle Zynda, "We're All Just Floating in Space," in *Finding Serenity: Anti-heroes, Lost Shepherds, and Space Hookers in Joss Whedon's* Firefly, ed. Jane Espenson (Dallas: BenBella, 2004), 85–96. For an expansive exploration existentialism in the Whedonverse, see *The Existential Joss Whedon: Evil and Human Freedom in* Buffy the Vampire Slayer, Angel, Firefly, *and* Serenity, ed. J. Michael Richardson and J. Douglas Rabb (Jefferson, N.C.: McFarland, 2007).

12. Jean-Paul Sartre, "Existentialism Is a Humanism," trans. Philip Maret, in *Existentialism from Dostoevsky to Sartre,* ed. Walter Kaufmann (New York: Meridian, New American Library, 1956), 290.

13. Ibid., 291.

14. Ibid., 295.

15. Existentialism seemingly falls into self-referential incoherence at this point. It certainly seems that Sartre wishes to affirm that it is good (or right) to lead an authentic life and bad (or wrong) to live in bad faith. But this entails a kind of objectivist account of value that he is attempting to deny. But if it cannot be (objectively) good to live authentically, why is it so important to not live in bad faith?

16. This analysis also seems to apply to Whedon's villains in the following way. Consider how Sartre would have to admit that both Angelus and Niska (Michael Fairman) lead authentic lives. Neither follows typical conventions in their villainy. Angelus doesn't simply feed upon human beings; rather, he strives to utterly destroy them (and nuns are his specialty). He believes it is a kind of art form, one that he more or less pioneered among vampires. (True, Liam/Angel is under the influence of a vampiric demon, but this could be interpreted as part of Angelus's facticity. That Angelus is a human turned to a vampire is analogous to the birth conditions of a human being. Thus, what's crucial for Sartre is what Angelus chooses to do about the facticity surrounding his vampiric essence.) Niska, as Zoe reminds us, has his own code, one that he lives by because it works best for him. He refuses to let anyone—including his wife—impinge upon how he chooses to do business. In this way, both are analogous to Sartrean heroes (but see the previous note). The fact that they are Whedonverse *villains* only furthers the claim that Joss is no thoroughgoing existentialist.

17. Plato, *Apology,* in *The Trial and Death of Socrates,* 2nd ed., trans. G.M.A. Grube (Indianapolis: Hackett, 1975), 38a.

18. Ibid., 28c.

19. Rawls argues that "human good is heterogeneous because the aims of the self are heterogeneous," and therefore a just society would be one that would allow each of its members to pursue their own version of the good while constraining them only to allow others in society the opportunity to do the same (see John Rawls, *A Theory of Justice* [Cambridge: Belknap Press of Harvard University Press, 1971], 554).

20. Ibid., 92–93. Rawls defines a set of primary social goods—such as "rights, liberties, powers and opportunities, income and wealth" (54)—that would form the basis of a just society. The first set of goods he identifies are those designed to protect basic liberties equally for all, including the right to participate within the political and social

system through voting, free expression and assembly, and with freedom of conscience and thought. The political system is designed to maintain these liberties for all and is simultaneously constrained through the rule of law from arbitrarily imposing on the individual. The second set of goods he is concerned with are economic. He argues that although inequalities will arise even in a just society, "the social order is not to establish and secure the more attractive prospects of those better off unless doing so is to the advantage of those less fortunate" (65). In this regard, a just society must provide a basic safety net for all its citizens so as to afford them a fair chance of achieving success at a variety of life plans germane to their skills and abilities.

"Look What Free Will Has Gotten You"

Isolation, Individuality, and Choice in *Angel*

Susanne E. Foster and James B. South

The "Jasmine arc" comprises six episodes at the end of season four of *Angel*.[1] These episodes detail, through a series of seemingly improbable events, the birth, rise, and death of a being called Jasmine (Gina Torres), a godlike creature brought into the world by Cordelia (Charisma Carpenter) and Angel's son, Connor (Vincent Kartheiser). Once born, Jasmine exerts a near magical force over humans, causing them to worship her and follow her commands. In this enthralled state, her followers experience peace within themselves and with others. But as Angel (David Boreanaz) and his team realize, as one by one they are freed from Jasmine's spell through contact with her blood, the peace and sense of fulfillment comes at a very high price. Among the significant philosophical issues raised by this sequence are three themes related to the human predicament. First, and fundamentally, is the way in which the subjective nature of the human perspective, the fact that the individual's unique set of experiences influences the way the world appears to her, makes problematic the nature of an individual's conception of the good life. Relatedly, the episodes dramatize the ways in which human subjectivity causes difficulties for the nature and possibility of community and love. Finally, in the portrayal of humans willing to give over to another being their own conception of the good, these episodes force us to confront the efficacy of human choice in the case of our most important commitments.

The Guiding Passage

Near the end of the arc, in an episode titled "Peace Out," Connor talks with Cordelia, who is in a coma. Connor has protected Cordelia and Jasmine, but at the expense of his ties to his father and the rest of Angel's group. This one-sided conversation represents what we will call the "guiding passage." Connor's words:

> You know—what this was all about? Protecting our baby—Jasmine —so she can be, and make this world the kind of place you wanted. And it is better. Not harsh and cruel—the way that Angel likes it so he has a reason to fight. 'Cause you know that's what he's about, him and the others. Finding reasons to fight. Like that's what gives their lives any meaning. The only damn thing! I'm not like them. I just—I want to stop. Stop fighting. I just want to rest. God, I want to rest. But I can't. It's not working, Cordy. I tried. I tried to believe. I wanted it. Went along with the—the flow. Jasmine, she's—she's bringing peace to everyone, purging all of their hate and anger. But not me. Not me! I know she's a lie. Jasmine. My whole life's been built on them. I just—I guess I thought this one was better.

Connor's words are moving. They move us because they evoke the pain and uncertainty of human life. We find ourselves thrust into the world, into a particular place and time, with a conception of the good, a set of values and goals, already given. From this necessarily limited perspective, we must act and give meaning to our lives by finding a position from which we can make choices and take responsibility for our actions. Yet the perspectival nature of human knowledge and the sense we have in retrospect that the choices we have made were made for reasons external to the choice—that is, who I am with all its local contingencies compels me to act based on my character and past experiences—undermine our sense of agency and threaten us with nihilism.

Even to the extent that we may be free to choose, our choice of actions is fraught with tensions. On the one hand, we must embrace our selves and the conception of the good that seems commensurate with our subjective perspective; that is, we must embrace our individuality. On the other hand, though, we also need to be recognized by others, to join a community, to love and be loved. One central aspect of a vision of the good is, then, the nature of love and concern and how we might connect to the other, whether that "other" is a group (humanity) or an individual. Such commitments, however, are possible only where a shared conception of the good is present. Thus, even under the best of circumstances, the individual is torn between the demands of individuality and the demands of conformity. In the Jasminic arc, the resolution of this tension takes one of three forms. One, which we shall call the *Jasminic conception*, privileges communal membership over the individual. The second, which we shall call the *Connoric conception*, privileges the individual over communal membership. Finally, the *Angelic conception* insists on maintaining the creative tension between the individual and communal membership and learning to live with the competing demands of each.

A Philosophical Problem

The guiding passage exemplifies a philosophical problem that emerges from human experience: the need to find a vision of the good life to call one's own, a vision that shapes one's life and can provide meaning to that life. As Aristotle teaches, whenever we act, we aim at an end or goal, and those goals are given to us by our conception of the good.[2] But how much direct influence on our conception of the good can we have? Given our limited perspective and social embeddedness, a vision of the good is always present to us, often outside of our control. Being born in a particular place and time, individuals are raised with a set of cultural assumptions, and if they find themselves in a culture with strong authoritarian tendencies like a cult, their ability to question the assumptions is reduced further. Consider Jasmine's followers. Once under her influence, they have a vision of the good that has usurped their own prior conception. People whose lives were following another direction, or, perhaps, were directionless, suddenly find a new meaning to their lives: they live to serve Jasmine. So, too, they find a meaningful death in being sacrificed to and for Jasmine. This sacrifice makes their previously solitary lives rich in meaning, subsumable into a grand plan for the betterment of humanity and the glorification of Jasmine. Though they say their former lives lacked meaning, they seem incapable of genuinely comparing the two conceptions.

Wherever Jasmine goes, the humans who come into contact with her are immediately enraptured. She is beautiful and kind, but the power of her seduction is based on a far stronger human motive: the need to belong and be loved. Jasmine is able to see the most intimate thoughts and needs of her followers. She knows their names, and she offers the right words of comfort and praise.[3] She relieves them of their individual burdens and troubles. Once her followers become a part of the "body Jasmine," their everyday cares slip away.[4] In short, she offers them purpose, and their apparently empty lives take on a new meaning. They live to serve her and the vision of the good that she provides. As her influence spreads, she also provides tremendous social benefits. Those who serve Jasmine live in harmony with the rest of her followers. Violence and crime disappear. So, too, will war, once her influence spreads. Government becomes unnecessary. Even those who, the viewer knows, most clearly belonged to a community with shared projects—the members of Team Angel—remark on the new level of meaning and purpose Jasmine gives to their lives. This is all the more startling to the viewer since, prior to Jasmine's birth, they had been making the world better by fighting demons and other dark forces. Now, though, from what the viewer can gather, all they do is hang around Angel's hotel, the Hyperion, waiting for Jasmine to call them to perform some task.

There is an even more puzzling feature of everyone's acquiescence to Jasmine's will. Her own articulation of the good for humanity seems both self-serving and trite: "You don't have to do anything except love one another, although a temple would be nice. Something massive and awe-inspiring, yet warm and nurturing, celebrating the gentle pleasures of a peaceful, precious coexistence" ("Peace Out"). Jasmine does little to merit the worship she receives. Her activity extends as far as appearing to those who have not seen her—in order to bring them into her community; gorging herself on the adoration, and occasionally the lives, of her followers; and giving direction for the quashing of insurrection against herself. But how can she command the devotion of so many? Her message is rhetorically bland and philosophically thin: "I want to thank you for allowing me to speak with you. I come to you not as a leader or divinity, but as your partner in a venture to make this the best of all possible worlds, without borders, without hunger, war, or misery. A world built on love, respect, understanding, and, well, just enjoying one another" ("Peace Out"). Even before the veil of Jasmine's beauty is lifted for the viewer, we are suspicious of her powers.

Seeing the Real Jasmine

Early in the arc, on one outing to eliminate vampires and other evildoers—soulless creatures who seem immune to Jasmine's charms—Jasmine takes Fred (Amy Acker) aside for a personal conversation. Later, Fred recalls Jasmine's invitation to name her: "I remember the first time she took me aside at that fight at the bowling alley. Me, pale, frail Winifred Burkle, sitting with a goddess, and she was asking me what her name should be" ("Sacrifice"). Fred, who had been fighting beside Angel for a season and a half, now finds her life's meaning in this simple interaction with Jasmine. As Fred and Jasmine sit in the bowling alley, a vampire injures Jasmine. Fred, feeling distraught that Jasmine has been injured while in her care, offers to wash the blood out of Jasmine's clothes. Back at the hotel, Fred scrubs and scrubs, but the more she scrubs the more distraught and frantic she becomes. Her exposure to Jasmine's blood breaks the spell. The next time she sees Jasmine, the goddess has been transformed. In place of the beautiful and benevolent creature, Fred sees a maggot-riddled monster. No longer part of the "body Jasmine," Fred is no longer part of the community. Since Fred is now an outsider, Jasmine directs that she be hunted down. Wes (Alexis Denisof) and Gunn (J. August Richards) want to bring her back alive so she can be made to see what she has rejected. From their perspective, it is inconceivable that Fred could have run away because she saw Jasmine for what she really is. If they can just get her back in Jasmine's presence, she will be able to be part of the community again. But for Fred, the thrall has been broken. The conception of the good provided by Jasmine is seen to be rootless. In returning to her previous conception of the good, Fred now finds herself outside the community of her friends. She can relate only to those outside Jasmine's influence. But, and this is crucial, she does return to her previous vision of the good, the one that had provided her life with meaning and purpose and shaped her choices and actions: the mission to make the world better by destroying one monster at a time.

What makes Connor's situation as evidenced in the "guiding passage" so extreme, then, is that he admits that he does not have a particular vision of the good and cannot make himself believe in any particular vision of the good. Having been raised in a demon dimension by an enemy of Angel, Connor was never given love and acceptance. His upbringing taught him that no one was to be trusted—no one would work unselfishly to meet his needs. As a result, Connor seems intrinsically situated outside any community, and he knows such visions for what they are—lies. And because he does not and cannot embrace a vision of the good, he is bereft of community and paralyzed into inactivity. What does it mean to say that any vision of a good life is a lie? There are two relevant features of human experience that underwrite the kind of claim that Connor makes in the "guiding passage."

First, there's the fact that any person's vision of the good arises from and is situated in her particular perspective, and thus no one can have a "God's-eye" view of the good. That is, the individual sees only that part of the good visible from her epistemological perspective, and what she sees is distorted—those parts of the good closest to her experience seeming larger, those farther seeming smaller than they might otherwise, and none of the elements connected to other goods the way they might objectively be. Connectedly, there's the fact that any individual's vision of the good is tied up with contingent features of that individual's history, both those within her control (e.g., results of personal choices) and those outside of her control (e.g., place of birth, sex, etc.). Hence, any particular vision of the good is largely determined by means that are not conducive to generating an objective truth.

Second, sharing a conception of the good, becoming part of a community that embraces a specific, but not particularized, vision of the good, means giving up the details of one's own vision generated by the particular circumstances of one's agency and experience. The process of entering a community, then, necessarily involves a measure of what Sartre, for example, would call "bad faith." According to Sartre, humans are beings whose existence precedes their essence. They have no given nature; hence there are, for them, no objective values. Through choosing to act, to value some particular set of goods, they create their own model of humanity. The person who accedes to a communal vision of the good with its corresponding set of values and goals, then, abandons the task of creating a particular model of the human. Further, people who act from communal visions abdicate responsibility for their actions.[5] This is true not only for those who have given themselves over to a cult but for those whose choices are dictated by affiliation or commitment to an ideal. Gunn and Wes do not choose to hunt Fred; Jasmine tells them to do it.

The most extreme manifestation of this abandonment of one's responsibility to create values and choose actions takes place when Jasmine confronts Angel in a bookstore. Fred fires a bullet through Jasmine into Angel. Contact with Jasmine's blood causes Angel to see the real Jasmine. Angel flees with an apologetic Fred, who knows the devastating psychological impact of being ripped from the body Jasmine. Meanwhile, Jasmine, seeing her blood on the floor of the bookstore, realizes the danger to her plans if the blood is not cleaned. She directs the owner of the store, a conspiracy theorist who has named his store the "Magic Bullet," to burn it down. He happily complies, asking Jasmine if he should stay in the store while it burns. She does not bother to answer him, and so he stands in the flames until he is consumed. Here, even the subjective drive for self-preservation has been surrendered to Jasmine's good. The later scenes in which Jasmine speaks and acts directly through her followers are merely physical manifestations of the psychological surrender present in the Jasminic model.

The Human Need for Love

A central component of any vision of the good is participation in community, which is only possible through some mode of love. This need for community is characterized well by Plato in his *Symposium*.[6] There Aristophanes relates a myth about the origin of love. According to him, the first humans were double our current state, having four feet, four arms, and the like. In this powerful state, humans challenged the gods, and, to put down the insurrection and prevent future rebellions, Zeus split each human in half, rearranging most of their parts into the current form of human beings. The lesson extracted by Aristophanes from this myth is that humans are partial creatures, forever separated from what could make them whole. The possibility of happiness, then, is limited by and dependent on finding the other self whether the other is conceived of as an individual or a community. Like the creatures in the myth, we go through life suffering in isolation, desperate to find another self or other selves. In the Aristophanic myth, the wretched half-humans began to die of loneliness. In pity for their suffering and to preserve the race, Zeus rearranged human genitalia so that some unity between split humans became possible. But no form of human love seems to heal completely the wounds of our isolation.

One conception of love and community present in this arc is the Jasminic one. As a demon from another world that had worshiped Jasmine eons ago characterizes her: "She is the devourer . . . the song . . . the peace . . . the whole . . . and you try to name her." And he continues, "We loved her first." When Wesley asks him to define love, the demon is blunt in his response: "Same as all bodies. Same as everywheres. Love is sacrifice" ("Sacrifice"). The demon's equation of love and devouring can be construed literally. Jasmine is the devourer, maintaining her energy by eating a certain number of her followers each day. Even those who are not literally devoured, though, are incorporated into the overarching vision of Jasmine. Toward the beginning of the arc, Jasmine replaces her followers' conception of the good with her own and redirects their activities to serve her own ends. As her power grows, her followers become little more than automata through which she senses and speaks and moves. The isolation endemic to our limited perspective is one that makes us susceptible to the seduction by an ersatz whole, one in which we give up our particular conception of the good for the sake of connectedness and community. This model is a portrayal of love as bad faith. The individual does not truly act, but Jasmine acts through the individual. There is no genuine community, only the submersion of one individual into another. And sacrifice on this account is not an individual's choice to give up some part of her own good to preserve another individual, but rather the taking away of her good by another for some communal and, therefore, impersonal image of the good.

Another conception of love and sacrifice present in the arc is the one dramatized by Connor's actions and choices. At this conception's root is the denial of the possibility of love as something given and able to be accepted by another. No matter how much Connor acts as if he is part of Jasmine's group, kneeling when Angel kneels before her and even allowing her to speak to him in his own mind, he is never able to find unity with the group—that is, to adopt Jasmine's conception of the good. No amount of wanting to love and work for Jasmine can bring him the connection he so craves, or the rest that he seeks. Though he asserts again and again that he is now part of something—that it is Angel and his team who are now outside ("Sacrifice")—the "guiding passage" shows his claim to be false. He cannot submerse himself within her vision and thus remains outside the body Jasmine. Connor's situation is extreme, but we all spend significant amounts of time feeling these moments of isolation. Connor's plight mirrors the Aristophanic myth in that in his experience of isolation, he knows that something is missing from his life. He has no genuine bond with other human beings. Connor's suffering and isolation are not redeemed, but remain meaningless.

The third form of love explored in the arc is more promising. At the end of the arc, Angel gives up his relationship to Connor in order that the boy be given a new past, free of the memories of the horrors of the Hell dimension in which he once lived and that have made him incapable of accepting and giving love. Where the Jasminic model of love involved the subsumption of the individual vision of the good under a communal vision, on the Angelic model, love is formed intersubjectively, each person giving and taking various elements to form a shared conception of the good. Although the members of Angel's Team—Fred, Wes, Gunn, Lorne—each have their own projects and concerns, which often cause tensions within the group, they are nonetheless able to work together and flourish as a kind of extended family based on some shared conception of the importance of the work they do.

On this third model, then, the uniqueness of the other is acknowledged. Projects and a conception of the good are shared. Like the demon mentioned above who espouses the Jasminic model, Angel can say that love is or can require sacrifice. Here, though, the sacrifice is not a matter of devouring another or of submerging an individual's good into a common vision, which would make choice meaningless. Angel's sacrifice is for the sake of a particular person, Connor, and is consistent with his own previous conception of the good and based on his genuine insight and knowledge of Connor's needs. On this model, the other is seen as individual and the good sought is particular. Its goal is both union with the beloved and the flourishing of the beloved. Sacrifice here risks failure because the other is not in our control and may choose either not to return the love or may fail to flourish from our sacrifice. In this case, what Angel sacrifices is precisely the possibility of a loving relationship with Connor or the possibility that Connor will know he has made this sacrifice. Though Angel's sacrifice fails to achieve a community of love with Connor, it succeeds to the extent that it provides Connor with the capacity to love and to choose a conception of the good and a meaningful path for his life, which he had previously lacked.

Freedom and Choice

Paralleling these three conceptions of love are three different conceptions of the reality and importance of human freedom and choice. From the Jasminic perspective, human freedom is an illusion. Choice, or at least significant choice, is controlled and determined by powers outside the agent. Skip (David Denman), a demon, articulates this view well in a conversation with Angel and his team: "You really think it stops with her, amigo? You have any concept of how many lines have to intersect in order for a thing like this to play out? How many events have to be nudged in just the right direction? Leaving Pylea. Your sister. Opening the wrong book. Sleeping with the enemy. Gosh, I love a story with scope." Indeed, in the case of Cordelia, Connor, and Jasmine, as Skip explains, the real powers running the show provided various misdirections and disinformation to provide the illusion of human choice. The possibility of genuine human choice—one not controlled by forces outside the agent—is called into question repeatedly.

Furthermore, this illusion of freedom is tied to elements destructive of the human good. At the beginning of the arc, Connor is torn between his mother's plea that he follow his own heart and let the innocent go and Cordelia's need for an innocent to be sacrificed in order to bring forth Jasmine's birth. Cordelia, fighting to bend Connor to her own will—or that of the powers working through her—argues that Darla (Julie Benz), Connor's mother, represents more of Angel's lies, lies designed to isolate Connor and take him away from the community of Cordelia and their child. The viewer knows that in fact Darla had sacrificed her own life to let Connor live and thus represents the efficacy of choice. Yet Cordelia explains Darla's appearance to Connor now by reference to magic, as if Connor's possibility for choice is being taken away by Angel. She adds the claim that it is by submitting to the powers, that is, by surrendering one's own choice and conception of the good, that life can become meaningful. The death of the innocent girl will raise the girl's life above the meaninglessness of ordinary life as she becomes part of the grand purpose of bringing Jasmine into the world. In other words, on this view, freedom, even if possible, is destructive of meaning and community since real meaning comes from submission to a higher plan. This stark juxtaposition of possibilities for meaning within human freedom is where all the issues we've discussed come into clearest focus. The most powerful statement of this contrast comes from Jasmine after her defeat: "No. No, Angel. There are no absolutes. No right and wrong. Haven't you learned anything working for the Powers? There are only choices. I offered paradise. You chose this! . . . And look what free will has gotten you" ("Peace Out").

Throughout the arc, we are presented with apparent choices. Various characters believe they have it within their power to choose one of two paths. But even if our choices, or our important choices at least, are not predetermined by a fate or the powers, humans may not be free. Connor's situation and his nihilism make it clear that genuine choice must rest on more than choosing under conditions that are underdetermined. Because he cannot find reasons to embrace a conception of the good or to enter a community, his choices are reduced ultimately to chance; that is, they are random. In the choice between completing Cordelia's wishes or recognizing the meaning of sacrifice as Darla describes it, Connor's choice to sacrifice the innocent does not seem to be the result of thought but rather simply an impulsive decision. He chooses and acts, and his reaction to the death of the girl makes it clear that he has not fully embraced the consequence of his choice. The "guiding passage" shows that he has no conception of the good guiding his choices. He keeps searching in vain for something to believe in, something to give his choices and his life meaning. As Nietzsche says: "Apart from the ascetic ideal, man, the human animal, had no meaning so far. His existence on earth contained no goal; 'why man at all?'—was the question without answer; the will for man and earth was lacking; behind every great human destiny there sounded as a refrain a yet greater 'in vain!' This is precisely what the ascetic ideal means: that something was lacking, that man was surrounded by a fearful void—he did not know how to justify, to account for, to affirm himself; he suffered from the problem of his meaning."[7] At the end of the arc, Connor's actions have not helped him achieve a vision of the good, and his choices remain arbitrary. Faced with the struggle between his father, Angel, and his daughter, Jasmine, he "chooses" Angel and crushes Jasmine's skull with a single blow. But, as Angel remarks: "Jasmine's dead. I brought back her name and her powers were destroyed. Connor killed her. I've never seen him like this. He wasn't hurt or angry, he just killed her. And his face, it—it was just blank, like he had nothing left" ("Peace Out"). In his choice of Angel over Jasmine, Connor has no reason for choosing one over the other—no vision of the good shaping his view of the world, and no illusions to comfort him. Like the suffering humanity discussed by Nietzsche,

Connor is on the edge of suicidal nihilism, and like that humanity, Connor simply wills. But this arbitrary choice is no choice at all, as is evident if we contrast it with Angel's choice at the end of the arc.

The third conception of choice present in this arc is articulated by Angel in response to Jasmine's taunt that he rejected her offer of paradise and that, as a result of his "free" choice, he has doomed humans to a life of war, strife, and competition. Angel explains that he's chosen to rid the world of Jasmine's power "because I could. Because that's what you took away from us. Choice." He continues: "Hey, I didn't say we were smart. I said it's our right. It's what makes us human." Angel as much as admits here that freedom may be at the root of isolation, suffering, and conflict since true freedom stems from a necessarily unique subjective perspective and its corresponding conception of the good. Embracing one's own conception of the good leaves open the possibility and probability of deep disagreements with others whose perspectives differ. Our choices will be at odds with one another. We will end up at war. But, meaningful choices, choices between things we value based on our subjective perspective, are fundamental to being human.

The Whedonverse never allows clear and easy answers. There is, of course, a standard philosophical objection to free will: namely, the determinist objection. On that view, our perspective is not of our own making but rather results from our having been born into a particular place and time; it is thrust upon us, as it were. And in being thrust into this place and time with its history of causes, all our thoughts, actions, and effects, down to the molecular level, are simply the result of all previous causal interactions. Like our perspective, our vision of the good is the result of external forces. But, if we are not responsible for our beliefs or vision of the good, then the difference between the Jasminic model and the Angelic model is whether the agent is controlled by a predetermined group vision or a predetermined individual vision of the good. It is significant that this is a concern not raised in the arc. It is as though Whedon and his colleagues simply do not care about this objection. Instead, their concern is with a second challenge to the Angelic conception of free choice: namely, the threat of other, more powerful "agents," whether those agents are "gods," as they often are in the Whedonverse, or, in our reality, social structures that threaten to annihilate individuality. For example, on many forms individuals are asked to identify their ethnicity by checking one box. This practice effectively denies the possibility of biracial parentage. It is a genuine question whether there can be real freedom under such situations. As we saw above, the demon Skip asserts that the lives of Angel's team have been controlled to bring about the birth of Jasmine. Is freedom of choice an illusion? Gunn asserts that it is not: "Then we'll kick it over and start a new game. Look, monochrome can yap all he wants about no-name's cosmic plan, but here's a little something I picked up rubbing mojos these past couple of years. The final score can't be rigged. I don't care how many players you grease, that last shot always comes up a question mark. But here's the thing—you never know when you're taking it. It could be when you're duking it out with the Legion of Doom, or just crossing the street deciding where to have brunch. So you just treat it all like it was up to you—the world in the balance—'cause you never know when it is" ("Inside Out"). It is, at the end of the day, unclear whether humans choose freely, but nonetheless we must act as if we do, both because our fate may be within our own power in spite of the Jasmine-like threat of social constraints and because embracing a conception of the good and acting on it is the only remedy to the paralysis of the nihilism that overcomes Connor.

The Price of Choice

Though our world is not one in which a goddess walks among us stripping us of our free will and particular conception of the good, we are nonetheless subject to the type of isolation and loneliness experienced by Connor, and in trying to come to terms with that from our necessarily limited perspectives, we find ourselves negotiating the challenge of connection with others with varying degrees of success. One way we find ourselves losing our individual identity is falling in with various forms of conformity. In the arc, the proprietor of the occult bookstore the Magic Bullet is an extreme example of our tendency to lose our self in a story that seems bigger than the lonely self and can provide our life with a larger meaning. While we might not all obsess over the Kennedy assassination, there remains a susceptibility in human nature to find ourselves lost by means of Sartrean "bad faith." John Stuart Mill, in *On Liberty*, shows us the stakes that the arc has dramatized:

> In our times, . . . every one lives as under the eye of a hostile and dreaded censorship. . . . [Instead of asking] what do I prefer? or, what would suit my character and disposition? or, what would allow the best and highest in me to have fair play, and enable it to grow and thrive? They ask themselves, what is suitable to my position? what is usually done by persons of my station and pecuniary circumstances? or (worse still) what is usually done by persons of a station and circumstances superior to mine? . . . It does not occur to them to have any inclination, except for what is customary. Thus the mind itself is bowed to the yoke: even in what people do

for pleasure, conformity is the first thing thought of; they like in crowds; they exercise choice only among things commonly done: peculiarity of taste, eccentricity of conduct, are shunned equally with crimes: until by dint of not following their own nature, they have no nature to follow: their human capacities are withered and starved: they become incapable of any strong wishes or native pleasures, and are generally without either opinions or feelings of home growth, or properly their own.[8]

Under these sorts of social conditions, it is not surprising that we are prone to developing a Jasminic conception of community, with its deformed requirements for love and its suppression of freedom. Nor should it be surprising that those who cannot conform feel forever trapped in isolation and separated from the human community, as Connor does. The challenge thrown down by this arc is to develop a conception of community that acknowledges the freedom and uniqueness of each of us. At the end of the arc, Angel chooses to make a new future for Connor without Connor's input or permission. He chooses for Connor the "ordinary" life of a teenager in a two-parent family, and Connor's memory of his hellish past is erased. It may be that Connor's brokenness, shown throughout the arc, makes this a good choice for Connor, and Connor's brokenness may preclude the possibility of his own participation in the choice through consent. But it dramatizes how fragile is an individual's connection to a community and meaningful projects. At the same time, Angel's choice provides us with an image of what genuine choice and love can look like in the Whedonverse. Angel's decision to withdraw connection from a person who is an essential part of his life and to do it for the good of that person, presents us with an example of free choice, but it inflects that example with the notion of loving sacrifice. Meaningful choice may be possible, but its price is dear.

Notes

1. These episodes are: "Inside Out," "Shiny Happy People," "Magic Bullet," "Sacrifice," "Peace Out," and "Home." As the title "Inside Out" would suggest, these episodes reorient the plot of the season in a complex way. Revealing that the Cordelia present throughout season four was not really Cordelia, but some other creature inside her making her direct things, forces the viewer to reinterpret Cordelia's prior actions.

2. Aristotle, *Nicomachean Ethics*, 1094a1–22 and 1112b11–13a2.

3. This feature of Jasmine's power is most evident in "Magic Bullet," where Angel asks her, "No, I mean, how is it that you always know exactly what each person needs to hear?" and Jasmine replies: "Just look into their hearts. And sometimes, it's right on their face."

4. The phrase "body Jasmine" will be used throughout the chapter to refer to the fact that she requires the submersion of an individual's will and action into her own.

5. Sartre's most helpful discussion of the notion of these issues appears in "Existentialism Is a Humanism," which can be found in *Existentialism from Dostoevsky to Sartre,* ed. Walter Kaufmann (New York: New American Library, 1975), 345–69. Sartre's extended discussion of bad faith occurs in *Being and Nothingness,* pt. 1, chap. 2.

6. Aristophanes' story in the *Symposium* appears at 189d–192e.

7. Friedrich Nietzsche, *On the Genealogy of Morals,* trans. Walter Kaufmann and R. J. Hollingdale (New York: Vintage, 1969), 162, emphasis in the original.

8. John Stuart Mill, *On Liberty,* ed. Elizabeth Rapaport (Indianapolis: Hackett, 1979), 58–59.

Aiming to Misbehave at the Boundary between the Human and the Machine

The Queer Steampunk Ecology of Joss Whedon's *Firefly* and *Serenity*

Lisa Hager

> Love. You can learn all the math in the 'verse, but you take a boat in the air you don't love, she'll shake you off just as sure as the turning of the worlds. Love keeps her in the air when she oughta fall down, tells you she's hurting 'fore she keens. Makes her a home.
> —Captain Malcolm "Mal" Reynolds (Nathan Fillion), *Serenity*

> Steampunk seeks to find a relationship with the world of gears, steel, and steam that allows machines to not only co-inhabit our world but to be partners in our journey. To be born, age, and die like we all must, that is not only true of humans, plants, rivers, animals but also of machines. This may be a crucial realignment of our relationship to the world, man-made and natural.
> —Professor Calamity, "My Machine, My Comrade," *Steampunk Magazine*

Joss Whedon's television series *Firefly* and the subsequent feature film *Serenity* (2005), based on the show, are well known among scholars and viewers alike for their mixing of genres.[1] Set in a future when humanity has colonized many worlds, *Firefly* tells the stories of *Serenity*'s nine-person crew as they attempt to make a life for themselves through various petty crimes and smuggling on the outer reaches of space, known as the Border planets. *Firefly* takes place as the known universe is recovering from a civil war in which the underdog, Border-planet-oriented Independents, known as "Browncoats," fought and were defeated by the hegemonic central-planet-based Alliance. In *Firefly,* the future is both extremely technologically advanced—with cyberpunk faster-than-light space travel and terraforming of moons having become the norm—and simultaneously retrofuturistic as much of the style for such technology and lack thereof outside of the central planets consistently recalls the American Old West.[2]

This play of contradictory generic influences shapes the *Firefly*-verse as a whole so that, as Barbara Maio remarks, its "style is defined in relationship with genres, and as a hybrid product that grows, incorporating different traditions."[3] Though much scholarly work on the show has focused on teasing out these myriad influences and exploring the implications of their use, especially in relation to cyberpunk and the Western, the show's mobilization of steampunk in its construction of the relationship between *Serenity* and crew has been largely neglected.[4] However, looking at *Firefly* in relation to steampunk aesthetics and ethics gives us a way to tease out the show's complex use of technology and its philosophical working out of a mutually sustainable relationship between humanity and machines in a postindustrial future. Indeed, as the similarity of sentiment between Mal's comments about his ship and Professor Calamity's description of his steampunk machines suggests, the connection between *Serenity* and her crew points toward a way of interacting, of living *with* technology, that borrows heavily from steampunk and posits an interactive and companionable relationship between the technological and the human. In this steampunk relationship, *Serenity*'s position as the crew's home environment also enables it to take on the subjectivity of a character within the show, as *Serenity* comes to stand in for the diverse crew as a whole. Thus *Firefly*, as a cultural artifact, asks us, as viewers, to consider the ethical implications of our own relationship with our natural and mechanical environments.

Living with Machines: Steampunk and the Mechanical

Steampunk is a hybrid mixture of various cultural movements and fiction genres, and it is this quality that lends itself to understanding *Firefly*'s heterogeneous style and especially its approach to technology. Appropriately enough, steampunk's evolution has been oddly circular and seemingly haphazard. Initially developed in the late 1980s and early 1990s by writers most well known for their cyberpunk novels, including William Gibson, Bruce Sterling, K. W. Jeter, and Tim Blaylock, steampunk looks to the past of the Victorian Industrial Revolution and its steam engines to understand our present world. Steampunk focuses on the Industrial Revolution and England's role, as the imperial and economic power of the nineteenth century, in developing so much of the technocultural infrastructure of our modern age. As a science fiction subgenre, it does so by imagining alternate nineteenth-century histories in which inventions like Charles Babbage's "Difference Engine" (an early computer) and zeppelins have flourished and become part of everyday life. Coupled with this interest in the age of steam, steampunk questions Victorian cultural assumptions through, as Margaret Rose terms it, "[evoking] an irreverent attitude toward history."[5] For steampunk, history is not some all-encompassing narrative, but a flexible, changeable, vulnerable story.

By focusing on such a pivotal time in the rise of industry, technology, and capitalism, steampunk's revision of history goes beyond simple wish fulfillment and thought experiments. Noting that the Victorians often hold a mirror to our modern culture, Steffen Hantke suggests that it is this likeness across historical distance that makes the nineteenth century such compelling material for steampunk: "What makes the Victorian past so fascinating is its unique historical ability to reflect the present moment."[6] Given that much of what seems "natural" to us was being hotly and often violently debated in the nineteenth century, from the regimented factory system of production to mechanical modes of transportation, the Victorian period offers us the chance to see our modern digital and information technosociety becoming itself and negotiating viable ethical stances in response to humanity's evolving relationship with the inanimate, the machine.

In changing the development of technology and exploring the implications of those changes for our present culture, steampunk unsettles the notion of history as an ontological narrative. As Karen Hellekson explains, steampunk "speculates about such topics as the nature of time and linearity, the past's link to the present, the present's link to the future, and the role of individuals in the history-making process . . . [making] readers rethink their world and how it has become what it has."[7] Consequently, when steampunk tweaks nineteenth-century history by adding its impossible inventions of clockwork and steam and examining the cultural implications of those results, it can also offer a critique of our twenty-first-century relationship with technology. Similarly, *Firefly*, in borrowing from steampunk in its depictions of the spaceship *Serenity*, not only comments on our potential future but also questions our present.

A Strange Little Bug and Her Crew: *Serenity* as a Queer Steampunk Environment

The interrelatedness of the crew with *Serenity* suggests the possibility of relations between the human and technological that work on the basis of interdependence, rather than the more traditional mastery of the machine by man. Not only does *Firefly* have, to borrow Michael Marek's term, an "ecology" as a series with its own mythic structure and visual vocabulary, but *Serenity* herself represents a steampunk ecological environment.[8] In envisioning *Serenity* as a steampunk ecological system, I propose that it is not only a steampunk environment but also an intensely queer steampunk environment in its resistance to fixedness and, crucially, in the connections it posits across the seemingly impassible divide between the living and the nonliving—a highly queer ethical relationship in both its strangeness and its subversion of the hegemonic power of the "normal."

Pointing toward the importance of queer theory in ecology, Timothy Morton argues that "life-forms constitute a *mesh,* a nontotalizable, open-ended concatenation of interrelations that blur and confound boundaries at practically any level: between species, between the living and the nonliving, between organism and environment."[9] Queer ecology flies in the face of the traditional demarcation between the living and the nonliving, and thus a queer steampunk ecology flagrantly crosses the line between the human and the machine. Consequently, inflecting steampunk with Morton's vision of queer ecology not only highlights steampunk's emphasis on the mutually interactive nature of the relationship between man and machine, but it also calls attention to how that relationship ultimately destabilizes many of Western thought's most basic ecological and biological definitions. In terms of *Firefly,* then, we can understand the machine, *Serenity,* and the human, the ship's crew, as relating to one another in a mutually dependent queer steampunk ecological ethical system that raises the possibility of a sustainable encounter with the wholly other that is companionable and interactive without reducing the other to sameness. Moreover, the nature of this relationship enables both crew and ship to resist totalizing narratives on both textual and metatextual levels.

Though *Serenity* is seemingly an advanced, modern piece of technology, its design and characterization position the ship as a steampunk character who is the tenth crew member. In the overall design of the ship, Whedon pushed his production designer, Carey Meyer, to strongly reference organic, lived-in forms. The goal was to give *Serenity,* classification Firefly, "an insect feel, an ugly duckling feel, really battered, run-through-the-wringer feel. . . . He [Whedon] wanted the spaceship to be another character on the show."[10] Aside from its visual design, the ship moves like the firefly for which its type is named. The landing gear consists of buglike legs that extend out and bend like legs to absorb the momentum of landing, and the ship's engine at full burn resembles a firefly's light. In being an inanimate object and yet moving and looking like an organic form, the ship itself moves between the living and nonliving, connecting both.

The interior design furthers this movement, particularly in regard to the engine room and function of the ship's mechanic, Kaylee Frye (Jewel Staite), both in relation to *Serenity* and the other crew members. Each of the ship's areas has a particular color scheme corresponding to its purpose. In this design scheme, the utilitarian areas like the bridge, the cargo hold, and hallways are consistently dark, gray, and coldly lit. In contrast, the kitchen, lounge, passenger quarters, and engine room—areas that make *Serenity* a home and give her a personality—are done in earth tones with warm lighting. In particular, it is the engine room that highlights *Serenity*'s steampunkiness and, simultaneously, her personality. This space, as Whedon notes, is "rusty and brown because that's very earthy and likable and real, and that's Kaylee's space—that was very deliberate."[11] An almost classic steampunk space with its aforementioned rustiness and exposed inner workings of various jerry-rigged and mismatched parts, *Serenity*'s engine room, the heart of the ship, is where Kaylee communicates with *Serenity* and, critically, where *Serenity* communicates with Kaylee.

Noticeably, the show firmly positions both participants in this relationship as active rather than merely asserting Kaylee's control over *Serenity*. Kaylee's mechanical talent is a sort of telepathic ability to talk with machines: "machines just got workings and they talk to me" ("Serenity"). Thus, it is the communication between Kaylee and *Serenity* that enables the former to keep the latter running and the latter to provide a home for the crew. Kaylee's mechanical intuition positions her as the steampunk inventor/ tinkerer who has created and continues to care for the unique machine, recalling Lev Grossman and Gary Moskowitz's description of steampunk: "Steampunk isn't mass-produced; it's bespoke and unique, and if you don't like it, you can tinker with it till you do."[12] As a steampunk machine, *Serenity* is thus never "done" and is always in a state of becoming, and Kaylee's tinkering makes that becoming possible. For example, when *Serenity* breaks down in "Out of Gas," Kaylee tells Mal: "I'm sorry, Captain. I'm real sorry. I shoulda kept better care of her. Usually she lets me know when something's wrong. Maybe she did and I wasn't paying attention." This comment positions *Serenity* as the active speaker and Kaylee as the inattentive listener who is usually much more aware of what is going on with the ship, turning the tables on the usual master/object relationship between mechanic and machine. This mechanic works with her machine, and the machine works with the mechanic.

Many have problematized Whedon's characterization of Kaylee's mechanical skill, citing the ways in which her skill is portrayed as stereotypical maternal instinct rather than hard-won knowledge. Noting this attempt to feminize Kaylee's mechanical acumen, Dee Amy-Chinn describes *Serenity* as Kaylee's "surrogate child."[13] However, Kaylee's identification with *Serenity* is more complex than a simple reproduction of the mother/child relationship because, as a steampunk tinkerer, her relationship with machines depends upon their subjectivity rather than objectivity. Whedon, in describing Kaylee's character, notes that "Kaylee is the soul of the ship . . . [she's] the thing that connects everybody."[14] Although clearly still playing off of the maternal, nurturing model of femininity, Whedon's description of her character highlights the extent to which her mechanical skill makes her part of the larger whole that is *Serenity*'s steampunk ecology. If Kaylee is the soul of this spaceship, then *Serenity* is not just a thing; it is a collective being who makes life possible for her crew—*Serenity* is home.

Kaylee is the character who not only connects the crew with this home but also makes clear the importance of valuing that home and the life it enables. As she tells Simon Tam (Sean Maher) in response to his absent-minded comment that *Serenity* is *luh-suh* (garbage): "You were being mean, is what. And if that's what you think of this life, then you can't think much of them that choose it, can you?" ("Safe"). Here, Kaylee insists on *Serenity* as metonymically standing in for both the crew members, who have chosen to make *Serenity* their home, and their life. Hence, when Simon, who still feels forced to take refuge on *Serenity* at this point, insults the ship, he insults the entire existence of everyone on it. *Serenity*, both the concept and ship, are choices that the individual must make to be a part of an interrelated system, a family that includes the animate and inanimate. Similarly, when River Tam (Summer Glau) seems to "become" *Serenity* in order to trick the bounty hunter Jubal Early in "Objects in Space," she is able to direct the crew and outwit Early.[15] As she tells Early: "You're talking to *Serenity*. And . . . Early, *Serenity* is very unhappy" ("Objects in Space"). By metaphorically becoming the ship, River can express and act on the gestalt wishes of the ship and its crew—to get rid of the intruder. Thus for both River and Kaylee, taking on the identity of ship proves also to be taking on the identity of whole, both ship and crew, to maintain the health and balance of the system.

The Alliance and Its Perfect World: The Dangers of Uniformity and Conformity

The diversity and interdependency of *Serenity*'s queer steampunk ecology stands in sharp contrast to the regulated modern design and ethos of the Alliance and its Core planets. As opposed to the warm earth tones and patchwork quality of *Serenity*'s design, the color scheme used for the Alliance is marked by its cool monotone grays, blacks, and whites. In the world of *Firefly*, the Alliance represents the dangers and safety of sameness, modernity, and central authority. The uniforms of its military are deliberately based on Nazi uniforms, and its ships are smooth-lined monoliths that are virtually indistinguishable from each other.[16] Though the Core planets, those most strongly identifying as Alliance planets and thus most closely under Alliance control, have all the benefits of sophistication and civilization, there is an underlying sense that they are too perfect, too clean. As Zoe Alleyne Washburne (Gina Torres) explains in "Ariel": "It's a Core planet. It's spotless, there's sensors everywhere, and where there ain't sensors, there's feds. All the central planets are the same." Zoe's intense dislike of the life-crushing similarity of all Core planets strongly echoes what steampunk maker Jake von Slatt has described as steampunk's "backlash against the sameness of design" found in modern design.[17] Indeed, there are strong parallels between the contemporary design principles evident in the products of technology companies like Apple, with its ultrasmooth and sleek iPods, and the clean, monotonous lines of Core cities and buildings, as exemplified in the hospital on Ariel. As Professor Calamity remarks, seemingly agreeing with *Serenity*'s first mate here: "The technology that sits by our side is too complicated, too swift to serve, too abstract to engage our senses. There is a nauseating sameness found in most of today's technologies (like the tree farm). Replication has replaced revelation. To know one is to know all, thus the value of one is none."[18] Technology, much like the life system it creates on the central planets, is too easy. It requires no work or thought on the part of the individual to function and, as such, does not lead to any sort of investment by or relationship with its user/tinkerer because it has no individuality, no history, no soul, no ethics.

Expanding on the danger of such an approach to the relationship between humans and technology, the plot of the film *Serenity* demonstrates how it leads to only one place: death. In the course of the film, River leads the crew to discover the Alliance's secret that has been literally driving River crazy. The crew learns from a holographic recording left by a member of the Search and Rescue Team on a planet named Miranda that, when terraforming the planet, the Alliance added a chemical, G-23 Paxilon Hydroclorate (Pax), to the air in order to "calm the population, weed out aggression." This attempt to "make people safer" led to 90 percent of the population becoming so calm and peaceful that they stopped doing anything: "they all just let themselves die." The other 10 percent of the population had the opposite response and became Reavers, people who have lost all touch with any sense of humanity and have become unthinkably violent animals who rape, eat, and wear the skins of their victims. They are sort of real-life bogeymen who haunt the universe in ships as maimed as their bodies and psyches, and it is only in the film that Whedon actually reveals what they look like (though the "survivor" in "Bushwhacked" gives viewers an inkling). They are the Alliance's return of the repressed, with unspeakable vengeance. In either case, the Alliance's quest for the perfect world demonstrates that humanity's flawed nature is bound up in its survival. To be a "perfect" citizen of the Alliance is to be dead.

As opposed to the embracing of difference and flaws that *Serenity*'s queer steampunk nature suggests, Pax represents not just the Alliance's fascist need for control but also its willingness to change the nature of humanity to do so. The wording of the Pax's purpose here is significant; the goal of the Pax was to make people safer both in terms of creating a less violent society and to control the unpredictable nature of life itself—a safer society and a safer type of people. Miranda's Pax homogenizes its people, resulting in extreme apathy and violence. *Serenity* and her crew represent a direct challenge to this hegemonic thinking. Consequently, when Mal asks the crew to join him in revealing the Alliance's dirty secret, he highlights their differences from one another as well as their shared place-ness: "You all got on this boat for different reasons, but you all come to the same place" (*Serenity*). Offering a clear contrast to the Alliance's quest for total sameness, *Serenity*'s crew members are still diverse individuals, even as they share a home and a life. They are all a part of *Serenity*.

Punking the Alliance: *Serenity*'s Queer Steampunk Critique

Importantly, the challenge that *Serenity* represents to the power of the Alliance is not some idealistic rebellion against an evil empire; instead, it is a questioning of the basic understanding of the nature of humanity, whose real value lies in the process, not in the result. Through the references and flashbacks to Mal's and Zoe's experiences in the war, *Firefly* makes clear that rebellion in its pure form is not possible. Fighting on the side of the Independents, Mal and Zoe would seem to be taking the side of a very American model of individual freedom.[19] Yet, the reality of war shows such ideals to be hollow. For example, when Zoe tells Simon about Serenity Valley when he first joins the crew, she describes the true horror of the battle, which happened after the fighting: "Wounded, and sick, and near to mad as can still walk and talk. Both sides left us there while they 'negotiated the peace.' For a *week*. And we just kept dying" ("Serenity" deleted scenes). The experience of this trauma, of this complete disillusionment, marks a person forever: "Once you've been in Serenity, you never leave. You just learn to live there" ("Serenity" deleted scenes). Zoe's point is meant not just in relation to herself and Mal, but to all of *Serenity*'s crew members. Zoe insists that the battle of Serenity Valley demonstrates the hollowness of any rebellion's claim to philosophical purity—that eventually all rebellions become co-opted by the powers that be because rebellions seek that power. Consequently, *Serenity*'s crew lives on the margins of the economic and military power that is the Alliance because not a single one of them "fits" in those worlds anymore and trying to rebel against it would only put a different power in place.

Yet *Serenity* and her crew do not simply give in to the control of the Alliance. They fight for the right to be the dissent within the system, and they recognize both the value and limitations of their dissent. On an ethical level, they, much like the work of steampunk contraptors to reimagine modern technology as personal, create an alternative way of life out of the existing legal and economic landscape. As smugglers, they may disobey the law, but they also, as the noted science fiction author Mercedes Lackey observes, "[keep] things from becoming intolerable on the fringes which would lead to a rebellion."[20] They are part of the system: one cannot smuggle unless there is an authority to deceive, and their smuggling serves a purpose in making sure the outer planets get some of the supplies they so desperately need. Their resistance to the Alliance is located not in violence, but in, as Matthew Hill argues, "refusing to play along and be defined by our fear and the signifiers of that which has injured us."[21] Thus, when Mal is forced to revisit the trauma of unimaginable death and horror on Miranda, he chooses to speak for those dead so as to prevent a second Miranda: "They [the Alliance] will try again. . . . They'll swing back to the belief that they can make people . . . better. And I do not hold to that" (*Serenity*). In telling the crew that he "aims to misbehave" and broadcast the report of the Mirandan Research and Rescue Team, he seeks to disturb the narrative of progress that the Alliance has worked so hard to make the only narrative of history, as River's dream education sequence at the film's beginning demonstrates. In disrupting the smoothness of the Alliance's writing of history by revealing what the Alliance has concealed, they—much like steampunk makers who retrofit current technologies—make visible the workings of modernity and tell an alternate history that asks us to question the ethics of our relationship with and use of technology.

However, Mal is very aware of the limitations of his and his crew's act, suggesting that any sort of punking, be it steam or otherwise, ultimately can only offer a critique and create possibilities. Consequently, in a deleted scene, Mal confirms that he is all too well aware of the likely outcome of the upheaval the broadcast has started: "'Verse wakes for a spell. Won't be long 'fore she rolls right over and falls back asleep. T'aint my worry."[22] Although

Mr. Universe proclaims earlier in the film that "you can't stop the signal," Mal here argues that people will eventually stop listening. The point of the act was not to change the world but rather to act according to one's personal ethical code and raise the question of the need for change. It is a moment, however small, of discursive freedom and variety when the master narrative's functioning is no longer smooth and untroubled. For a moment, though, they have offered an alternative narrative, a redesign, a punk, of the Alliance's version of truth and humanity.

Even at the end of the film, when we, as viewers, expect the happy ending or at least the satisfyingly sentimental ending, *Serenity* punks such an ontology—in much the same way as her crew momentarily disturbed the Alliance's historical narrative. *Serenity* and her crew have been, in Zoe's words, "tore up plenty," but they have put themselves back together again physically and emotionally. Even Zoe, who has lost her husband, Wash, says that *Serenity* will "fly true." For the film's final scene, we then cut to Mal and River on the bridge, and Mal gives the speech about love that begins this essay. This all seems like a fine, if a bit elegiac, ending to a Hollywood film. But *Serenity* has the last word. As they leave the planet, a panel, more than likely the primary buffer panel that flew off at the beginning of the film, again flies off the ship, and the last words of the film are Mal again asking, "What was that?" Offering one of Whedon's Hong Kong–style moments in which our expectations as viewers are frustrated by *Firefly*'s wry humor, the scene defuses the emotion of the ending and leaves the film with unfinished, ongoing feel. Despite being fixed up with the help of the Alliance, *Serenity* here asserts her otherness but also her personality, her refusal to be "fixed," to be made in any way into the perfect machine. In much the same way as her crew avoids being caught up in the rebellion/authority dynamic with the Alliance, *Serenity* refuses to be fixed even within the narrative of the Hollywood movie, with its happily-ever-after ending in which all is explained and settled. She remains always in process as a queer steampunk ecological system.

Through the portrayal of the interdependent relationship between *Serenity* and crew and their shared philosophical avowal of process over result, *Firefly* suggests a queer steampunk ecological ethics, a way of relating to technology, that refuses the simplistic, reductive relationships of modernity or complete Luddism. *Serenity* represents a middle ground that is always in process, always on the journey to becoming. That becomingness ultimately posits an ethical stance that refuses product-oriented ideas of value. What *Firefly* then asks us to consider is how our supposed mastery of machines reflects our desire to master the messiness of life rather than embracing the process of living, with its failures and imperfections. In doing so, we might move toward an understanding of technology as a partner on a journey and thus see the permeability of the boundaries between the animate and inanimate.

Notes

1. Please note that I use the name *Firefly* throughout this essay to indicate the world created in both the television series and its feature film, *Serenity.* Though there are differences between the two that are worth exploring, the basic system of relations between the crew and its ship remains stable throughout both incarnations of the *Firefly*-verse.

2. Though the mechanism for faster-than-light travel (FTL) is not explicitly discussed in *Firefly, Serenity* regularly travels between planets that are great distances apart in the matter of a few days, thus indicating the necessity of some sort of FTL capability.

3. Barbara Maio, "Between Past and Future: Hybrid Design Style in *Firefly* and *Serenity,*" in *Investigating* Firefly *and* Serenity: *Science Fiction on the Frontier,* ed. Rhonda Wilcox and Tanya R. Cochran (New York: Tauris, 2008), 202.

4. Cyberpunk is a subgenre of science fiction characterized by dystopian futures in which humanity has become fully enmeshed within technology, often to the point of almost complete abjection. Cyberpunk works include William Gibson's *Neuromancer* (1984), Neal Stephenson's *Snow Crash* (1992), and, more recently, *The Matrix* films (1999; 2003).

5. Margaret Rose, "Extraordinary Pasts: Steampunk as a Mode of Historical Representation," *Journal of the Fantastic in the Arts* 20, no. 3 (2009): 321. Some critics, such as Jess Nevins, argue that this questioning does not purpose any solutions: "Like the punks, steampunk rarely offers a solution to the problems it decries—for steampunk, there is no solution—but for punk and steampunk the criticism must be made before the change can come." Steampunk texts like *Firefly* do begin to describe what that solution might look like (Jess Nevins, "The Nineteenth Century Roots of Steampunk," *New York Review of Science Fiction* 21, no. 5 [245] [2009]: 5).

6. Steffen Hantke, "Difference Engines and Other Infernal Devices: History According to Steampunk," *Extrapolation: A Journal of Science Fiction and Fantasy* 40, no. 3 (1999): 245.

7. Karen Hellekson, "Toward a Taxonomy of the Alternate History Genre," *Extrapolation* 41 (2000): 254–55; Nevins, "The Nineteenth Century Roots of Steampunk," 5.

8. Michael Marek, "Firefly: So Pretty It Could Not Die," in *Sith, Slayers, Stargates, and Cyborgs: Modern Mythology in the New Millennium,* ed. David Whitt and John Perlich, Popular Culture and Everyday Life series, no. 19 (New York: Peter Lang, 2008), 101.

9. Timothy Morton, "Guest Column: Queer Ecology," *PMLA* 125, no. 2 (March 2010): 275–76.

10. Joss Whedon, Firefly: *The Official Companion,* vol. 2 (London: Titan, 2007), 34.

11. Joss Whedon, Firefly: *The Official Companion,* vol. 1 (London: Titan, 2006), 10.

12. Lev Grossman and Gary Moskowitz, "A Handmade World," *Time* 174, no. 23 (2009), http://search.ebscohost.com/login.aspx?direct=true&db=aph&AN=45616897&site=ehost-live.

13. Dee Amy-Chinn, "'Tis Pity She's a Whore: Postfeminist Prostitution in Joss Whedon's Firefly?" *Feminist Media Studies* 6, no. 2 (2006): 177.

14. Joss Whedon, Serenity: *The Official Visual Companion* (London: Titan, 2005), 16.

15. Marek, "Firefly: So Pretty It Could Not Die," 116.

16. Whedon, Firefly: *The Official Companion,* 1:196.

17. Peter Bebergal, "The Age of Steampunk: Nostalgia Meets the Future, Joined Carefully with Brass Screws," *Boston Globe,* August 26, 2007, www.boston.com/news/globe/ideas/articles/2007/08/26/the_age_of_steampunk/ .

18. Calamity, "My Machine, My Comrade," no. 25.

19. For an excellent discussion of trauma and *Firefly,* see Matthew B. Hill, "'I Am a Leaf on the Wind': Cultural Trauma and Mobility in Joss Whedon's *Firefly,*" *Extrapolation* (University of Texas at Brownsville) 50, no. 3 (Fall 2009), http://search.ebscohost.com/login.aspx?direct=true&db=aph&AN=48548609&site=ehost-live.

20. Mercedes Lackey, "*Serenity* and Bobby McGee," in *Finding Serenity: Anti-Heroes, Lost Shepherds and Space Hookers in Joss Whedon's* Firefly, ed. Jane Espenson (Dallas: BenBella, 2004), 67.

21. Hill, "I Am a Leaf on the Wind," 504.

22. Whedon, Serenity: *The Official Visual Companion,* 155.

Shepherd Book, Malcolm Reynolds, and the Dao of *Firefly*

Roger P. Ebertz

What is the good life? Reflective human beings have been asking variations of this question for millennia. Many associate the question with philosophy, remembering Socrates' remark that the unexamined life is not worth living. Others turn to religion for a vision of the good life. Some turn to ethics looking for rules for good living. In this essay, I explore the borderlands between philosophy, religion, and ethics, where the question of the good life is discussed, with a particular view to Joss Whedon's television series *Firefly* and the sequel film, *Serenity*.[1] Like many films and television series, *Firefly/Serenity* not only tells a story, but suggests a vision of what makes a life good and worth living. In this essay, I tease out this vision, exploring the characters of Shepherd Book (Ron Glass) and Malcolm Reynolds (Nathan Fillion), and the life of the crew on board the ship *Serenity*.

Thinking about the Good Life: A Framework

Before we look specifically at *Firefly/Serenity*, let me suggest three very different ways of thinking about what constitutes a good life. First, one might think of the good life as a life of enjoyment and happiness. One's goal is to acquire material goods and enjoy the pleasure and security these goods can provide. If one succeeds at this goal, one's life is good. In tension with this in many people's minds is a second view according to which the good life is a life in which a person does what is right, follows the rules of morality. According to this approach, to live well, or in other words to live a good life, one should seek to discover the rules of morality and live by them. Some religious people think about life this way and look to their religious faith for the rules that, if followed, can make one's life good. Others look to philosophical concepts of duty, such as those of Immanuel Kant, for rules for living. The good life is all about being moral. Finally, I suggest a third way of seeing the good life. According to this approach, neither individual satisfaction and happiness nor following moral rules make a life good. Unlike the view that looks for rules by which to determine how to live, this third way finds the goodness of life in a state of being. This approach also rejects the individualism of the first way and affirms that a good life can be found only in relationship, above all to other humans, but to the world around us as well. One's life is made good not just by acquiring goods and material security, or by simply following the rules, but by being the kind of person who contributes to the particular community in which one lives.

The Good Life as Goods, Security, and Happiness

In my courses, when I ask my students what they consider a good life, many name things they would like to have or do that they believe would lead to happiness. As one approaches the vision of the good life in *Firefly/Serenity,* one's first thought might be that it is a vision of individualistic hedonism.[2] Malcolm Reynolds is a renegade who has left behind society, engages in missions that violate the laws, and looks for jobs that will secure his life on the ship. The most brazen hedonist in the series, however, is Jayne Cobb (Adam Baldwin). Always ready to go where the money leads, taking advantage of opportunities for pleasure as they arise, Jayne has little regard for either religion or morality. Jayne is clearly out for pleasure. In the "Jaynestown" episode, it becomes clear that Jayne has betrayed associates to pull off a heist that will make him rich. In "Heart of Gold," Jayne is the first to take advantage of the "services" at the brothel they have come to help.

But the very depiction of Jayne's character casts a critical shadow on his approach to life, and hedonism is not the prevailing vision of the series. Although Mal sees a place for Jayne in a gunfight, he never really trusts him ("Out of Gas"). The rejection of hedonism is also expressed clearly in *Serenity: Better Days,* one of the comic books written by Whedon to fill in the gap between the series and the movie sequel. In this story, the crew of the ship has managed to secure a significant amount of loot, enough to set them fantasizing about what they would do with it all. But their dreams are dashed when their newfound wealth is stolen from them. Inara (Morena Baccarin) sees that the thieves knew just where to look for the goods, evidence that perhaps it was an inside job. To Mal, Inara says: "All those fantasies about what the crew wants to do with their lives. . . . But you . . . you're doing it. You get by and the crew stays together. You get rich . . . then everything does change." Mal replies, "This is where I am Inara, ain't a place of wishes."[3] For

Mal, the good life has more to do with life on the ship right now, not dreams of things that might bring pleasure and security.

The Religion and Ethics of Shepherd Book

If the hedonistic vision is rejected, perhaps rules are the key to the good life. In some people's minds, it is religion that provides the rules. Religion and spirituality are more pervasive in *Firefly/Serenity* than one might initially expect. Inara's subtle Buddhism, Mal's early religious faith and later rejection of God, and River's (Summer Glau) abilities to hear the dead all touch on spirituality. But the most obvious representative of religion on board the ship is Shepherd Derrial Book. In various scenes, other characters look to Book for the religious and ethical voice, expecting him to speak and act according to the Bible.

To some extent, the character of Shepherd Book remains mysterious throughout the series. But there are enough clues to piece together a sketch of his beliefs and ethical views. Shepherd Book is a Christian. In an interview, Ron Glass reports that he discussed with Whedon the possibility of making Book Buddhist, an option that would reflect Glass's personal beliefs more closely. But Whedon was set on making Shepherd Book a "fundamentalist Christian guy."[4] Book is not, however, a stereotypical fundamentalist. He has a less literal way of interpreting the Bible than most fundamentalists, and he wears vaguely clerical-looking clothes, looking somewhat like a Catholic or Anglican priest or monk.

We get our first glimpse of Book as he wanders around Persephone's Eavesdown docks looking for a ship on which to travel. After turning down one ship, Book seems ready to pass right by the spaceship *Serenity* when Kaylee (Jewel Staite) grabs his attention with her startling claim, "You're gonna come with us." The two banter a bit about ships, but Kaylee turns the conversation to deeper questions, "So, uh, how come you don't care where you're going?" Book replies, "'Cause how you get there is the worthier part." Kaylee asks him if he is a missionary, and he responds: "I guess . . . I'm a Shepherd, from the Southdown Abbey. Book, I'm called Book. Been out of the world for a spell. Like to walk it a while, maybe bring the word to them as need it." He wants to travel, share the Word with others. The scene gives us an important clue to Book's approach to life: it is the journey that matters, not the goal ("Serenity").

As would be expected, the Bible is central to Book's religion. When Kaylee is injured in the episode "Serenity," Book stands by her bed, Bible in hand. In "Shindig," as Badger (Mark Sheppard) comes threateningly onto the ship, Book stands and reads the Bible. In "Jaynestown," Book discovers River Tam cutting up his Bible. Alarmed, he asks what she is doing. "Bible's broken," she says, "contradictions, false logistics—doesn't make sense." River specifically refers to the stories of the Garden of Eden and Noah's ark, apparently wanting to find ways to make these stories consistent with the scientific theories of the day. "Give me that, River," Books says, "you don't fix the Bible." In "Bushwhacked," when the crew of *Serenity* is considering whether to board a drifting ship on a humanitarian mission, Shepherd Book appeals to the story of the Good Samaritan. In "Heart of God," Book takes up a hammer and volunteers to reinforce the brothel against an expected attack, saying, "Been following the footsteps of a carpenter for some time now," a clear reference to the New Testament depiction of Jesus.

Book's religious life includes other interesting elements as well. As Book becomes a part of the community on board *Serenity,* he finds himself wanting to help. In one scene, we find him talking with Inara, wondering aloud how he can contribute to the ship's life. In an intriguing bit of dialogue, Inara suggests, "You could always pray that they make it back safely." When Book replies that the captain wouldn't want his prayers, Inara responds, "Don't tell him. . . . I never do." This scene is interesting not just because it suggests that prayer is a part of Book's religion, but because it also suggests that prayer is a part of Inara's spirituality. At several other times in the series, we see Book apparently standing and praying. In various episodes, we get clues about the religious order from which Book has come.[5]

Recall that one way to think about what constitutes a good life is to determine what is morally right and to define the good life in terms of this standard. If one is thinking along these lines, one might expect Shepherd Book to be a voice for the rules, and by virtue of that, the voice for living the good life. As one digs into Book's character, however, one discovers a more nuanced understanding of morality and the good life than a simple focus on rules might suggest.

There are indeed times when the crew of *Serenity* expects Shepherd Book to speak for morality, to be concerned about the rules. Inara clearly expects Book to be judgmental when they first meet in "Serenity." When he comes into her shuttle, she asks, "So. Would you lecture me on the wickedness of my ways?" Book responds with humor: "I brought you some supper, but if you'd prefer a lecture, I've got a few catchy ones prepped. Sin and hellfire . . . one has lepers."[6] In "War Stories," Book picks up a semiautomatic weapon to help the crew rescue Mal. Zoe challenges him, "Preacher, don't the Bible have some pretty specific things to say about killing?" Book responds: "Quite specific. It is, however, somewhat fuzzier on the subject of kneecaps." In both of these scenes, Book is expected to be a defender of the rules, a role he brushes off with humor. In "Our Mrs. Reynolds," Book is more serious as a guardian of morality. The attractive Saffron (Christina Hendricks) has come aboard the ship claiming to be Mal's wife, having been married the evening before in a local ceremony that Mal was too ignorant and drunk to understand. Now his "wife," Saffron, is on board, ready to take up her wifely role. Mal denies that they are married and refuses to have anything to do with her. But the Shepherd recognizes that Saffron's sensuality is powerful and that Mal could easily go astray, warning him: "If you take sexual advantage of her, you're going to burn in a very special level of hell. A level they reserve for child molesters and people who talk at the theater." Again, one should not miss the humor; nevertheless, Book is here acting as a kind of guardian of morality.[7]

Yet Shepherd Book's approach to ethics goes beyond adherence to rules. He is expected to be the rule keeper, but his words and behavior suggest that he does not think that following the rules is what is ultimately important. He is willing to take up arms when he believes it is necessary for some sufficiently worthy good. He is more concerned that Inara be respected as a person than that she be condemned as a prostitute.[8] In fact, Book is strikingly and consistently nonjudgmental—toward Inara, toward others, even toward the Reavers. Interestingly, it is Mal, not Book, who is judgmental with regard to Inara's "whoring," motivated, no doubt, by Mal's unspoken affection for her. Book is consistently respectful toward Inara, even though other crew members suggest that it is odd to have a Companion and a preacher on the same ship.

What does seem to be at the heart of Shepherd Book's ethics is personal concern for others. Book frequently praises crew members and passengers on the ship. "That's a rare gift," he says to Kaylee with regard to her ability to keep the ship running ("Serenity"). In "The Train Job," Book recognizes Simon's bravery and dedication to his sister, how Simon gave up his career and family and risked his life to save his sister. To Mal, he says, "That young man's very brave." Then he turns to Mal and praises him as well, "Not many would take them in." In short, Book's version of Christian faith does not issue in an ethics of rules, but as an ethics of respect and concern for others. Like the carpenter he follows, Book's approach to life goes beyond following rules to something deeper. Similarly, the vision of the good life in *Firefly/ Serenity* goes deeper than either maximizing happiness or following the rules.

Before we leave the topic of Shepherd Book's religion and ethics, there is an additional important dynamic in Book's spirituality that will be helpful to point out. As his character unfolds, Book is both a man of faith and a man of doubt. On the one hand, Book articulates the idea that one must have faith. When River complains that Book's Bible is broken and doesn't make sense, Book explains: "It's not about making sense. It's about believing in something and letting that belief be real enough to change your life. It's about faith. You don't fix faith, River. It fixes you" ("Jaynestown"). In another place, Book says: "I don't care what you believe. Just believe it" (*Serenity*). For Book, faith is crucial. But it is the faith itself, not the object of one's faith, that matters most.[9] But Book, the believer, is not beyond doubt and questioning. Two scenes stand out. In one, the pilot episode ("Serenity"), we find Book talking with Inara. Book laments that he has been away from the abbey for only two days and "I've beaten a lawman senseless, I've fallen in with criminals. I watched the captain shoot the man I swore to protect. And I'm not even sure if I think he was wrong." Interrupting Inara's response, he says, "I believe I just . . . (a pained smile) I think I'm on the wrong ship." Inara responds in a way that reflects her own spirituality: "Maybe. Or maybe you're exactly where you ought to be." In "Out of Gas," when the whole crew is facing death as the result of diminishing oxygen, River senses that Book is afraid. He admits that he is, even when River reminds him that his Bible says he should not be afraid. In both of these scenes, we see Book struggling with doubt.

Book and Mal

Near the beginning of this essay, I indicate that Joss Whedon had insisted that the Book character be a Christian fundamentalist. Whedon explains, "Shepherd Book is somebody I would probably get along famously with, except we don't agree about anything." Whedon says Book serves as "a voice for the other side."[10] This is a significant clue to the vision of *Firefly*, a clue that I would like to pursue first by considering the relationship between Malcolm Reynolds and Shepherd Book.

From the beginning, Captain Reynolds is critical of Book's religion. His attitude surfaces in numerous places but perhaps is most clearly expressed in "Train Job." When Mal asks Book what he's doing on a ship with brigands instead of being off saving heathens, Book responds that there are plenty of heathens right here. Mal replies: "If I'm your mission, Shepherd, best give it up. You're welcome on my boat. God ain't." On the surface, at least, Mal has little time for religion. Mal says: "I ain't looking for help from on high. That's a long wait for a train don't come" (*Serenity*).

What is at the root of Mal's attitude toward religion? An important key is found in the opening battle scene from Whedon's *Firefly* pilot, "Serenity."

Mal and Zoe are in the midst of battle, badly outnumbered, refusing to give up the Valley of Serenity. Mal tries to rally his beleaguered troops. Before charging out, he reaches into his shirt and pulls out a cross on a necklace and kisses it. Moments later, he learns that the rebel forces have given up and ordered Mal and the other rebel forces to surrender. The "angels" (air cover from the rebel forces) and God have both failed him. In the series, as we travel along with Malcolm Reynolds, captain of *Serenity,* we see a man who has given up on God and given up on fighting military battles to defend what is right. He is a man who has seemingly given up on belief in anything.[11] On the edge of the 'verse, he has found a life where at least he can be free. In a sense, then, Shepherd Book and Malcolm Reynolds are opposites with regard to religion. Malcolm Reynolds is a man who once believed, but who has given up on faith. Shepherd Book, a man who was not always a Shepherd, emphasizes the importance of faith, faith in something, faith in anything. But in spite of the contrast between them, they also appreciate and respect one another. When the Shepherd wants to say last words over the Reaver victims, Mal concedes that it doesn't hurt to show respect for the dead.[12] Book, on the other hand, admires the captain for knowingly keeping Simon and River, wanted criminals, on board the ship.

Yin and Yang, Shepherd and Captain

What are we to make of the relationship between Mal and Book? The answer, I believe, can be conceptualized in terms of the ancient concepts of yin and yang. According to Chinese philosophical tradition, in particular Daoism, nature, or "the Dao" (often translated as "the way"), consists of contrasting forces interacting in a continuously changing balance. As one author puts it: "The Chinese view of the cosmos, Earth, human beings, the rhythms of day and night, the seasons, the phases of the day—indeed all life, came under the dynamic power of yin and yang in all phenomena."[13] Yin represents the cold and dark, the passive, the feminine. Yang speaks of light and warmth, the active, the masculine. Westerners may see hints of hierarchical thinking in these contrasts, but Chinese thought emphasizes the need for both yin and yang, and the interaction between the two. The two are dependent on one another, "complementary, rather than oppositional." They are "alternating, even 'pulsating' creative forces representing the interplay between spiritual and physical, emotion and intellect, passivity and activity, the yielding and the firm, resistance and generation. Rather than opposition between the two, there is polarity in unity, like two sides of one coin—a harmonized unity of opposites."[14] Unlike Platonic idealism, in which perfect reality is understood as unchanging, the ancient Chinese concepts of yin and yang suggest that if there is perfection at all, it is not in some unchanging world, but in the constant interaction of opposing forces in the world. And in this process, each is made real by the presence of its "opposite." As is stated in the Daodejing, one of the most ancient Daoist texts: "Recognize beauty and ugliness is born. Recognize good and evil is born."[15] On this view, opposites depend upon one another.

In several ways, the relationship between Shepherd Book and Malcolm Reynolds is much like that of the yin and the yang. As yin and yang stand in complementary tension, Book and Reynolds complement one another in dynamic, yet taut, harmony. One dimension of this complementarity is manifested in their attitudes toward religion: Shepherd is a person of faith while the captain is one who has given up on faith. And there is even more to it than this. In the well-known symbol used to express yin and yang in Chinese thought, one finds two parts, one predominantly white, the other predominantly black. In the middle of each, one finds a bit of the opposite: a white dot in the midst of the black, a black dot in the midst of the white. Even in the yin, there is yang. Even in the yang, there is yin. The same is true of Book and Reynolds. Although Book is a person of faith, he also doubts. Even in his doubt, his rejection of religion, Mal is driven to believe.

There is another aspect of the characters of Book and Mal that seems consistent with yin and yang, and the Dao in which they are combined. The Dao is always mysterious. As the Daodejing begins, "The Dao that can be named is not the Dao."[16] Dao is beyond total understanding. Both Book and Mal are mysterious as well. Book is shrouded in a mysterious past. No one really knows who he is and where he came from. Why does he know so much about weapons, about the Alliance, about Adelai Niska (Michael Fairman)? Why do Alliance forces treat him with respect? Who the hell is he, anyway!? This mysterious past has its representation in the present, also. Book is a Shepherd, but the crew never knows quite what to expect, what Book is up to. Malcolm Reynolds is mysterious as well. Just when we have him figured out as the pragmatic, ruthless captain of *Serenity*, he shows compassion for a crew member or a person in need. When he would be justified in ejecting Simon and River, or Jayne, from the ship, he allows them to stay aboard, affirming almost familial loyalty to them. In an early conversation, Inara asks Book why he is so fascinated by Mal. "Because he is something of a mystery," he replies, and asks her in turn, "Why are you?" "Because so few men are," she says. Both Book and Inara find Malcolm Reynolds fascinating precisely because they can't seem to figure him out ("Serenity"). Like yin and yang, Mal and Book stand in a mysterious, complementary relationship to one another.[17]

Malcolm Reynolds and the Crew of *Serenity*

Let's return now to the question with which we began: What is the good life? I sketched three different approaches to thinking about a good life. According to the first, the good life is a life of individual happiness and satisfaction through the acquisition of things which can bring security and comfort. We have considered Jayne as the best representative of this view on board the ship *Serenity*. The second approach focuses on following the moral rules, the key to good living. With a view to this notion of the good life and the thought that religion is the source of the appropriate rules, it was natural to consider Shepherd Book, the character who most represents religion in the series. In spite of the crew's assumptions that as a Christian he will uphold the rules of the Bible, Book's ethics does not focus on rules as much as on concern for others. Like Book's ethics, the vision of the good life that is suggested in the *Firefly/Serenity* series goes beyond both pleasure and rules. It is to that third approach to the good life that we turn: community with others.[18]

Although the word "community" feels a bit too tame for the interaction on board *Serenity*, it is difficult to find a better word. In a sense, they are a family, tied together by a mysterious bond in spite of their quarrels and differences. Malcolm Reynolds says it himself at the end of "Our Mrs. Reynolds" when he confronts Saffron after she double-crosses him and tries to highjack his ship: "You got all kinds of learnin' and you made me look the fool without tryin', and yet here I am with a gun to your head. That's 'cause I got people with me. People who trust each other, who do for each other, and ain't always lookin' for the advantage." Certainly there are times when this "trust" among the crew breaks down. Yet Mal is right—when things get difficult, the crew and passengers of *Serenity* "do for each other." Out of their differences, the same differences that produce tensions, each one brings something to the community. Even Jayne, the crew member who seems least trustworthy, has a role to play, as a fighter and sharpshooter. He contributes a very practical mind. When the crew is going to leave Mal behind on *Serenity* as it runs out of oxygen, Jayne makes sure the oxygen will last as long as possible for the captain's benefit ("Out of Gas"). River, the troubled young savant who brings endless trouble to the ship, saves the day on more than one occasion with her psychic abilities and hidden talents in sharpshooting and martial arts. Inara the "Companion," the ship's ambassador of respectability, proves to be crucial in several episodes. And clearly Simon, with his medical knowledge and abilities, and Kaylee, with her ability to work mechanical wonders, play important roles.

Life on *Serenity* is what it is because of each of these individuals. But there is also a constant threat that one or more will leave or be rejected. Jayne constantly implores Mal to get rid of Simon and River, both for the money and to make life easier on board the ship. Jayne betrays Mal and by all rights should be left behind. The complex relationship between Mal and Inara eventually results in Inara leaving the ship. In spite of all of these tensions, the members of the community are held together. Why? One key factor seems to be Malcolm Reynolds himself. In spite of his rough exterior, Mal is a person of moral character. How can a thief be a person of moral character? If one understands goodness as following the proper rules, then clearly Mal falls short. And he definitely has his personal weaknesses. But in many ways, he displays goodness and virtue. When Book asks him why it is that he keeps Simon and River on board, he says, "Only because it's the right thing to do" ("The Train Job").[19] When Mal discovers that the medicine he has just stolen will result in the suffering of people who were expecting the medicine, he changes course, at significant risk to his own life, to return the medicine. "There's others who need this more," he says. At the end of the episode, he implies that he had no choice but to do what he did ("The Train Job"). On the other hand, when they contemplate theft of medicine from the hospital, sensitive Kaylee is concerned that people in the hospital need the medicine. But Simon assures them all that since it is an Alliance facility, the medicine will be quickly replaced and no one will suffer. The people on the outer planets, who will eventually get the medicine, will benefit. The crew is stealing from the rich to sell to the poor. Mal, as their leader, is a Robin Hood character. In other episodes, Mal disdains a man who made money using slaves ("Shindig") and says a planet on which women are subject to the desires of men is dumb ("Our Mrs. Reynolds"). When Atherton claims that Inara is "mine," Mal counters: "Yours? She don't belong to nobody!" ("Shindig"). According to the rules of this planet, Atherton has paid the price of an escort for the evening. Mal, however, doesn't care about these rules; Inara is not something to be owned. And when he wins the duel with Atherton, Malcolm has mercy on him. Instead of following the rules of the culture, he lets Atherton live.

There are two additional elements of Mal's character that I believe are also important to understanding the dynamics on *Serenity*. First, Mal is open to "the other." In this regard, I believe Mal reflects Whedon himself, when Whedon tells us that Book is a voice from the "other side." Throughout the series, Mal is a force that holds together disparate elements. As we have seen, Book and Mal stand to one another as "other." Educated Simon and his sister, River, stand in opposition to Jayne, the pragmatic hedonist. There is a constant tension between Mal and Inara, fueled by unspoken affection, over the legitimacy of Inara's profession. Mal has not selected a bunch of people like himself. Whether intentionally or not, the community that has come together is a mixture of very different people, so different at times that one might be tempted to say they are "opposites." And yet, they are held together, in large part, because of Mal's loyalty to them. And this loyalty is the second element I want to emphasize. Mal has more than enough reason to eject Jayne into space ("Ariel"). Yet he keeps Jayne on board as part of the crew. Life would be much simpler if Mal were to follow Jayne's advice and get rid of River and Simon. Yet speaking to Jayne, Mal says of River and Simon: "This is my boat. They're part of my crew. No one's getting left. Best you get used to that" ("Ariel"). And although Mal seems to have an ambiguous relationship with Book at times, in the end, he sees Book also as part of his crew—up to the preacher's last breath (*Serenity*).

The Dao of *Firefly*

As we watch *Firefly*, we find ourselves cheering for this diverse group of "brigands." Somehow, there is something good about what they have going. As they steer their course between the evils of the Alliance on the central planets and the Reavers on the outer edges of the 'verse, we wish them the best. We want them to survive and even flourish. When Inara or Book is off ship for an episode, there is something missing. And in the end, I find myself mourning the deaths of both Book and Wash (Alan Tudyk) in *Serenity*, the film sequel.

What is it that is good about their life together? It is just that. It is their life together that is good. The words used to describe the relationship between yin and yang earlier in this essay, could describe life on *Serenity* as well. The ship's crew, including its various passengers, constitutes "alternating, even 'pulsating' creative forces representing the interplay between spiritual and physical, emotion and intellect, passivity and activity, the yielding and the firm, resistance and generation." Although they are at times "oppositional," they are also always moving toward an equilibrium in which the power of each is brought into the creation of the community, not in a way in which individuality is thwarted and subjected to tyranny (this would be the way of the Alliance), but in a way that appreciates the diversity and builds upon it. On board *Serenity*, we find both believing and doubting; we witness both extreme sensitivity and insensitivity; we see violent impulses and passivity in the face of danger. Like every other member of the crew, Shepherd Book plays an important role in the Dao of *Firefly*, not as the representative of religion, but as the voice from the other side, the side of faith as opposed to doubt, a voice for the touch of faith one finds in Malcolm Reynolds himself.[20] Mal, on the other hand, is the other for Shepherd Book, representing something hidden, never fully revealed, in Book's past and ongoing journey. The balance is not just between Book and Mal, but between all the members of the crew. Each of the characters is a mix as an individual, and each is different from the others. And together, they pulsate with life, the life of *Serenity*. Like Daoism itself, the *Firefly/Serenity* series communicates the value of being open to the other, of learning from differences, and of working with, rather than against, others. It illustrates the importance of balance between the active and the passive, between the light and the dark, between the "masculine" and "feminine." It is a vision of the good life from which we can all learn.

In two parallel scenes, Book and Mal affirm the goodness of life on board *Serenity*. In the episode "Safe," Book is badly injured. They manage to take him for treatment at an Alliance facility. Back on the ship, as Book lies in the infirmary, Mal expresses his amazement that the Alliance has allowed Book to come and go. Someday, Book suggests, he will explain. At this point, he seems to want to rest. Before he does, he says to Mal, "It's good to be home." In a very similar scene in "Out of Gas," it is Mal who almost dies. At the end of the episode, surrounded by his crew, Simon tells him he must rest. Mal admits that the doctor is right. "You all gonna be here when I wake up?" he asks. Book replies for them all, "We'll be here." Mal closes his eyes and says, "'kay," and with a smile, "That's good." In these two scenes, Book and Mal suggest that they have found the good life here on board *Serenity*, among those who are bound together on this tiny island in the sky.

The good life, according to the *Firefly/Serenity* series, has at least two elements. One of these is freedom. *Serenity* flies beyond the bounds of the Alliance, the government that would encompass and control everyone and everything. There is a political libertarian theme in *Firefly* that I have not discussed. I leave this for further exploration later. The other element of the good life is not easy to spell out. It is community, but not just community. It is a special community that begins with openness to the other. It is made possible by trust and loyalty, even if these virtues are not always fully lived out.[21] It is a community in which a diverse group of individuals find they need one another, learn to depend upon one another, and come to value one another as persons. Like yin and yang, apparent opposites in creative tension, the members of the crew, which includes everyone on board in the end, create a life worth living. In the midst of a life that is certainly not peaceful, they find serenity. As Whedon expresses it in the theme song for the series: "Take my love, take my land, Take me where I cannot stand, I don't care, I'm still free, You can't take the sky from me . . . Since I found Serenity." *Serenity* is more than just a ship: it's family, it's home, it's a way of life.

Notes

I want to thank Dean Kowalski for his helpful and suggestive comments. They have greatly improved this essay.

1. In this essay, I use the phrase "the *Firefly/Serenity* series" or simply "*Firefly/Serenity*" to refer to the entire series, including both the television series and the film *Serenity*. There is also the possibility of confusion between the film, entitled *Serenity*, and the pilot episode of *Firefly*, also entitled "Serenity." In keeping with the style of placing the names of episodes in quotations marks, I refer to the pilot episode of *Firefly* as "Serenity." When I refer to the film, I italicize *Serenity*.

2. Although hedonism, the quest to maximize pleasure, is not identical with the view that focuses on security and happiness, it is an example of such a view. I will use it to represent the more general approach that emphasizes aiming at maximizing goods as the key to a good life.

3. Joss Whedon, *Serenity: Better Days* (Milwaukie, Ore.: Dark Horse, 2008). This graphic novel lacks page numbers.

4. Joss Whedon, *Firefly: The Official Companion*, vol. 1 (London: Titan, 2006), 166, quoted in Wikipedia, "Derrial Book."

5. Before coming on board, he had been at Southdown Abbey ("Serenity"), and later Book spends time away from the ship, at Bathgate Abbey ("Ariel"). In "Out of Gas," we find the crew members sitting around the table, laughing as they listen to Book tell stories from his life in the abbey. It seems clear that he is part of an order of monks that do not marry. In another episode, Book frightens River when he has his hair untied, apparently in accordance with the rules of his order.

6. Early on in the series, Book does seem a bit taken aback by Inara's profession, but as I argue, he always treats her with respect, a respect that grows over the course of the series.

7. Even here, one could argue that it is the welfare of Saffron about which Book is concerned, not some rules concerning sexual activity.

8. In doing so, Book is far closer to doing "what Jesus would do" than many Christians.

9. A similar idea comes out in an interesting dialogue between Book and Mal. When Mal faces a challenge, Book tells him: "Only one thing is gonna walk you through this, Mal. Belief." Mal replies: "You know I always look to you for counsel . . . but sermons make me sleepy, Shepherd. I ain't looking for help from on high. That's a long wait for a train don't come." To which Book responds, " . . . When I talk about belief, why do you always assume I'm talking about God?"

10. Joss Whedon, *Serenity: The Official Visual Companion* (London: Titan, 2005), 11, quoted in Wikipedia, "Derrial Book."

11. But as I show below, Mal remains, in a way, a very moral person.

12. Although it may well be that Mal, the pragmatist, allows Book to perform his rites merely to keep him occupied.

13. Jeaneane Fowler and Merv Fowler, *Chinese Religions: Beliefs and Practices* (Brighton: Sussex Academic Press, 2008), 47–48.

14. Ibid., 51–52.

15. Lao-Tzu, *Tao Te Ching*, trans. Stephen Addiss and Stanley Lombardo (Indianapolis: Hackett, 1993), 2.

16. This is an alternative translation. Addis and Lombardo translate this verse, "Tao called Tao is not Tao" (ibid., 1).

17. In this essay, I am emphasizing the way in which yin and yang complement one another and the similar complementary relationship between Mal and Book. Readers might want to explore the comparison further, asking in what ways Book has the characteristics of yin and Mal of yang.

18. For more on understanding Whedon's vision of the good life via community, please see Dean Kowalski, "Plato, Aristotle, and Joss on Being Horrible," in this volume.

19. Are we to take Mal at face value here? Does he mean it is the morally right thing to do? Or does he mean it is the pragmatically right thing to do?

20. See Eric Greene, "The Good Book," in *Serenity Found: More Unauthorized Essays on Joss Whedon's* Firefly *Universe*, ed. Jane Espenson (Dallas: BenBella, 2007), 79–93. Greene suggests that each of the crew members represents something of Malcolm Reynolds. Greene's suggestion and my discussion in this section portray Mal almost as a "hub" of the ship's life, the center, holding the other characters together. This image, however, is in tension with the image of Mal and Book as yin and yang, an image that suggests that each is held together by something more mysterious. Readers may want to reflect on these two images, asking if one or the other more accurately portrays Mal's role on board the ship.

21. The following words of Simon to Jayne are illustrative: Jayne is badly injured and Simon stands over him in the infirmary. Simon says, "You're in a dangerous line of work, Jayne. Odds are, you'll be under my knife again. Often. So I want you to understand one thing very clearly. No matter what you do, or say, or plot . . . no matter how you come down on us, I will never ever harm you. You're on this table you're safe. 'Cause, I'm your medic, and however little we may like or trust each other, we're on the same crew. Got the same troubles, same enemies and more than enough of both. Now we could circle each other and growl, sleep with one eye open but that thought wearies me. [Simon injects something into Jayne with a hypodermic needle.] I don't care what you've done. I don't know what you're planning on doing, but I'm trusting you. I think you should do the same, 'cause I don't see this working any other way" ("Trash").

Acknowledgments

We would like to thank Mark Conard and Anne Dean Watkins at the University Press of Kentucky for the opportunity to compose this volume and, more importantly, for the professional license to craft it as we wished. Conard and Watkins are to be commended for their faith in volume editors. We are incredibly grateful for Tim Minear's involvement in the project. We are encouraged by his affirmation that Joss's voice remains distinct throughout the Whedonverse, assuming one searches for it carefully enough, which bolsters the basic presupposition of this book. And, of course, we are indebted to the contributing authors for their high-quality efforts. Each essay appears here in print for the first time. Some authors crafted multiple drafts of their chapters, and not one of them complained—as far as we know, at least.

Dean A. Kowalski would like to thank his volume coeditor, Professor Evan Kreider. Evan's unusually extensive knowledge of the Buffyverse and his willingness to become quickly an equally adept expert on *Dollhouse*—to say nothing of his wise counsel—were great boons to this project. He is also indebted to former student Jamon Schroeder for introducing him to the 'verse and suggesting a book project containing material from *Firefly*. Crafting a volume centered around the good life provided Kowalski the opportunity to reflect on (although lacking Haymer's "floaty island" from "Trash") what makes his life good—the loving support he receives from his wife, Patricia, and the Aristotelian friendship he enjoys with the likes of Joe Foy, among others, quickly come to mind. His life has also been enriched in immeasurable ways by his two children. The joys of fatherhood are indeed difficult to adequately describe, but he looks forward to the day when he can share the Whedonverse with them. Accordingly, it is to his children that he dedicates this book: To Nicholas and Cassie—No power in the 'verse can stop my love for you.

S. Evan Kreider would like to thank his lovely and compassionate wife, Jacqueline—sine qua non. (He would also like to remind her that the frilly pink, hoop-skirt dress birthday present was just a joke.)

Appendix

A History of the Whedonverse

Whedon's Television Credits (Creator and Executive Producer)

BUFFY THE VAMPIRE SLAYER (1997–2003)

Season One

No.	Episode title	Air date	Writer(s)
1.01	Welcome to the Hellmouth	03.10.97	Joss Whedon
1.02	The Harvest	03.10.97	Joss Whedon
1.03	Witch	03.17.97	Dana Reston
1.04	Teacher's Pet	03.24.97	David Greenwalt
1.05	Never Kill a Boy on the First Date	03.31.97	Rob Des Hotel, Dean Batali
1.06	The Pack	04.07.97	Matt Kiene, Joe Reinkemeyer
1.07	Angel	04.14.97	David Greenwalt
1.08	I Robot . . . You Jane	04.21.97	Ashley Gable, Thomas A. Swyden
1.09	The Puppet Show	05.05.97	Dean Batali, Rob Des Hotel
1.10	Nightmares	05.12.97	Joss Whedon, David Greenwalt
1.11	Out of Mind, Out of Sight	05.19.97	Joss Whedon, Ashley Gable, Thomas A. Swyden
1.12	Prophecy Girl	06.02.97	Joss Whedon

Season Two

No.	Episode title	Air date	Writer(s)
2.01	When She Was Bad	09.15.97	Joss Whedon
2.02	Some Assembly Required	09.22.97	David Tyron King

Season Two (*continued*)

No.	Episode title	Air date	Writer(s)
2.03	School Hard	09.29.97	Joss Whedon, David Greenwalt
2.04	Inca Mummy Girl	10.06.97	Matt Kiene, Joe Reinkemeyer
2.05	Reptile Boy	10.13.97	David Greenwalt
2.06	Halloween	10.27.97	Carl Ellsworth
2.07	Lie to Me	11.03.97	Joss Whedon
2.08	The Dark Age	11.10.97	Dean Batali, Rob Des Hotel
2.09	What's My Line?: Part One	11.17.97	Howard Gordon, Marti Noxon
2.10	What's My Line?: Part Two	11.24.97	Marti Noxon
2.11	Ted	12.08.97	David Greenwalt, Joss Whedon
2.12	Bad Eggs	01.12.98	Marti Noxon
2.13	Surprise	01.19.98	Marti Noxon
2.14	Innocence	01.20.98	Joss Whedon
2.15	Phases	01.27.98	Dean Batali, Rob Des Hotel
2.16	Bewitched, Bothered, and Bewildered	02.10.98	Marti Noxon
2.17	Passion	02.24.98	David Tyron King
2.18	Killed By Death	03.03.98	Dean Batali, Rob Des Hotel
2.19	I Only Have Eyes for You	04.21.98	Marti Noxon
2.20	Go Fish	05.05.98	David Fury, Elin Hampton
2.21	Becoming: Part One	05.12.98	Joss Whedon
2.22	Becoming: Part Two	05.19.98	Joss Whedon

Season Three

No.	Episode title	Air date	Writer(s)
3.01	Anne	09.29.98	Joss Whedon
3.02	Dead Man's Party	10.06.98	Marti Noxon
3.03	Faith, Hope & Trick	10.13.98	David Greenwalt
3.04	Beauty and the Beasts	10.20.98	Marti Noxon
3.05	Homecoming	11.03.98	David Greenwalt
3.06	Band Candy	11.10.98	Jane Espenson
3.07	Revelations	11.17.98	Douglas Petrie
3.08	Lovers Walk	11.24.98	Dan Vebber
3.09	The Wish	12.08.98	Marti Noxon
3.10	Amends	12.15.98	Joss Whedon

No.	Episode title	Air date	Writer(s)
3.11	Gingerbread	01.12.99	Jane Espenson, Thania St. John
3.12	Helpless	01.19.99	David Fury
3.13	The Zeppo	01.26.99	Dan Vebber
3.14	Bad Girls	02.09.99	Douglas Petrie
3.15	Consequences	02.16.99	Marti Noxon
3.16	Doppelgangland	02.23.99	Joss Whedon
3.17	Enemies	03.16.99	Douglas Petrie
3.18	Earshot	09.21.99	Jane Espenson
3.19	Choices	05.04.99	David Fury
3.20	The Prom	05.11.99	Marti Noxon
3.21	Graduation Day: Part One	05.18.99	Joss Whedon
3.22	Graduation Day: Part Two	07.13.99	Joss Whedon

Season Four

No.	Episode title	Air date	Writer(s)
4.01	The Freshman	10.05.99	Joss Whedon
4.02	Living Conditions	10.12.99	Marti Noxon
4.03	The Harsh Light of Day	10.19.99	Jane Espenson
4.04	Fear Itself	10.26.99	David Fury
4.05	Beer Bad	11.02.99	Tracey Forbes
4.06	Wild at Heart	11.09.99	Marti Noxon
4.07	The Initiative	11.16.99	Douglas Petrie
4.08	Pangs	11.23.99	Jane Espenson
4.09	Something Blue	11.30.99	Tracey Forbes
4.10	Hush	12.14.99	Joss Whedon
4.11	Doomed	01.18.00	Marti Noxon, David Fury, Jane Espenson
4.12	A New Man	01.25.00	Jane Espenson
4.13	The I in Team	02.08.00	David Fury
4.14	Goodbye, Iowa	02.15.00	Marti Noxon
4.15	This Year's Girl	02.22.00	Douglas Petrie
4.16	Who Are You?	02.29.00	Joss Whedon
4.17	Superstar	04.04.00	Jane Espenson
4.18	Where the Wild Things Are	04.25.00	Tracey Forbes
4.19	New Moon Rising	05.02.00	Marti Noxon
4.20	The Yoko Factor	05.09.00	Douglas Petrie
4.21	Primeval	05.16.00	David Fury
4.22	Restless	05.23.00	Joss Whedon

Season Five

No.	Episode title	Air date	Writer(s)
5.01	Buffy v. Dracula	09.26.00	Marti Noxon
5.02	Real Me	10.03.00	David Fury
5.03	The Replacement	10.10.00	Jane Espenson
5.04	Out of My Mind	10.17.00	Rebecca Rand Kirshner
5.05	No Place Like Home	10.24.00	Douglas Petrie
5.06	Family	11.07.00	Joss Whedon
5.07	Fool for Love	11.14.00	Douglas Petrie
5.08	Shadow	11.21.00	David Fury
5.09	Listening to Fear	11.28.00	Rebecca Rand Kirshner
5.10	Into the Woods	12.19.00	Marti Noxon
5.11	Triangle	01.09.01	Jane Espenson
5.12	Checkpoint	01.23.01	Douglas Petrie, Jane Espenson
5.13	Blood Ties	02.06.01	Steven S. DeKnight
5.14	Crush	02.13.01	David Fury
5.15	I Was Made to Love You	02.20.01	Jane Espenson
5.16	The Body	02.27.01	Joss Whedon
5.17	Forever	04.17.01	Marti Noxon
5.18	Intervention	04.24.01	Jane Espenson
5.19	Tough Love	05.01.01	Rebecca Rand Kirshner
5.20	Spiral	05.08.01	Steven S. DeKnight
5.21	The Weight of the World	05.15.01	Douglas Petrie
5.22	The Gift	05.22.01	Joss Whedon

Season Six

No.	Episode title	Air date	Writer(s)
6.01	The Beginning: Part One	10.02.01	Marti Noxon
6.02	The Beginning: Part Two	10.02.01	David Fury
6.03	Afterlife	10.09.01	Jane Espenson
6.04	Flooded	10.16.01	Douglas Petrie, Jane Espenson
6.05	Life Serial	10.23.01	David Fury, Jane Espenson
6.06	All the Way	10.30.01	Steven S. DeKnight
6.07	Once More, with Feeling	11.06.01	Joss Whedon
6.08	Tabula Rasa	11.13.01	Rebecca Rand Kirshner
6.09	Smashed	11.20.01	Drew Z. Greenberg
6.10	Wrecked	11.27.01	Marti Noxon
6.11	Gone	01.08.02	David Fury

No.	Episode title	Air date	Writer(s)
6.12	Doublemeat Palace	01.29.02	Jane Espenson
6.13	Dead Things	02.05.02	Steven S. DeKnight
6.14	Older and Far Away	02.12.02	Drew Z. Greenberg
6.15	As You Were	02.26.02	Douglas Petrie
6.16	Hell's Bells	03.05.02	Rebecca Rand Kirshner
6.17	Normal Again	03.12.02	Diego Gutierrez
6.18	Entropy	04.30.02	Drew Z. Greenberg
6.19	Seeing Red	05.07.02	Steven S. DeKnight
6.20	Villains	05.14.02	Marti Noxon
6.21	Two to Go	05.21.02	Douglas Petrie
6.22	Grave	05.21.02	David Fury

Season Seven

No.	Episode title	Air date	Writer(s)
7.01	Lessons	09.24.02	Joss Whedon
7.02	Beneath You	10.01.02	Douglas Petrie
7.03	Same Time, Same Place	10.08.02	Jane Espenson
7.04	Help	10.15.02	Rebecca Rand Kirshner
7.05	Selfless	10.22.02	Drew Goddard
7.06	Him	11.05.02	Drew Z. Greenberg
7.07	Conversations with Dead People	11.12.02	Jane Espenson, Drew Goddard
7.08	Sleeper	11.19.02	David Fury, Jane Espenson
7.09	Never Leave Me	11.26.02	Drew Goddard
7.10	Bring on the Night	12.17.02	Marti Noxon, Douglas Petrie
7.11	Showtime	01.07.03	David Fury
7.12	Potential	01.21.03	Rebecca Rand Kirshner
7.13	The Killer in Me	02.04.03	Drew Z. Greenberg
7.14	First Date	02.11.03	Jane Espenson
7.15	Get It Done	02.18.03	Douglas Petrie
7.16	Storyteller	02.25.03	Jane Espenson
7.17	Lies My Parents Told Me	03.25.03	David Fury, Drew Goddard
7.18	Dirty Girls	04.15.03	Drew Goddard
7.19	Empty Places	04.29.03	Drew Z. Greenberg
7.20	Touched	05.06.03	Rebecca Rand Kirshner
7.21	End of Days	05.13.03	Douglas Petrie, Jane Espenson
7.22	Chosen	05.20.03	Joss Whedon

ANGEL (1999–2004)

Season 1

No.	Episode title	Air date	Writer(s)
1.01	City of	10.05.99	Joss Whedon, David Greenwalt
1.02	Lonely Hearts	10.12.99	David Fury
1.03	In the Dark	10.19.99	Doug Petrie
1.04	I Fall to Pieces	10.26.99	Joss Whedon, David Greenwalt
1.05	RM W/A VU	11.02.99	David Greenwalt, Jane Espenson
1.06	Sense and Sensitivity	11.09.99	Tim Minear
1.07	Bachelor Party	11.16.99	Tracey Stern
1.08	I Will Remember You	11.23.99	David Greenwalt, Jeannine Renshaw
1.09	Hero	11.30.99	Howard Gordon, Tim Minear
1.10	Parting Gifts	12.14.99	David Fury, Jeannine Renshaw
1.11	Somnambulist	01.18.00	Tim Minear
1.12	Expecting	01.25.00	Howard Gordon
1.13	She	02.08.00	David Greenwalt, Marti Noxon
1.14	I've Got You under My Skin	02.15.00	David Greenwalt, Jeannine Renshaw
1.15	The Prodigal	02.22.00	Tim Minear
1.16	The Ring	02.29.00	Howard Gordon
1.17	Eternity	04.04.00	Tracey Stern
1.18	Five by Five	04.25.00	Jim Kouf
1.19	Sanctuary	05.02.00	Tim Minear, Joss Whedon
1.20	War Zone	05.09.00	Garry Campbell
1.21	Blind Date	05.16.00	Jeannine Renshaw
1.22	To Shanshu in L.A.	05.23.00	David Greenwalt

Season 2

No.	Episode title	Air date	Writer(s)
2.01	Judgment	09.26.00	Joss Whedon, David Greenwalt
2.02	Are You Now or Have You Ever Been?	10.03.00	Tim Minear

No.	Episode title	Air date	Writer(s)
2.03	First Impressions	10.10.00	Shawn Ryan
2.04	Untouched	10.17.00	Mere Smith
2.05	Dear Boy	10.24.00	David Greenwalt
2.06	Guise Will Be Guise	11.07.00	Jane Espenson
2.07	Darla	11.14.00	Tim Minear
2.08	The Shroud of Rahmon	11.21.00	Jim Kouf
2.09	The Trial	11.28.00	David Greenwalt, Doug Petrie, Tim Minear
2.10	Reunion	12.19.00	Tim Minear, Shawn Ryan
2.11	Redefinition	01.16.01	Mere Smith
2.12	Blood Money	01.23.01	Shawn Ryan, Mere Smith
2.13	Happy Anniversary	02.06.01	Joss Whedon, David Greenwalt
2.14	The Thin Dead Line	02.13.01	Jim Kouf, Shawn Ryan
2.15	Reprise	02.20.01	Tim Minear
2.16	Epiphany	02.27.01	Tim Minear
2.17	Disharmony	04.17.01	David Fury
2.18	Dead End	04.24.01	David Greenwalt
2.19	Belonging	05.01.01	Shawn Ryan
2.20	Over the Rainbow	05.08.01	Mere Smith
2.21	Through the Looking Glass	05.15.01	Tim Minear
2.22	There's No Place Like Plrtz Glrb	05.22.01	David Greenwalt

Season 3

No.	Episode title	Air date	Writer(s)
3.01	Heartthrob	09.24.01	David Greenwalt
3.02	That Vision Thing	10.01.01	Jeffrey Bell
3.03	That Old Gang of Mine	10.08.01	Tim Minear
3.04	Carpe Noctem	10.15.01	Scott Murphy
3.05	Fredless	10.22.01	Mere Smith
3.06	Billy	10.29.01	Tim Minear, Jeffrey Bell
3.07	Offspring	11.05.01	David Greenwalt
3.08	Quickening	11.12.01	Jeffrey Bell
3.09	Lullaby	11.19.01	Tim Minear
3.10	Dad	12.10.01	David H. Goodman
3.11	Birthday	01.14.02	Mere Smith
3.12	Provider	01.21.02	Scott Murphy
3.13	Waiting in the Wings	02.04.02	Joss Whedon
3.14	Couplet	02.18.02	Tim Minear, Jeffrey Bell
3.15	Loyalty	02.25.02	Mere Smith
3.16	Sleep Tight	03.04.02	David Greenwalt

Season 3 (*continued*)

No.	Episode title	Air date	Writer(s)
3.17	Forgiving	04.15.02	Jeffrey Bell
3.18	Double or Nothing	04.22.02	David H. Goodman
3.19	The Price	04.29.02	David Fury
3.20	A New World	05.06.02	Jeffrey Bell
3.21	Benediction	05.13.02	Tim Minear
3.22	Tomorrow	05.20.02	David Greenwalt

Season 4

No.	Episode title	Air date	Writer(s)
4.01	Deep Down	10.06.02	Steven S. DeKnight
4.02	Ground State	10.13.02	Mere Smith
4.03	The House Always Wins	10.20.02	David Fury
4.04	Slouching toward Bethlehem	10.27.02	Jeffrey Bell
4.05	Supersymmetry	11.03.02	Elizabeth Craft, Sarah Fain
4.06	Spin the Bottle	11.10.02	Joss Whedon
4.07	Apocalypse, Nowish	11.17.02	Steven S. DeKnight
4.08	Habeas Corpses	01.15.03	Jeffrey Bell
4.09	Long Day's Journey	01.22.03	Mere Smith
4.10	Awakening	01.29.03	David Fury, Steven S. DeKnight
4.11	Soulless	02.05.03	Elizabeth Craft, Sarah Fain
4.12	Calvary	02.12.03	Jeffrey Bell, Steven S. DeKnight, Mere Smith
4.13	Salvage	03.05.03	David Fury
4.14	Release	03.12.03	Steven S. DeKnight, Elizabeth Craft, Sarah Fain
4.15	Orpheus	03.19.03	Mere Smith
4.16	Players	03.26.03	Jeffrey Bell, Elizabeth Craft, Sarah Fain
4.17	Inside Out	04.02.03	Steven S. DeKnight
4.18	Shiny Happy People	04.09.03	Elizabeth Craft, Sarah Fain
4.19	The Magic Bullet	04.16.03	Jeffrey Bell
4.20	Sacrifice	04.23.03	Ben Edlund
4.21	Peace Out	04.30.03	David Fury
4.22	Home	05.07.03	Tim Minear

Season 5

No.	Episode title	Air date	Writer(s)
5.01	Conviction	10.01.03	Joss Whedon
5.02	Just Rewards	10.08.03	David Fury, Ben Edlund
5.03	Unleashed	10.15.03	Sarah Fain, Elizabeth Craft
5.04	Hell Bound	10.22.03	Steven S. DeKnight
5.05	Life of the Party	10.29.03	Ben Edlund
5.06	The Cautionary Tale of Numero Cinco	11.05.03	Jeffrey Bell
5.07	Lineage	11.12.03	Drew Goddard
5.08	Destiny	11.19.03	David Fury, Steven S. DeKnight
5.09	Harm's Way	01.14.04	Elizabeth Craft, Sarah Fain
5.10	Soul Purpose	01.21.04	Brent Fletcher
5.11	Damage	01.28.04	Steven S. DeKnight, Drew Goddard
5.12	You're Welcome	02.04.04	David Fury
5.13	Why We Fight	02.11.04	Drew Goddard, Steven S. DeKnight
5.14	Smile Time	02.18.04	Joss Whedon, Ben Edlund
5.15	A Hole in the World	02.25.04	Joss Whedon
5.16	Shells	03.03.04	Steven S. DeKnight
5.17	Underneath	04.14.04	Elizabeth Craft, Sarah Fain
5.18	Origin	04.21.04	Drew Goddard
5.19	Time Bomb	04.28.04	Ben Edlund
5.20	The Girl in Question	05.05.04	Steven S. DeKnight, Drew Goddard
5.21	Power Play	05.12.04	David Fury
5.22	Not Fade Away	05.19.04	Jeffrey Bell, Joss Whedon

FIREFLY (2002)

No.	Episode title	Air date	Writer(s)
1.01	Serenity, Part 1	12.20.02	Joss Whedon
1.02	Serenity, Part 2	12.20.02	Joss Whedon
1.03	The Train Job	09.20.02	Joss Whedon, Tim Minear
1.04	Bushwhacked	09.27.02	Tim Minear
1.05	Shindig	11.01.02	Jane Espenson
1.06	Safe	11.08.02	Drew Z. Greenberg
1.07	Our Mrs. Reynolds	10.04.02	Joss Whedon

1.08	Jaynestown	10.18.02	Ben Edlund
1.09	Out of Gas	10.25.02	Tim Minear
1.10	Ariel	11.15.02	Jose Molina
1.11	War Stories	12.06.02	Cheryl Cain
1.12	Trash	Not aired	Ben Edlund, Jose Molina
1.13	The Message	Not aired	Joss Whedon, Tim Minear
1.14	Heart of Gold	Not aired	Brett Mathews
1.15	Objects in Space	12.13.02	Joss Whedon

DOLLHOUSE (2009–2010)

Season 1

No.	Episode title	Air date	Writer(s)
1.01	Ghost	02.13.09	Joss Whedon
1.02	The Target	02.20.09	Steven S. DeKnight
1.03	Stage Fright	02.27.09	Maurissa Tancharoen, Jed Whedon
1.04	Gray Hour	03.06.09	Sarah Fain, Elizabeth Craft
1.05	True Believer	03.13.09	Tim Minear
1.06	Man on the Street	03.20.09	Joss Whedon
1.07	Echoes	03.27.09	Elizabeth Craft, Sarah Fain
1.08	Needs	04.03.09	Tracy Bellomo
1.09	Spy in the House of Love	04.10.09	Andrew Chambliss
1.10	Haunted	04.24.09	Jane Espenson, Maurissa Tancharoen
1.11	Briar Rose	05.01.09	Jane Espenson
1.12	Omega	05.08.09	Tim Minear
1.13	Epitaph One	Not aired	Joss and Jed Whedon, Maurissa Tancharoen

Season 2

No.	Episode title	Air date	Writer(s)
2.01	Vows	09.25.09	Joss Whedon
2.02	Instinct	10.02.09	Michele Fazekas, Tara Butters
2.03	Belle Chose	10.09.09	Tim Minear
2.04	Belonging	10.23.09	Maurissa Tancharoen, Jed Whedon
2.05	The Public Eye	12.04.09	Andrew Chambliss
2.06	The Left Hand	12.04.09	Tracy Bellomo

2.07	Meet Jane Doe	12.11.09	Maurissa Tancharoen, Jed Whedon, Andrew Chambliss
2.08	A Love Supreme	12.11.09	Jenny DeArmitt
2.09	Stop-Loss	12.18.09	Andrew Chambliss
2.10	The Attic	12.18.09	Maurissa Tancharoen, Jed Whedon
2.11	Getting Closer	01.08.10	Tim Minear
2.12	The Hollow Men	01.15.10	Michele Fazekas, Tara Butters, Tracy Bellomo
2.13	Epitaph Two: Return	01.29.10	Maurissa Tancharoen, Jed Whedon, Andrew Chambliss

Whedon's Film Credits (Director or Screenwriter)

Toy Story (1995, screenwriter)
Alien Resurrection (1997, screenwriter)
Titan A. E. (2000, screenwriter)
Serenity (2005, director and screenwriter)
Dr. Horrible's Sing-Along Blog (2008, director and screenwriter)
The Cabin in the Woods (2012, screenwriter)
The Avengers (2012, director and screenwriter)

Contributors

David Baggett is professor of philosophy at Liberty University and editor of *Tennis and Philosophy: What the Racket Is All About* (2010). His seventh book, *Good God: The Theistic Foundations of Morality* (with Jerry L. Walls), was published in 2011. Dave swears by his pretty flowered bonnet he's not in his bunk.

Patricia Brace is professor of art history at Southwest Minnesota State University. With cowriter Robert Arp, she has contributed chapters to Lost *and Philosophy: The Island Has Its Reasons* (2007); True Blood *and Philosophy* (2010); *The Philosophy of David Lynch* (2011); and *The Ultimate* Lost *and Philosophy: Think Together, Die Alone* (2011). She also contributed an essay to Dexter *and Philosophy: Mind over Spatter* (2011). A longtime resident of the Whedonverse, she used the nom de plume "Wesley's Wench" on the spoiler boards, and she still ships Spuffy (forever!).

Roger P. Ebertz is professor of philosophy and chair of the Department of Philosophy and Religion at the University of Dubuque. His research interests include epistemology, ethical theory, and environmental philosophy; and he has recently edited *Environmental Perspectives* (2009). Two instances of "crazy, random happenstance" have shaped his interest in philosophy and popular culture: the spelling of his last name and glimpsing Dean Kowalski's first syllabus for a course on philosophy and film. He now teaches "philosophy at the movies" regularly and was a contributing author to *Steven Spielberg and Philosophy* (2008).

Susanne E. Foster is associate professor of philosophy at Marquette University. Her primary work is in virtue theory and environmental ethics. This article is her first philosophical work drawing on popular culture. For a woman who hadn't watched television since the turn of the millennium, she considers this a giant step forward.

Joseph J. Foy is assistant professor in the Department of Political Science, Law, and Philosophy at the University of Wisconsin–Parkside. Specializing in popular culture as democratic theory, Foy edited the John G. Cawelti Award–winning book *Homer Simpson Goes to Washington: American Politics through Popular Culture*; and he coedited *Homer Simpson Marches on Washington: Dissent through American Popular Culture*. He also edited *SpongeBob SquarePants and Philosophy: Soaking up Secrets under the Sea* and is coediting the forthcoming *Homer Simpson and the Promise of Politics: Popular Culture as Political Theory*. He has contributed essays to *The Philosophy of* The X-Files, *Steven Spielberg and Philosophy*, TrueBlood *and Philosophy*, *The Rolling Stones and Philosophy*, and several other volumes. When he is not editing and writing, Foy spends his time being a dad to his wonderful two-year-old son, Connor, whom he often tells to "live as though the world were as it should be to show it what it can be."

Jason D. Grinnell is assistant professor of philosophy at Buffalo State College. His primary philosophical interests are in bioethics and professional ethics, as well as ancient philosophy. This is his first foray into the world of philosophy and popular culture, but he wants to be an achiever. Like Bad Horse.

Lisa Hager is assistant professor of English and women's studies at the University of Wisconsin–Waukesha. Her current book project looks at the relationship between the New Woman and the Victorian family. She is a regular book reviewer for *English Literature in Transition 1880-1920*, and has published articles in *Nineteenth-Century Gender Studies*, *Women's Writing*, and *Children's Literature Association Quarterly*. In her spare time, she plays with dinosaurs in a place called "This Land" and is looking forward to her surprising but inevitable betrayal.

Gary Heba is associate professor of English at Bowling Green State University, with interests in visual rhetoric, multimedia communication, and film. He has authored "Everyday Nightmares: The Rhetoric of Social Horror in the *Nightmare on Elm Street* Series," in the *Journal of Popular Film and Television*, and coauthored, with Robin Murphy, "Go West Young Woman! Hegel's Dialectic and Women's Identities in Western Films" in *The Philosophy of the Western* (2010).

DEAN A. KOWALSKI is associate professor of philosophy at the University of Wisconsin–Waukesha. He is the author of *Classic Questions and Contemporary Film: An Introduction to Philosophy* (2004) and has edited and contributed essays to *The Philosophy of* The X-Files (2007) and *Steven Spielberg and Philosophy* (2008). He has also contributed essays to *James Bond and Philosophy* (2006) and *The Philosophy of Martin Scorsese* (2007). When he is not busy "Muldering out" the truth—which *is* out there—he subtly works toward the grammatical acceptance of such Joss phraseology as "uncomfortableness," "corpsified," and "creepifying"; such speak would make him decidedly shiny, he conjures.

S. EVAN KREIDER is associate professor at the University of Wisconsin–Fox Valley and contributing author for *The Philosophy of* The X-Files (2007). His philosophical interests include ethics and aesthetics, and his papers have appeared in the *International Journal of Applied Philosophy* and *Philosophical Papers*. At least, this is what the tattoo on his lower back tells him.

ROBIN MURPHY is assistant professor of English at East Central University. Her main research interests are civic literacy, trauma rhetoric, pop culture studies, and feminist theory. She serves on the review board of *Computers and Composition Online* and the *Journal for Undergraduate Multimedia Projects* and teaches a caboodle of different writing classes. She recently coauthored, with Gary Heba, "Go West, Young Woman!: Hegel's Dialectic and Women's Identities in Western Films," in *The Philosophy of the Western* (2010). Murphy often looks to the sky to remember who she is.

JAMES B. SOUTH is chair of the Philosophy Department at Marquette University. He is the editor of Buffy the Vampire Slayer *and Philosophy* (2003) and coeditor of *James Bond and Philosophy* (2006), and has written several essays on movies, comic books, and popular music. He primarily does research in late medieval and Renaissance philosophy but is making increasingly regular forays into writing about popular culture. Despite what some people may think, he has never received an invitation to join the Evil League of Evil.

AMY H. STURGIS is the author of four books and the editor of six others, most recently *The Intersection of Fantasy and Native America: From H. P. Lovecraft to Leslie Marmon Silko* (2009) and *The Demon of Brockenheim* (forthcoming). A frequent speaker at universities and genre conventions across North America, Sturgis was honored with the Imperishable Flame Award for Tolkien/Inklings Scholarship in 2006. In 2009 and 2011, she received the Sofanaut Award for her regular "History of the SF Genre" segments on the U.K.-based *StarShipSofa*, which became the first podcast ever to win a Hugo Award in 2010. Although her alma mater, Vanderbilt University, claims that Sturgis has a Ph.D. in intellectual history, she prefers to think that she has a Ph.D. in horribleness.

TAIT SZABO is assistant professor of philosophy at the University of Wisconsin–Washington County. He is the author of "Strange Love or: How I Learned to Stop Worrying and Love Porn," appearing in *Porn and Philosophy* (2010). Despite his professional interest in sexual ethics, he reports having a happy and healthy love life.

Index

Abbot, Carl, 29
actives. *See* dolls
Adam (character), 122
Allen, Woody, 14
Alliance, 9–10, 12, 19–20, 25, 27–28,
  30–32, 34–36, 39–49, 82, 92–93,
  97, 100, 105, 108, 142–43, 156–57,
  159, 161, 182, 187–91, 201, 203–5
Alpha (character), 59–60, 114, 144–45
Angel (character), 15, 50, 73–74, 76, 80–
  84, 92–93, 121, 125–28, 136–38,
  142–43, 146, 151, 156, 159–60,
  162–63, 168–73, 175–78, 180
Aquinas, Thomas, 16
arête. See virtue
Aristophanes, 173–74
Aristotle, 17, 71, 84, 93–95, 98–99, 170
  on excellence, 90–91
  on friendship, 78–80
  on wisdom, 90
asceticism, 137–38
autonomy, 10, 18, 40, 49–50, 56, 66–67,
  105, 115, 119, 128, 151–52, 163
  See also freedom

Badger (character), 16, 30, 196
Ballard, Paul, 58, 62–63, 65, 113–15,
  162–63
beauty, 12, 117–18, 125–26, 128–29, 171,
  201

Being and Time, 152
Berlin, Isaiah, 25, 32–36
Bible, 196–97, 202
Book, Shepherd, 13, 31, 39, 41, 44, 48,
  83, 106, 108, 194, 196–205
Border worlds, 34
Bradbury, Ray, 29–30
Brink, Topher, 56–57, 63, 113
Brown, Helen Gurley, 119
Browncoats, 28, 34, 43, 48, 50, 182
Buddhism, 196
Burkle, Winifred ("Fred"), 81–82, 84,
  156, 171–73, 175
Buzz Lightyear, 81, 158, 160

Camus, Albert, 10, 13
capitalism, 26, 119, 184
categorical imperative, 91
Chase, Cordelia, 72, 80–81, 84, 117,
  125–30, 168, 176–77
Christianity, 20, 34, 134, 136, 138,
  145–46, 196, 198–99, 202
Cinderella, 118–19
Cobb, Jayne, 12, 24, 33, 41, 48, 82–83,
  88–89, 92–98, 100, 107, 111, 195,
  201–4
coercion, 19, 33–34, 55–61
"Companions," 17, 48, 103, 105–15, 198,
  202
Connor, 168–70, 172–74, 180